THE ART LIFE
On Creativity and Career

STUART HORODNER

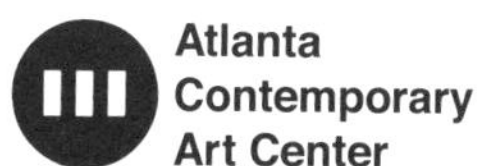
Atlanta
Contemporary
Art Center

The Art Life: On Creativity and Career

Published by
Atlanta Contemporary Art Center
535 Means Street NW
Atlanta, GA 30318
www.thecontemporary.org

Distributed by
D.A.P./Distributed Art Publishers, Inc.
155 Sixth Avenue, 2nd Floor
New York, NY 10013
www.artbook.com

ISBN 978-1-4507-9065-9

Editors: Stuart Horodner and Stacie Lindner
Design: Susan Bowman
Printing: Davis Direct, Montgomery, AL

Cover: Jennie C. Jones, Making *Out of the Blue – Sonny Red, Blue Note LP #4032*, 2009, *Red Bird Blue,*
Jun 26–Aug 16, 2009, Atlanta Contemporary Art Center

CONTENTS

CHAPTERS

PREFACE

I was very lucky. My parents exposed me to art early and often, and when I wanted to spend a significant amount of time drawing in my bedroom, I was encouraged. I watched my father (a specialist in the restoration of old photographs and a Sunday painter), cut out pictures from various publications and put them into manila folders with categories including faces, animals, still life, and sports. He called these his "swipe files," and he used them to inspire and inform his pictorial efforts. When I came across the collages of Romare Bearden, Max Ernst, Hannah Hoch and, then later, the photo-generated works by Barbara Kruger and Mark Tansey, I realized that scavenging and saving images was an invaluable practice. My own daily ritual of pasting choice items gathered from magazines, newspapers, and journals into black-bound sketchbooks provides me with several pleasures, from the physicality of arranging things on a page and gluing them down, to the space-saving satisfaction of keeping a "best of" collection in a condensed and manageable size. One of the things I appreciate most about curating is the hunter-gatherer aspect, and the combining of like elements or the pairing of strange bedfellows to establish new relationships and unpredictable outcomes.

At The Cooper Union and at Rutgers University, I had the privilege to study with professors including Dore Ashton, Leon Golub, Hans Haacke, Reuben Kadish, Irving Petlin, Martha Rosler, and Jack Whitten; add to these august figures the ongoing presence of my artist friends and our seemingly endless conversations with bottomless cups of coffee. The distinct energies and ethics of these individuals and the heady period in New York in the late 1970s and 1980s constituted my truest academy.

In the years after graduate school, I worked in a shopping mall selling limited edition prints; wrote for magazines and journals; co-owned and directed a storefront commercial gallery; developed exhibitions at universities and art centers; taught classes and served as guest lecturer at numerous schools; and organized a hotel art fair. These activities have often overlapped as a way to construct a livelihood, but also reflect my ambition to be a person who says "yes" when interesting offers come my way. One job informed how I did another, and they each provided me with a laboratory to try out different approaches to the task at hand. In this regard, I have always felt in sync with John Cage, who in the foreword to his 1961 book, *Silence: Lectures and Writings*, states:

> For over twenty years I have been writing articles and giving lectures. Many of them have been unusual in form—this is especially true of the lectures—because I have employed in them means of composing analogous to my composing means in the field of music. My intention has been, often, to say what I had to say in a way that would exemplify it: that would, conceivably, permit the listener to experience what I had to say rather than just hear about it. This means that, being as I am engaged in a variety of activities, I attempt to introduce into each one of them aspects conventionally limited to one or more of the others.[1]

Certain opportunities have required my relocating: from New York to Lewisburg, Pennsylvania; then to Portland, Oregon; and most recently to Atlanta, Georgia. I did not set out to be nomadic nor did I have a calculated plan of getting from one position to another. I've tried to pursue new challenges in unique contexts with dedicated colleagues. Each of these circumstances has helped to establish my voice and clarify my understanding of how contemporary art can operate, and who and how it serves.

In my position as Artistic Director at the Atlanta Contemporary Art Center, I function as a producer, advocate, explainer, and host. I am charged with creating exhibitions and public programs that present artists and arts professionals whose works are recognized for their uniqueness of vision, rigor of research, way with materials, and capacity to generate discourse. I hope that my curatorial offerings transform the lives of those who encounter them, as decades of involvement with ideas, objects, and events have most certainly enriched and empowered mine.

The thoughts on making and the marketplace gathered here are a synthesis of numerous lectures, panels, and workshops, originally unified by the *Artist Survival*

Skills series, later renamed *Creative Lives & Careers*. This shift of language is meant to acknowledge that we must lay claim to something beyond surviving, and dedicate ourselves to finding the tools and strategies that will help us thrive. This book has been conceived and shaped with that goal in mind.

NOTES

1. John Cage, "Forward," *Silence: Lectures and Writings* (Cambridge and London: MIT Press, 1967, First published 1961 by Wesleyan Univ. Press, Middletown, CT), ix.

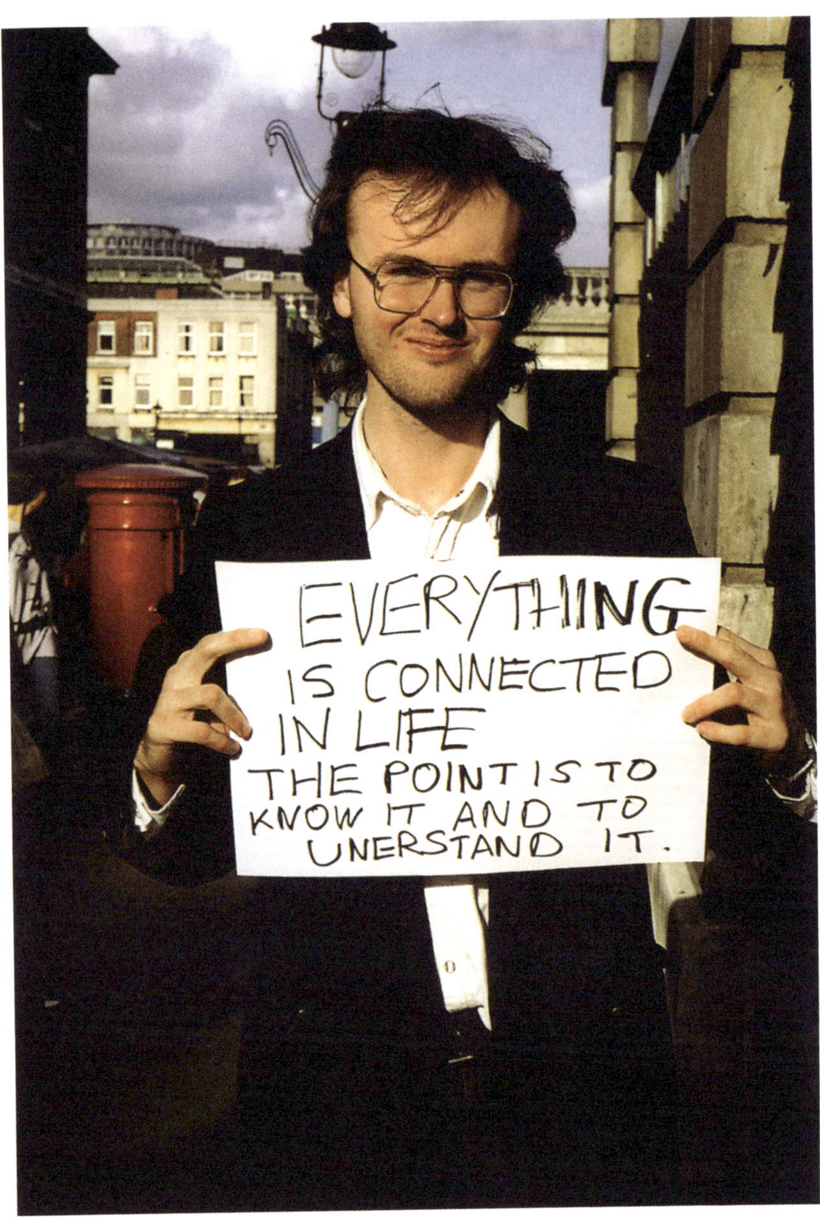

Gillian Wearing
Signs that say what you want them to say and not Signs that say what someone else wants you to say: Everything is connected in life. The point is to know it and to understand it.
1992–1993

INTRODUCTION

You have to start somewhere. I choose to begin with painter Thomas Nozkowski quoting writer Edward Dahlberg, who said, "It is presumptuous to assume we can do anything to help another person and it is vulgar not to try."[1]

This statement is meant to assert two things. First, that the goal of this collection of selected and solicited texts and images is to be of assistance. The various opinions revealed within these pages might serve as a compass for orienting yourself as you deal with the practical and philosophical matters that shape every art life. Second, that artists have always relied on their predecessors and peers for inspiration and confirmation, quoting them in casual or formal situations in order to prove points about one topic or another. Using what others have said makes history an active part of the present and affirms the user's position as part of the continuum.

There is a range of voices represented here, primarily those of visual artists, but also participants in the fields of literature, film, music, design, education, and food. I believe that their unique experiences are relevant to others, like the message written on a card held by one man in Gillian Wearing's photo series, *Signs that say what you want them to say and not Signs that say what someone else wants you to say.*

You give yourself a creative life—pursuing those questions and aesthetic conditions that mean the most to you. What are you interested in? Landscape and gender and nuclear power are each worthy subjects and there are plenty more. Do you aspire to exhibit in museums or public spaces or virtual realms? Your job is to figure out how to best engage these distinct contexts. Your studio may be a large industrial space or a second bedroom or the kitchen table, where you can work days or nights while wearing your favorite sweatpants and drinking tea as music blasts or silence is maintained. You might produce five or fifty objects a year, using bronze or oil paint or folded paper, and these can be large or tiny, made to last for centuries or a few weeks. Maybe you've been a printmaker for several years and all of a sudden you decide to make videos. OK. You might be influenced by Pop Art or Minimalism or Feminism or Fluxus. How are you using these various histories to your advantage? Does Edward Hopper or Gordon Matta-Clark or Agnes Martin or David Hammons inspire you? If not, who does? Do you like reading memoirs or murder mysteries or Roland Barthes? Try to understand the reasons for your choices, and if you feel the need to shift gears, indulge that impulse. Grant yourself the permission to acquire new skills, travel to biennials, buy a new computer, start a reading group. Risk not knowing what will happen when you do.

Others give you a career—the dealers, curators, critics, collectors, and administrators who have their own expectations about what you do and how you do it. They are invested in your output and development because what you do affects what they do. Like you, they put their time, zeal, reputations, and finances on the line every day. Your relationships with these interested parties can result in teaching jobs, grants, residencies, exhibitions, reviews, and sales. There can also be rejection letters, awkward studio visits, schmoozing at openings, and the deafening silence of no interest at all. That Thursday evening you once spent calmly applying gesso to a canvas can suddenly become filled with anxiety about an upcoming group show. Did you say the wrong thing to the museum director at that dinner party? Do you have good documentation of the performance where you repeatedly rolled down that hill in LA? Will preparators be able to follow the instructions for de-installing your inflatable sculptures? Are you ready for all this?

If you stay vigilant and find ways to make yourself necessary, you'll be nurtured by your immediate community and the art world beyond that. But this is a competitive and emotional business, and your career is subject to the egos, ambitions, and whims of numerous people. You will expect others to do the right thing (i.e.,

>

Stuart Horodner
Notebook
Aug 2006

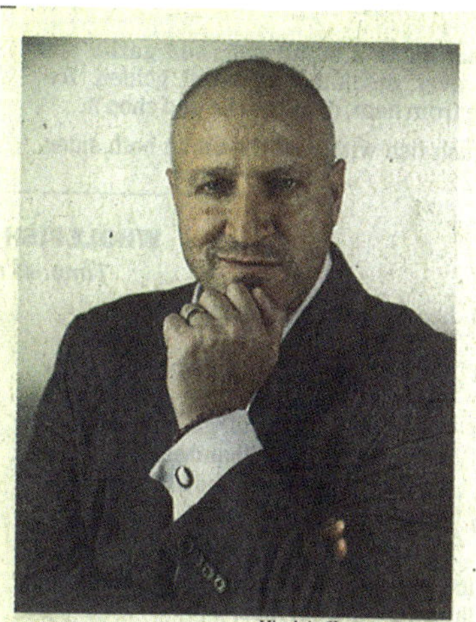

Virginia Sherwood/Bravo

MOVING ON Tom Colicchio built his reputation at Gramercy Tavern.

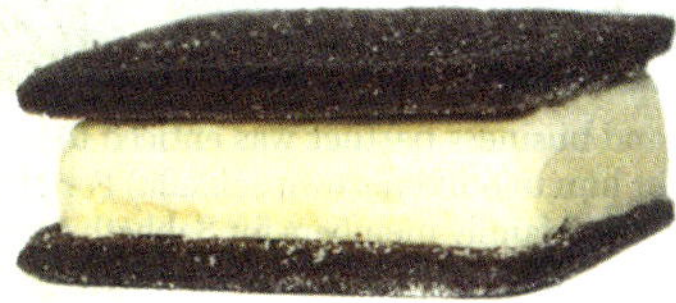

'Wichcraft

60 E. 8th St., nr. Broadway, and various Manhattan addresses; 212-780-0577; $3.50

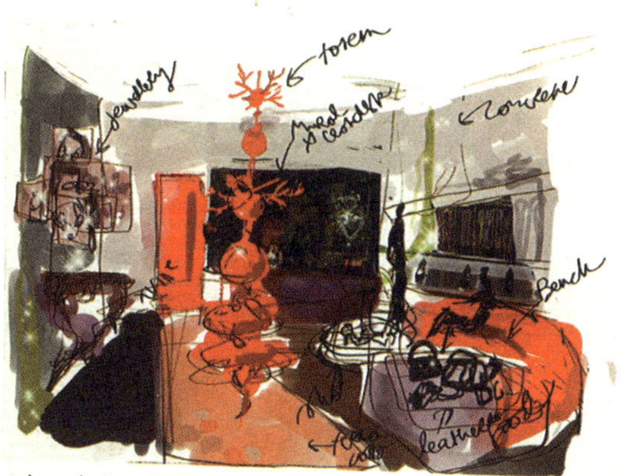

A rendering of Christian Lacroix's Las Vegas boutique

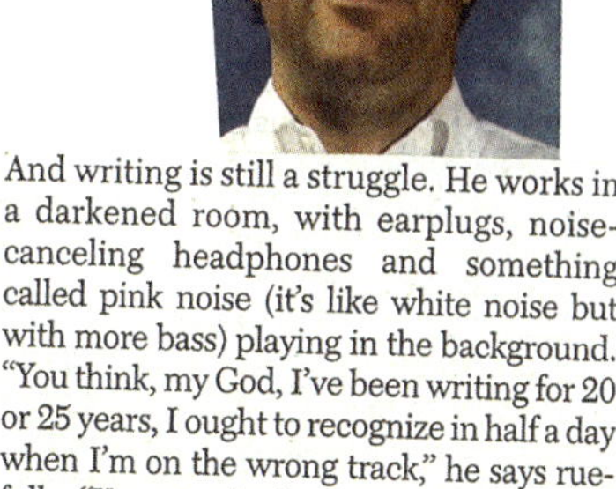

And writing is still a struggle. He works in a darkened room, with earplugs, noise-canceling headphones and something called pink noise (it's like white noise but with more bass) playing in the background. "You think, my God, I've been writing for 20 or 25 years, I ought to recognize in half a day when I'm on the wrong track," he says ruefully. "You wonder how on earth you ever wrote anything that didn't suck."

You can cut down on fear and embarrassment and disappointment, but you can never quite go cold turkey. "The double bind, the problem of consciousness mixed with nothingness, never goes away," Fran-

give you what you want), and some will and some won't. You can only keep at it, be pro-active and receptive, and try to be generous whenever possible. You are trying to get from no, to maybe, to yes.

A creative life and a career are not the same thing, but they are not mutually exclusive either. Ideally, one can construct a satisfying and sustainable merging of the two. In this pursuit, it may help to remember this comment by Franz Kline: "The real thing about creating is to have the capacity to be embarrassed."[2]

The analytic and inspirational entries included here have been taken from their original contexts in books, catalogues, newspapers, magazines, websites, e-mails, and transcripts of public presentations. Many of the contributors have taken part in exhibitions and programs at the Atlanta Contemporary Art Center from 2007 to 2011, and others have been included to represent provocative historical and contemporary viewpoints by a range of influential figures. They address the fact that a life in the arts can be simultaneously rewarding, frustrating, doubt-filled, joyful, and uncertain. It is a process that can feel as daunting as the task described by the title of a 1996 Martin Kersels sculpture, *Attempt to Raise the Temperature of a Container of Water by Yelling at It.* And yet, thousands of artists persist every day, motivated by a private insistency and the promise of satisfaction and recognition. I agree with Peter Schjeldahl who says, "Art is very silly and it is very free. The freedom is there to be used. It takes somebody with a lot of ambition and stamina to use it."[3]

This anthology is not a guide to professional practices. It will not tell you if or how to approach galleries or where to apply for funding. There are numerous good books and on-line resources that address these issues.[4] Instead, I have tried to construct a meditation on why one makes art at all and how to fuel the effort over time. Each chapter contains a brief introduction and an accumulation of interview fragments, lists, edited essays, and questions. They deal with the internal rationales regarding motivation, influence, subjects, and process, and the external conditions of community, criticism, career, and success. The entries are meant to establish calls and responses—those in one chapter may resonate with others nearby or in other chapters. I have resisted the impulse to explain the reasons for the selections too much, except to say that they ring true to me as profound and precise. Comments made by established practitioners exist side by side with those by up-and-comers. Illustrations appear throughout the book, including works of art that comment on the chapter content in their own way, as well as images of artists in action—producing, installing, thinking, and being social.

The publication of this book does not mean that the project is finished. The process of seeking relevant data goes on. I will continue to peruse publications looking for words and images that inspire me, and when I find them, my scissors and glue stick will be nearby. You may have your own method for stockpiling information—on bookshelves, in filing cabinets, on laptops. We need all the help we can get to continue nourishing our art lives and taking the risks that push us forward. We are alone together and in good company. It is up to each of us to find new ways of *making it*—in our respective studios and out in the world.

NOTES

1. Thomas Nozkowski, in *Letters to a Young Artist*, Peter Nesbett, Shelley Bancroft, and Sarah Andress, eds. (New York: Darte Publishing, 2006), 46.

2. Franz Kline, in Musa Mayer, "Stern Conditions," *Night Studio: A Memoir of Philip Guston by His Daughter* (New York: Alfred A. Knopf, 1988), 67.

3. Peter Schjeldahl, in "On Art and Artists: Peter Schjeldahl," in MaLin Wilson, ed., *The Hydrogen Jukebox: Selected Writings of Peter Schjeldahl*, 1978-1990 (Berkeley and Los Angeles: Univ. of California Press, 1991), 175.

4. Suggested publications include Jackie Battenfield, *The Artist's Guide: How to Make a Living Doing What You Love* (Philadelphia: Da Capo Press, 2009); Heather Darcy Bhandari and Jonathan Melber, *Art/Work: Everything You Need to Know (and Do) As You Pursue Your Art Career* (New York: Free Press, 2009); Michael Markowsky, *Arts in Store: Rethinking the Relationship between Art and Business* (Self-published, 2009); and Linda Weintraub, *In the Making: Creative Options for Contemporary Art* (New York: Distributed Art Publishers, 2003).

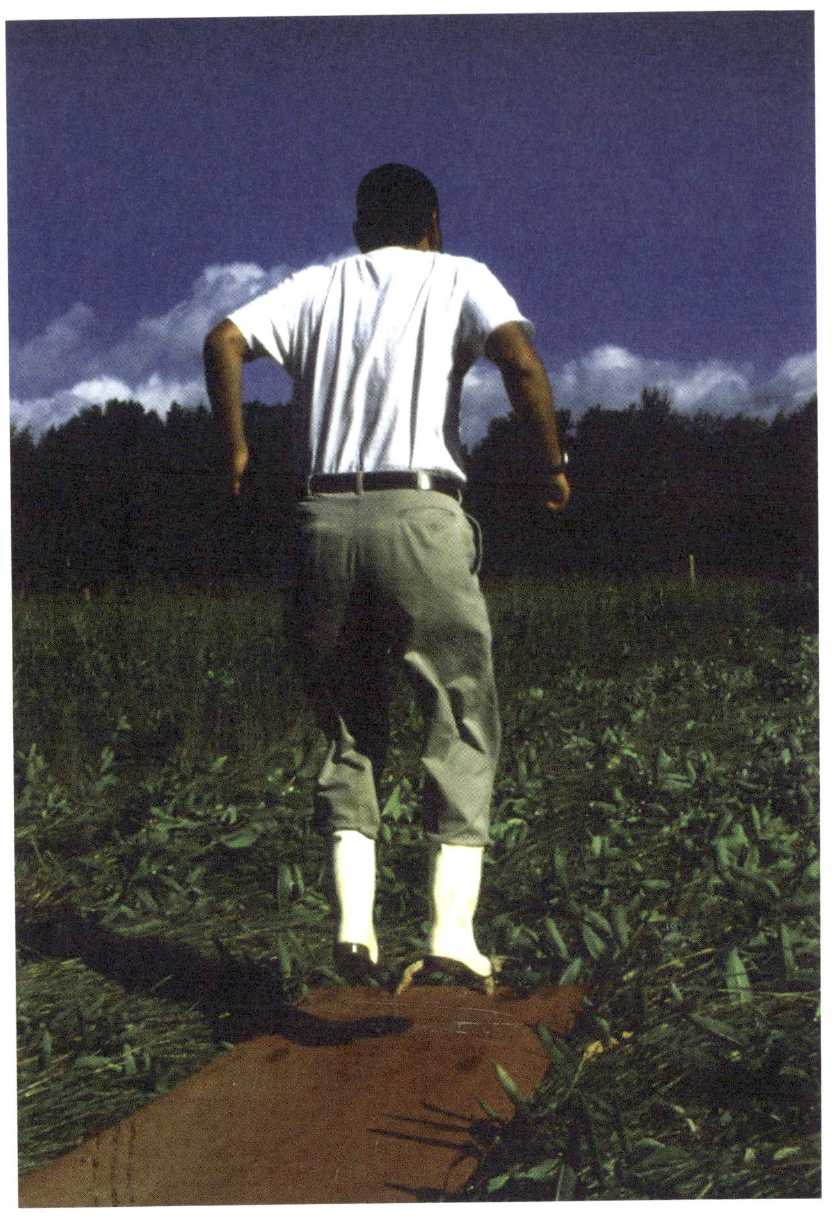

Daniel Bozhkov
Making Larry King crop sign,
How To Fly Over A Very Large Larry
2002–2003

1. MOTIVATION

In Dennis Oppenheim's sculpture *Theme for a Major Hit* (1974), motorized marionettes perform a jerky dance as the phrase "It ain't what you make, it's what makes you do it," repeats on a soundtrack. Do you know why *you* make art?

Are you trying to express yourself or solve problems? Mel Chin's *Operation Paydirt/ Fundred Dollar Bill Project* is an initiative dedicated to eradicating the lead-contaminated soil in New Orleans and others cities across the United States. Children complete Fundreds (fun hundred dollar bill templates), and become collaborators along with schools and art institutions in a nationwide exercise in community awareness and social change.

Do you like spending time alone or working with others? The Guerrilla Girls are the self-appointed "Conscience of the Art World." Since 1985, these anonymous feminists have produced sardonic posters, stickers, books, and public actions to expose the sexism, racism, and corruption in gallery and museum practices.

Do you hope to receive the respect and admiration of family members, friends, artists, audiences? Leo Castelli said, "My main motivation was to do something that would remain, something of lasting value, and especially something that would help the artists to go on with their work. Thousands of people have seen shows in my gallery, and I like to think that these shows have had their impact on the development of art."[1]

Do you have any other choice? In 1939, at the age of eighty-five, Bill Traylor suddenly began to draw silhouettes of humans and animals, filling them in with pencils or poster paints. He said, "It just come to me."[2]

You might be clear about your motives from the outset or question them repeatedly, asking, "Why do I keep doing this?" Your answers may change over time. Maybe you take great pleasure in wielding power tools and making repetitive gestures. Is this your way of dealing with *horror vacui*? Do you have legacy issues?

The following entries reveal the drive to transgress boundaries and venture into the unknown. This can feel like both a blessing and a curse, but it must be done. As Brian Bell and David Yocum, of bldgs, stated when proposing an ambitious architectural intervention for our main gallery, "This is Plan A. There is no Plan B. There is a Plan C but it is much more complicated—you really don't want to hear it."[3]

Charles Bukowski
The first thing writing must do is save your own ass.[4]

Francis Picabia
Why do you write?
I don't really know and hope I never know.[5]

Wayne Koestenbaum
Why do I want to write poems? Because I want to say what it's like inhabiting a decent male body in this decade.[6]

Tony Conrad
For me, music and art just crap out when they don't step across into non-polite spaces and outlaw territory. The job of an artist is to discover laws to violate that haven't been made yet.[7]

Joan Didion
I write entirely to find out what I'm thinking, what I'm looking at, what I see and what it means. What I want and what I fear.[8]

Arnold Glimcher
More than anything else in the world, I would like to be an artist. I'm a dealer because that's as close to the mark as I can get, but they are the people I admire, and theirs is the achievement which is paramount in cultural history.[9]

>
Stuart Horodner
Notebook
May 2005

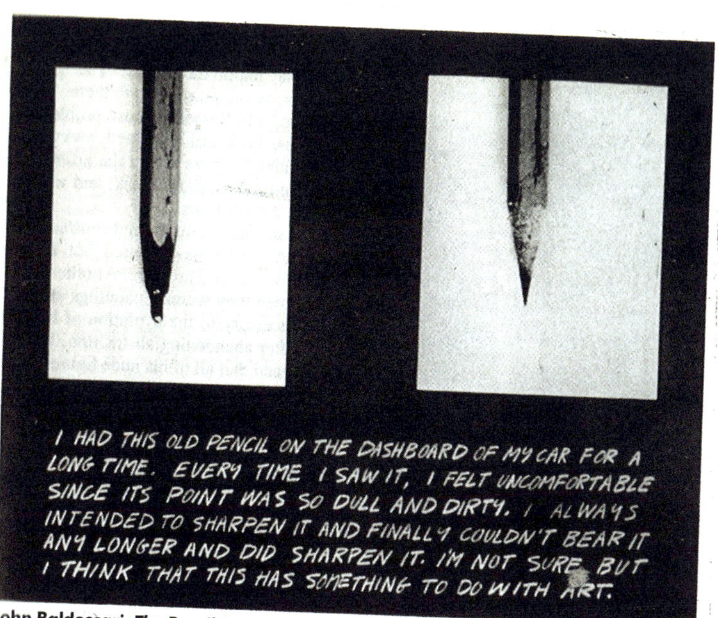

John Baldessari, *The Pencil Story*, 1972-73, two type-R prints with pencil on board, 22 by 27¼ inches. San Francisco Museum of Modern Art.

WASHINGTON, May 25 — Newly released documents show that detainees at Guantánamo Bay, Cuba, complained repeatedly to F.B.I. agents about disrespectful handling of the Koran by guards and, in one case in 2002, said that they had flushed a Koran down a toilet.

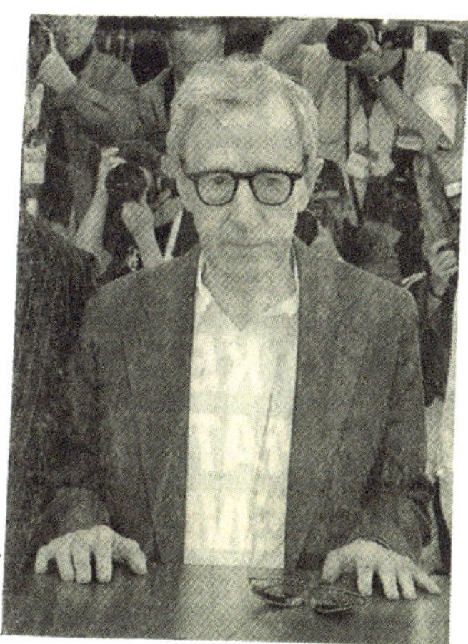

. He described his filmmaking career as the equivalent of giving a mental patient finger-painting or basket-weaving to keep them occupied.

"It's not habit. It's not for the money. It's a distraction. In my regular life, I'm consumed by depression, anxiety and terror. When I'm making a movie I get to live in a fantasy of beautiful women and charming men speaking amusing dialogue. Then when I return to real life, it's a terrible time."

Someone asked if the movie's dark conclusion implied Allen was cynical about justice.

"I think that I'm cynical in general, but for me cynical is reality, with a different spelling."

Marlene Dumas

I paint because I am afraid / to be dead while still alive.[10]

Julian Schnabel

I want my life to be embedded in my work, crushed into my painting, like a pressed car. If it's not, my work is just some stuff. When I'm away from it, I'm crippled. Without my relationship to what might seem like these inanimate objects, I am just an indulgent misfit. If the spirit of being isn't present in the face of this work, it should be destroyed because it's meaningless. I am not making some things. I am making a synonym for the truth with all its falsehoods, oblique as it is. I am making icons that present life in terms of our death. A bouquet of mistakes.[11]

Andy Moon Wilson

One of my big lifetime goals is to make a drawing that causes someone to throw up just from looking at it.[12]

Keith Richards

I'm not here just to make records and money. I'm here to say something and to touch other people, sometimes in a cry of desperation: "Do you know this feeling?"[13]

Orhan Pamuk

[...] the question we writers are asked most often, the favorite question, is: Why do you write? I write because I have an innate need to write! I write because I can't do normal work like other people. I write because I want to read books like the ones I write. I write because I am angry at all of you, angry at everyone. I write because I love sitting in a room all day writing. I write because I can only partake in real life by changing it. I write because I want others, all of us, the whole world, to know what sort of life we lived, and continue to live, in Istanbul, in Turkey. I write because I love the smell of paper, pen, and ink. I write because I believe in literature, in the art of the novel, more than I believe in anything else. I write because it is a habit, a passion. I write because I am afraid of being forgotten. I write because I like the glory and interest that writing brings. I write to be alone. Perhaps I write because I hope to understand why I am so very, very angry at all of you, so very, very angry at everyone. I write because I like to be read. I write because once I have begun a novel, an essay, a page, I want to finish it. I write because everyone expects me to write. I write because I have a childish belief in the immortality of libraries, and in the way my books sit on the shelf. I write because it is exciting to turn all life's beauties and riches into words. I write not to tell a story but to compose a story. I write because I wish to escape from the foreboding that there is a place I must go but—just as in a dream—can't quite get there. I write because I never managed to be happy. I write to be happy.[14]

Michelle Williams **Interview with Lynn Hirschberg**

LH: If you quit acting, what else would you do?

MW: That's the problem: I profoundly don't know how to do anything else. Except...I could be a pie baker. I like to bake blackberry pie. I am pretty proud of my pie skills. Pie could be my future.[15]

Eileen Myles

No one asked me to have a life like this, to be a poet. It was my idea. I mean and I would definitely say poetry is a very roundabout way to unite both work and time. A poet is a person with a very short attention span who actually decides to study it. To look. To draw that short thing out. It's an odd, feudal idea. Finally what you see is the thing you have in common with everyone else. That's the great riddle. It's not about poetry at all. Like Jimmy Schuyler once said, the writing the poem part is easy, it's the rest of the time that's the problem.[16]

Kiki Smith

I think the thing about making things is that you have a proof. You have some proof every day that something has been accomplished, that something's different. If you can make something as that proof it has a lot of power.[17]

Kerry James Marshall

I mean when the moon comes up in the evening and it's full, it's an amazing thing. And that's a phenomena that we don't have to explain; we just recognize it for what it is. It has a certain authority and a certain presence, just because it is. When there's a tornado, we may be terrified by it, but it's fascinating nonetheless because it is what it is, not because we know anything about it per se, but because we respond to what it is. That's what I mean by a phenomenological existence. So when artists make things, I think we attempt to make things that have the same kind of authority, or the same kind of presence, as things like the moon, like the sun, like a tornado, like a rock—where you see it and you know it.[18]

Marina Abramović

All the aggressive actions I do to myself I would never dream of doing in my own life—I am not this kind of person. I cry if I cut myself peeling potatoes. I am taking the plane, there is turbulence, I am shaking. In performance, I become, somehow, like not a mortal. All my insecurities—having a fat body, skinny body, big ass, long nose, a guy, being abandoned, whatever—aren't important. [...] What makes it art? Context and intention. The sense of purpose I feel to do something heroic, legendary, and transformative; to elevate viewers' spirits and give them courage. If I can go through the door of pain to embrace life on the other side, they can too.[19]

Roger Ebert

Werner Herzog and Errol Morris have been friends for a very long time, from the days in the 1970s when Morris saw Herzog's first films at the Univ. of Wisconsin and decided to become a filmmaker. Errol told Herzog of a film he wanted to shoot, but kept delaying. Herzog told him he needed more self-discipline. He added: "If you make this film, I'll eat my shoe."

That led to a famous evening at the Pacific Film archive in Berkeley, at which Herzog sat on the stage and did indeed eat his shoe. He was assisted in its preparation by the famous chef Alice Waters—perhaps suggesting that you can find everything you don't want at Alice's Restaurant. The meal was the subject of a famous documentary by Les Blank titled *Werner Herzog Eats His Shoe*.[20]

David Humphrey

We artists should not underestimate the importance of the stories we tell ourselves about how art will make a difference. These motivational fictions describe the ways a work might interact with the world to justify our extravagant, and potentially narcissistic, labors: that our art has transformational potential. A work might be understood as being critical of society or sanctuary from it, for instance, or a Trojan horse sent to the enemy as a nasty gift to unsettle their deeply entrenched frames of mind. We need renewable encouragement to make fresh work year after year in the face of uncertain rewards.[21]

Mike Kelley Interview with John Miller

JM: I remember when you first started doing the arrangements on the blankets and the afghans, and you joked that they were like Haim Steinbach's sculpture.

MK: That's true. I was thinking a lot about Haim Steinbach when I did them, Except I was trying to put all the things into them that I felt Haim left out of his. What I saw Haim Steinbach doing was working with this ideal—art about the commodity in terms of a classical notion of perfection. To do that you have to separate the objects from the world, put them on a stage or in a frame, like theatre or a movie. They are out of this world, that's how his shelves function. Then the objects never change, they're fetishized as being perpetually brand new. They're not allowed to wear out. What I wanted was to have something that was worn yet not nostalgic.[22]

Peter Schjeldahl Interview with Robert Storr

RS: I want to ask about the choices you make of who to write for and what kind of freedom that gives you. You have written for the art magazines—for all of them really—and also for the *New York Times* as well as for the wide circulation "glossies." I was wondering how the decision to write for one or another came about?

PS: Usually I was asked in the first place. In a way, as a writer, I don't feel that I work for publications so much as I work for editors. I write a lot for *Art in America*, when I do write for the magazines, because Betsy Baker is the editor. And when I wrote for the *Times*, I was very lucky because the editor of the Arts and Leisure section then was Seymour Peck, who I think a lot of New York writers will pay homage to. I once figured out my two criteria for an editor. One is that he let me do anything I want and two that he not let me make a fool of myself unwittingly. And also that he be a very good word craftsman, who is openly thrilled by good writing. I'll knock myself out to please an editor like that.[23]

Bob Dylan

A song is like a dream, and you try to make it come true. They're like strange countries that you have to enter. You can write a song anywhere, in a railroad compartment, on a boat, on horseback—it helps to be moving. Sometimes people who have the greatest talent for writing songs never write any because they are not moving.[24]

Hélène Cixous

Writing: a way of leaving no space for death, of pushing back forgetfulness, of never letting oneself be surprised by the abyss. Of never becoming resigned, consoled; never turning over in bed to face a wall and drift asleep again as if nothing had happened; as if nothing could happen.[25]

Padgett Powell

Would you rate yourself as more tired than you used to be or as a person who still has all the get-up-and-go that it takes?[26]

NOTES

1. Leo Castelli, in Alan Jones and Laura de Coppet, *The Art Dealers: The Powers Behind the Scene Tell How the Art World Works* (New York: Clarkson N. Potter, 1984), 109.

2. Bill Traylor, in Jane Livingston and John Beardsley, *Black Folk Art in America 1930–1980*, Exhibition catalogue (Corcoran Gallery of Art, Washington, DC, 1982), 139.

3. Brian Bell and David Yocum, e-mail to author, Nov 13, 2008.

4. Charles Bukowski, in Suzanne Lummis, "Charles Bukowski, 1920–1994," *Los Angeles Times* (Apr 10, 1994), http://articles.latimes.com/1994-04-10/books/bk-44148_1_charles-bukowski, accessed Jun 18, 2011.

5. Francis Picabia, "Survey," in "You Bunch of Idiots: Dada, 1919–1921," *I am a Beautiful Monster: Poetry, Prose, and Provocation*, Translated by Marc Lowenthal (Cambridge and London: MIT Press, 2007), 180, from "Réponse à l'enquête," in Littérature 12 (Feb 1920), 2.

6. Wayne Koestenbaum, in Peter Halley, "Wayne Koestenbaum," *Index Magazine* (1999), http://www.indexmagazine.com/interviews/wayne_koestenbaum.shtml, accessed Jun 18, 2011.

7. Tony Conrad, in Brian Duguid, "Tony Conrad," *EST* (Jun 1996), http://media.hyperreal.org/zines/est/intervs/conrad.html, accessed Feb 21, 2011.

8. Joan Didion, "*Why I Write*," *New York Times Magazine* (Dec 5, 1976).

9. Arnold Glimcher, in Jones and de Coppet, *The Art Dealers*, 173.

10. Marlene Dumas, in *Marlene Dumas: Measuring Your Own Grave*, Exhibition brochure (The Menil Collection, Houston, 2009), n.p.

11. Julian Schnabel, "1978: Madrid," *CVJ: Nicknames of Maitre D's & Other Excerpts from Life* (New York: Random House, 1987), 146.

12. Andy Moon Wilson, conversation with author, Jun 2010.

13. Keith Richards, in Liz Phair, "Stray Cat Blues," *New York Times Book Review* (Nov 14, 2010): 11.

14. Orhan Pamuk, "My Father's Suitcase: The Nobel Lecture," *Other Colors: Essays and a Story*, Translated by Maureen Freely (Toronto: Alfred A. Knopf Canada, 2007), 415.

15. Michelle Williams, in Lynn Hirschberg, "Heart to Heart: Michelle Williams & Ryan Gosling," *W* (Oct 2010): 142.

16. Eileen Myles, *Inferno (A Poet's Novel)* (New York: O/R Books, 2010), 108.

17. Kiki Smith, in Art21, "Kiki Smith: Learning by Looking: Witches, Catholicism, and Buddhist Art," *Art21*, http://www.pbs.org/art21/artists/smith/clip1.html, accessed May 17, 2011.

18. Kerry James Marshall, in Art21, "Kerry James Marshall: RHYTHM MASTR," *Art21*, http://www.pbs.org/art21/artists/marshall/clip2.html, accessed May 17, 2011.

19. Marina Abramović, in Judith Thurman, "Walking Through Walls: Marina Abramović's Performance Art," *The New Yorker* (Mar 8, 2010). http://archives.newyorker.com/?i=2010-03-08#folio=024, accessed Aug 8, 2010.

20. Roger Ebert, "Roger Ebert's Journal: Werner & Errol & the Images in Their Caves," *Chicago Sun Times* (Sep 13, 2010), http://blogs.suntimes.com/ebert/2010/09/werner_errol_the_images_in_the.html, accessed Feb 21, 2011.

21. David Humphrey, "Hi, My Name is Artwork," *Blind Handshake* (New York: Periscope, 2009), 25.

22. Mike Kelley, in John Miller, *Mike Kelley*, Edited by William S. Bartman and Miyoshi Barosh (New York: A.R.T. Press, 1992), 19.

23. Peter Schjeldahl, in "On Art and Artists: Peter Schjeldahl," in MaLin Wilson, ed., *The Hydrogen Jukebox: Selected Writings of Peter Schjeldahl, 1978–1990* (Berkeley and Los Angeles: Univ. of California Press, 1991), 170–171.

24. Bob Dylan, "Oh Mercy," *Chronicles: Volume One* (New York: Simon & Schuster, 2004), 165.

25.Hélène Cixous, "Coming to Writing," in Hélène Cixous, *"Coming to Writing" and Other Essays*, Edited by Deborah Jenson (Cambridge, MA: Harvard Univ. Press, 1991), 3.

26. Padgett Powell, *The Interrogative Mood* (New York: HarperCollins, 2009), 48.

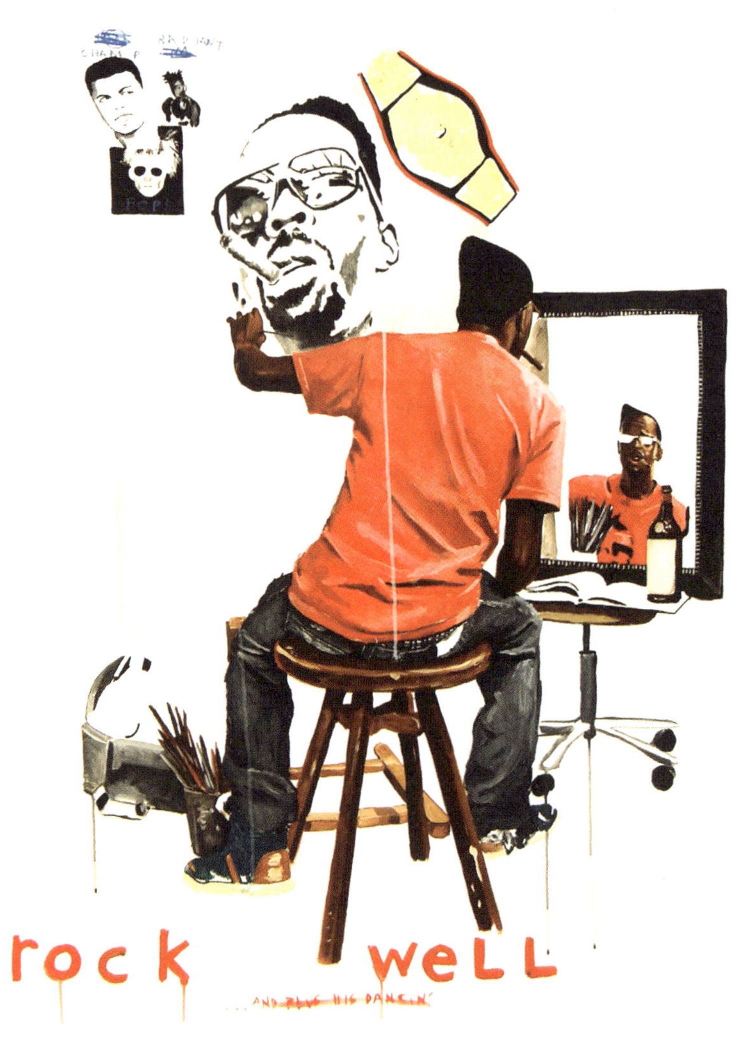

Fahamu Pecou
Rock...Well (Radiant Pop Champ)
2010

2. INFLUENCE

Books, artworks, places, and people that we know (or know about) influence our ideas and activities. They inform us about what is possible or permissible, and provide role models to test ourselves against. When asked about his affinity to Picasso's painterly style in the late 1930s, Arshile Gorky replied, "If he drips, I drip."[1] When Fahamu Pecou set out to portray himself in *Rock…Well (Radiant Pop Champ)* (2010), an interpretation of Norman Rockwell's famous 1960 *Triple Self-Portrait* for the cover of *The Saturday Evening Post*, he depicts a cigar smoking realist watched over by his personal wise men—Muhammad Ali, Andy Warhol, and Jean-Michel Basquiat.

As freshman art students at The Cooper Union, Hans Haacke made us buy Lucy Lippard's *Six Years: The Dematerialization of the Art Object from 1966 to 1972*, as required reading for his sculpture class. I was unaware of the possibilities beyond traditional forms and sanctioned art spaces, and this reference book jump-started my interest in site specificity, durational performance, archives, and ephemera. It introduced me to Eleanor Antin, Mel Bochner, Douglas Huebler, On Kawara, Richard Long, Joseph Beuys, and many others. I must credit Lippard's presentation of fragments of text, artworks, documents, and interviews with providing me an inclusive overview of the conceptual practices that were taking place in the years after my birth and before my bar mitzvah.

I've always been drawn to the example of multi-taskers, perhaps because they have given me the confidence to pursue different creative outlets at the same time. I'm encouraged by artists who write, musicians who draw or paint, film directors who act, and so on. Maybe it's because I have not always known what I wanted to do until I found myself doing it.

Frank O'Hara was a poet, critic, and curator at The Museum of Modern Art. His work expresses the belief that a profound engagement with art and literature, and the cultivation of love and friendship, is evidence of a life fully lived. I wholeheartedly agree. This section of his poem "Having a Coke With You" (1966) is a fine example:

I look
at you and I would rather look at you than all the portraits in the world
except possibly for the *Polish Rider* occasionally and anyway it's in the Frick
which thank heavens you haven't gone to yet so we can go together the first time
and the fact that you move so beautifully more or less takes care of Futurism
just as at home I never think of the *Nude Descending a Staircase* or
at a rehearsal a single drawing of Leonardo or Michelangelo that used to wow me
and what good does all the research of the Impressionists do them
when they never got the right person to stand near the tree when the sun sank
or for that matter Marino Marini when he didn't pick the rider as carefully
as the horse
it seems they were all cheated of some marvelous experience
which is not going to go wasted on me which is why I'm telling you about it [2]

Alice Neel's portraits of family members, neighbors, businessmen, and the creative community combine a coloring book certainty and a hint of caricature. I cherish any opportunity to see them. In her nude self-portrait at age eighty, she turned her observational acumen and curiosity on herself, depicting a piercing gaze, cascading flesh, and kinetic right foot. This no-nonsense painting has always reminded me to embrace audacity and candor.

Leon Golub was my mentor. He was a painter, educator, and agitator who was constantly tilting at windmills in the form of powerful political figures and the agencies that were responsible for war, torture, and corruption. Golub saw art-making as a heroic and idealistic enterprise fraught with contradictions and hurdles. He was more than capable of dealing with these while keeping a healthy sense of humor.

Brad Cloepfil Interview with Stuart Horodner

SH: How has life in Oregon affected your work?

BC: Two things. If you want to look for architecture that was evocative and powerful here in the Pacific Northwest, you didn't look at buildings. You looked elsewhere, at the dam system on the Columbia River, at the silos in eastern

Oregon built out of laminated 2 x 10s. Some of the old log flumes that go for miles still exist. There are other forms of architecture that are more interesting constructions and more bold. That's empowering and liberating because you don't have to worry about it being judged by your faculty, or the architectural community or your own sense of propriety. You can just go be moved, surprised and emboldened by these things that were not done intentionally per se. In a way, it was like the old days with Charles Moore looking at vernacular architecture. This is looking at civil engineering, 10 miles of snow fence and starting to understand that kind of power, that certain built acts can really move you. It gets into the sublime. It's real, they're not intellectual ideas, it's like landscape. You go out on the Columbia River Gorge, or the Wallowa Canyon or Hell's Canyon and you are awed and moved by the purity of form and space.[3]

Jørgen Leth

For me, poetry has a strong link to my filmmaking. My films learn from my poetry. In poetry, you're free. You start in the corner and you don't know where it leads you. I have no message, I have nothing I want to tell, I just start and see where it leads, and it's a big surprise and relief if it's good. That's the ideal state for filmmaking. I like the idea of chance coming into filmmaking, in shooting, in editing, and I do make space in my rules of game for chance. William Burroughs, Andy Warhol and John Cage are major influences for my work. Godard is the only cineastic influence.[4]

Morton Feldman

I'll tell you how I got my opening. I got it from Kafka. I read an article once on Kafka, and I was very fond of Kafka. You'll notice Kafka's first sentences: "Someone has been telling lies about Joseph K." You know that's Kafka, you are in the world of Kafka. We were all reading Kafka in New York at about twenty, twenty-one, fantastic thing. I took that idea and I put it into my own music. Kafka definitely influenced my feeling of how to begin a piece. Immediately in the atmosphere.[5]

Karyn Olivier

I often think of Tony Hepburn who was my ceramics professor at grad school. I vividly remember the day he came into my studio and said, "Everything in here is dead; there's no life in these objects. Stop using clay for the next month." It was a startling command—scary, really. My only true experience with art-making at that time was through clay. It took me a few days to realize that he wanted me to focus on the ideas—not to worry myself with questions like, "How can I make this out of clay knowing the material's limitations?" It cannily forced me to see that it was possible to develop an idea for a work without first and foremost thinking about how it might be achieved through the use of clay—maybe another material would actually make more sense, conceptually, to use. The idea, material and process work in concert with each other, of course, but it's ok to focus on just the conceptual framework initially, too. I now teach (in a sculpture department), but each semester I find myself quoting Tony for the benefit of the students as much as for myself—"the quality of the questions you ask yourself is in direct correlation to the quality and sophistication of the work produced." It resonates today with the same intensity it did twelve years ago.[6]

Tony Tasset

When I was a kid I always drew and I had books on Norman Rockwell, Walt Disney and the fantasy illustrator Frank Frazetta. Then I went to art school and of course rejected all those kitschy works. Recently I've realized those guys really influenced me because even if their message was pabulum, pro-American propaganda, and soft-core teenage fantasy, they did have a great power to communicate. I am probably more influenced by pop-culture these days than art. I want to make art like a Philip Roth novel or a Bob Dylan album.

I do not want to individuate my own touch, instead I want to honor the everyday and connect myself to other people, not separate myself. I see pumpkin carving, and snowman making as populist traditions of figurative sculpture making—contemporary ephemeral totem. And although their images are often used to sell things, the vernacular traditions themselves are not capitalist driven. I want to take something as common as a snowman and see if I can charge it with the emotional complexity of a Giacometti or a Rodin. When I made my first sad snowman I built a real sad snowman in my front yard as a model to look at. We had had one of those big Chicago snows and there were snowmen up and down the street, but only mine had a sad frown. After only one night my snowman had been knocked down while all the other smiling snowmen on the street were still intact. I theorized that there was something sacrilegious or unpatriotic about my Prozac deprived Frosty. When my snowman got knocked down I knew I was on to something.[7]

Mike Kelley

The most frightening media things I can remember from my childhood was a puppet show on a children's TV program about a puppet in one of these little prosceniums who was supposed to be on an endless stairway and falls off into nothingness. You just hear the voice: "Oooooooo..." For years that has been my ideal. If I could make something that moving, that could have you frightened for the

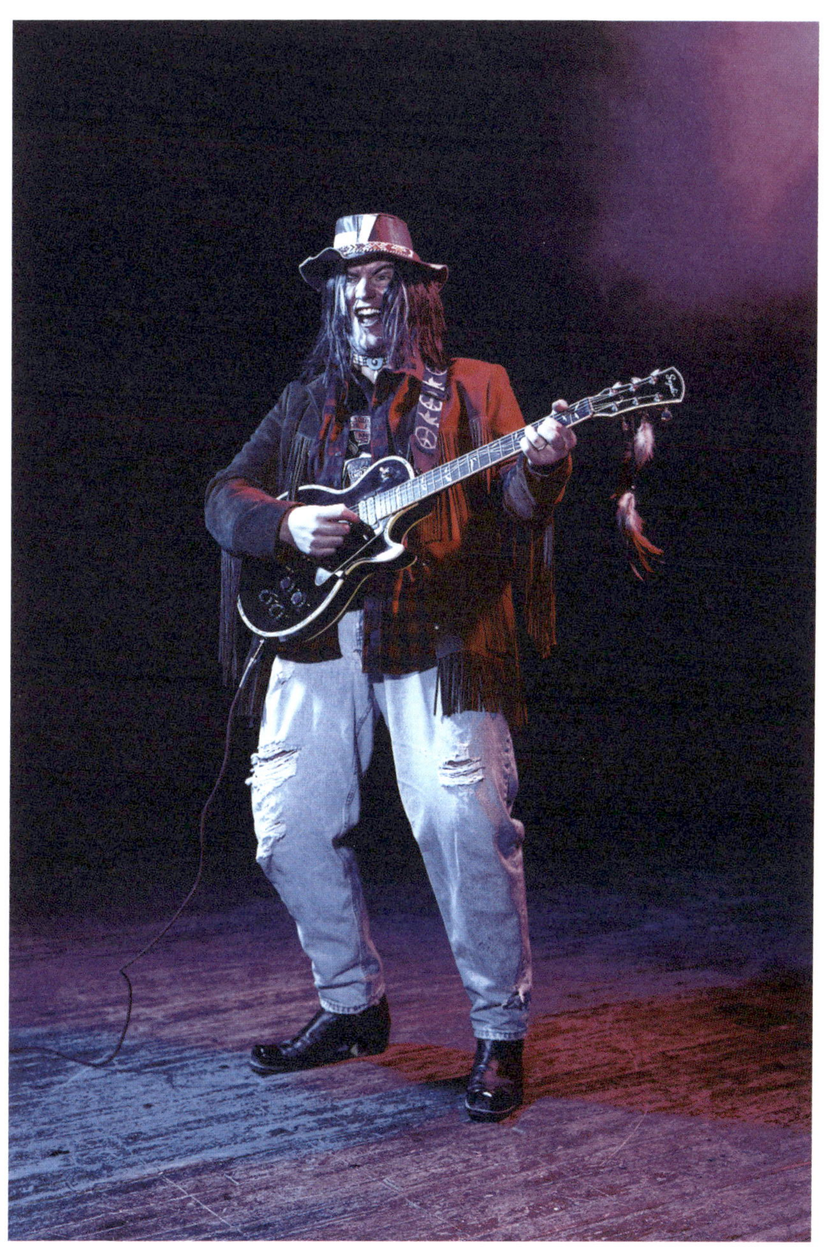

Tony Tasset
Neil Young
1997

rest of your life, and all it was was a piece of clay that falls off a piece of cardboard ... That so much emotion could be invested in this piece of shit—that's amazing.[8]

Tom Friedman

When I think about artists who have influenced me recently, I don't distinguish much between one or the other. I think everything I see and consider influences me in some way. It's interesting because art, visual art, doesn't affect me that much for some reason. It could have something to do with the mystery of it, that I feel I've already gone through it. Music is something that has that mystery for me. It really affects me, and I feel I've been more influenced by music than visual art. It's really odd that I don't get much out of looking at art, because I make objects and I hope people enjoy looking at them.[9]

Matt Bryans

I've always read a lot. To me, my newspaper works reminds me of George Orwell's character Winston's job in *1984*. His book *Why I Write* stays with me... "a generation of the unteachable is hanging upon us like a necklace of corpses." Graham Greene, William Golding, J.G. Ballard. Too many to mention. I like portable knowledge, but I also like libraries. That's why writers get through to me, and move with me through my life more than any "visual" artists ever have. No idea what THAT says about why I need to make things.[10]

Craig Drennen

My own circulation through the art world brought me two moments where I was usefully dislocated by aberrant paintings. The first was Jonathan Borofsky's 1980 installation at Paula Cooper Gallery, which I saw only in reproduction. In this instance it was not the ping-pong table, the trash bags, nor the accumulation of drawings on the floor that astonished me—it was the largish figure painting in the center of the room propped up by means of a single stick. The second case came years later when, as a museum worker in New York City, I was assigned the duty of installing Rauschenberg's *Monogram* combine from 1959 only to be beguiled by the lumpy glory of paint on a dead goat's nose.[11]

Byron Kim

My role models were Ad Reinhardt and Robert Smithson. Lately, I have been likely to take on a new one every year: Paul Farmer, Jane Goodall, Fred Rogers even.[12]

WILL.I.AM Interview with Steve Marsh

SM: A lot of poets and songwriters are trying really hard to say something nobody's said before.

W: No, no, no. There's no such thing as never said it before. Everything has been said. Anything that you can say, somebody's said it already. It's *how* you say it.[13]

Allan Kaprow

Pollock, as I see him, left us at the point where we must become preoccupied with and even dazzled by the space and objects of our everyday life, either our bodies, clothes, rooms, or if need be, the vastness of Forty-Second Street. Not satisfied with the suggestion through paint of our other senses, we shall utilize the specific substances of sight, sound, movements, people, odors, touch. Objects of every sort are materials for the new art: paint, chairs, food, electric and neon lights, smoke, water, old socks, a dog, movies, a thousand other things that will be discovered by the present generation of artists. Not only will these bold creators show us, as if for the first time, the world we have always had about us but ignored, but they will disclose entirely unheard-of-happenings and events, found in garbage cans, police files, hotel lobbies; seen in store windows and on the streets; and sensed in dreams and horrible accidents. An odor of crushed strawberries, a letter from a friend, or a billboard selling Drano; three taps on the front door, a scratch, a sigh, or a voice lecturing endlessly, a blinding staccato flash, a bowler hat—all will become materials for this new concrete art.[14]

Jasper Johns

The idea did come to me that I should have to mean what I did. Then, accompanying that was the idea that there was no reason to mean what other people did. So, if I could tell that I was doing what someone else was doing, then I would try not to do it, because it seemed to me that de Kooning did his work perfectly beautifully and there was no reason for me to help him with it.[15]

Beck

I think in pop music there's certain stones or markers that are unavoidable. There's this part of the minerals of the geology of how we operate and grow in music. That would be The Beatles, Neil Young, Dylan, Joni Mitchell, Sly Stone, James Brown, Aretha, David Bowie...everybody knows them. They're beyond being taken for granted. What can you possibly say about them that hasn't been said already? So you move from there and try to get into your own thing, your own life. But I'm not concerned with things that are revelations, just things that are more contributions to the grander scheme—this thing that was set in motion so long ago. I mean how can we fool ourselves and pretend that we are some driving force to it. It's like there's a car going down the hill at sixty miles an hour, and you're just running along pretending you're pushing it. By all your efforts and might, you are some sort of martyr for the cause of keeping it moving. Well, it's moving and it's going

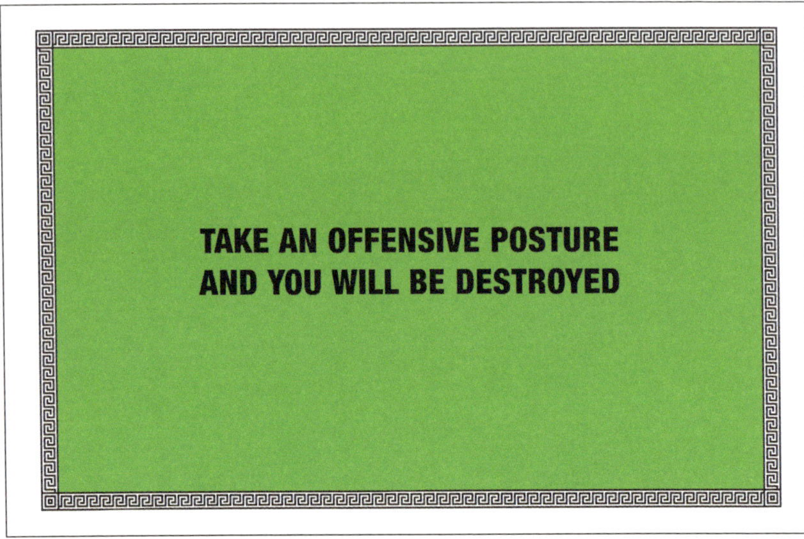

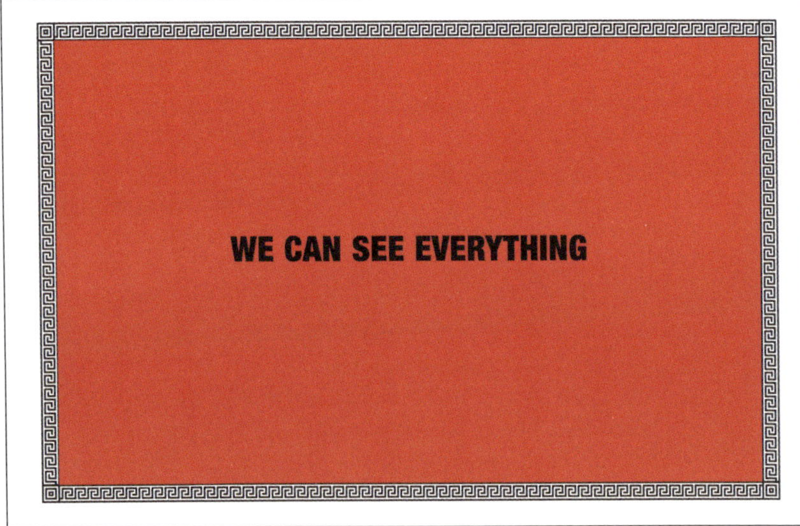

Susan Silton
by power of suggestion,
which in favorable circumstances
becomes instruction, #4, #5
2006

to outpace all of us someday. And I'm going to step back and let some kids fuck it up and make it cooler than any of us ever did. That's just the cycle of things.[16]

Jennie C. Jones

"It's taken me all my life to learn what not to play."

I think I love that quote from Dizzy [Gillespie] so much because learning what not to play is understanding the power in the sparse, understanding the weight and power of empty space, like a rest in music. Over the years my work has become more about removal and reduction—pairing things down to the critical elements.[17]

R.B. Kitaj

I'd like to try, not only to do Cézanne and Degas over again after Surrealism, but after Auschwitz, after [the] Gulag.[18]

Andy Warhol

I want to be like Matisse.[19]

Susan Silton Interview with Stuart Horodner

SH: I'm going to go right to the question that you hate the most, and we'll see where that leads us. Who or what have been the most significant influences on you?

SS: I'll tell you why I hate that question: Because that changes about every five seconds. The answer to that question changes depending on my mood that day.

Probably my earliest influence in terms of a creative process, it sounds so hokey, but my grandfather was a humongous stamp collector from the old country. Austria. All of the paraphernalia, the accoutrements of stamp collecting were incredibly influential to me as a child sitting on his knee—tweezers, hinges, and stamps themselves. And he had books, endless amounts of books of stamps. And I remember being old enough to know about the Holocaust, but not really understanding what that was, and remembering his countless books of stamps bearing the picture of Hitler on them. And in a variety of colors and shapes and sizes and just being dazzled by both the politics of it and the strangeness of this Austrian Jew, some of whose family was lost in the Holocaust, collecting these stamps of Hitler. And being aware of the formalist qualities of the stamps themselves and the pictures on the stamps, as well as the political weight of that and the disjuncture of this man, this Jew, old Jew, collecting these stamps of this person, this historical figure who obviously lived very large in his life.

SH: I find it amazing that the first work of yours that I ever saw came through the mail.[20]

Tom Waits Interview with Tom Waits

TW: List some artists who have shaped your creative life.

TW: Okay, here are a few that just come to me for now: Kerouac, Dylan, Bukowski, Rod Serling, Don Van Vliet, Cantinflas, James Brown, Harry Belafonte, Ma Rainey, Big Mama Thorton, Howlin Wolf, Lead Belly, Lord Buckley, Mabel Mercer, Lee Marvin, Thelonious Monk, John Ford, Fellini, Weegee, Jagger, Richards, Willie Dixon, John McCormick, Johnny Cash, Hank Williams, Frank Sinatra, Louis Armstrong, Robert Johnson, Hoagy Carmichael, Enrico Caruso.[21]

Anya Liftig

Somebody who is really influential to me is the character of Mary Richards on *The Mary Tyler Moore Show*. In terms of video, William Wegman videos are really influential. And I would also say writers like A.J. Liebling and Joseph Mitchell. If you put these things together you are like, "What is she talking about?" And really strong visual images like Dunkin' Donuts are very important to me. And Walter Matthau. But probably the person that is very, very important to me above all is Peter Sellers. I would probably say the thing that I think about most is *The Party*. Peter Sellers in *The Party* and that sort of blind silent stupidity.[22]

Willem de Kooning

In a piece on Arshile Gorky's memorial show—and it was a very little piece indeed—it was mentioned that I was one of his influences. Now that is plain silly. When, about fifteen years ago, I walked into Arshile's studio for the first time, the atmosphere was so beautiful that I got a little dizzy and when I came to, I was bright enough to take the hint immediately. If the bookkeepers think it necessary continuously to make sure of where things and people come from, well then, I come from 36 Union Square [Gorky's studio]. It is incredible to me that other people live there now. I am glad that it is about impossible to get away from his powerful influence. As long as I keep it with myself I'll be doing all right. Sweet Arshile, bless your dear heart.[23]

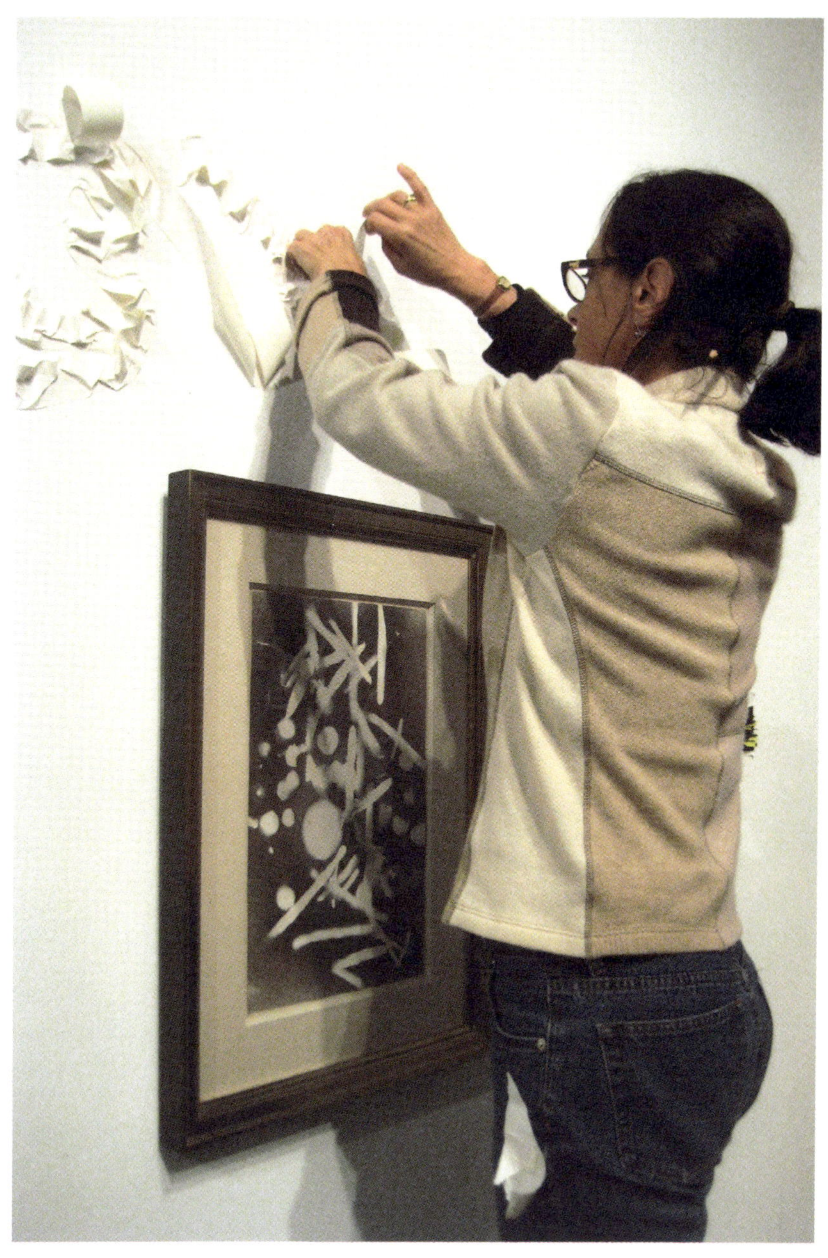

Rebecca Smith
Making *Birthday*
2008

David Smith

Do you think you owe your teachers anything, or Picasso or Matisse or Brancusi or Mondrian or Kandinsky?[24]

Rebecca Smith Interview with Michael Coffey

MC: Your work, *Birthday*, was a commissioned "response" to a specific artwork by your father, David Smith. Can you describe how you made it?

RS: I began by thinking about horizon lines and "traveling lines." I'd worked with traveling lines before, and they relate to my interest in Australian Aboriginal art in which lines traversing major areas of a painting, cave drawing or even body painting are commonly found.

I started out by doing some sketchbook drawings with a lot of lines and different colors of tape traveling the whole wall in many layers, not on top of each other but rising up the wall. That's how I first conceived of it, and I planned to edit many of the tape lines out when I worked on the real thing. I also thought of putting pieces of paper on the wall, echoing the frame of the pictorial work. I also had planned on stenciling my hand with spray paint because one of the associations with David's spray drawing is its relationship to early human spray drawings in caves: people would blow pigment through a hollow plant stem to stencil their hand prints on a wall. That was always a plan.

When I got to the real wall at the Atlanta Contemporary Art Center, I realized it would be just too loud and domineering to have many, many stripes in a Navaho blanket effect on this wall, so I decided to simply make notations for the orientations of things instead. One of the first things I made was the long blue line about a foot and half off the floor. Another very early move was the purple or lavender drape. It's like tape without a sticky side. Then I placed my father's spray drawing at around that point. I did those rising horizontals as a way to note where, potentially, the beginning of these lines could be. I thought that I would extend the colored tape lines further but as I was working on it, it seemed excessive, and I decided I wanted to leave a lot of the space empty. The piece seemed to speak so clearly at that point that I didn't want to embellish; in fact, I took some things away. I did want the white tape—I'd never used white tape before—and I thought it would be really interesting to do that. And I wanted to embellish with that, and have it be really baroque, and kind of demented and travel all the way across the 30 foot wall. It ended up traveling towards the [spray] drawing and then I decided to make a kind of flourish and a sort of nesting riff around the [spray] drawing.

Eventually I realized I was coming to the end of the wall and how was I going to end the white tape? At this point I should say that in doing this—and it was two and a half days to make this work—I was really excited and a little bit apprehensive about "meeting" my father in this form, but as I was making the piece I realized that whatever meaning was going to come out of it was just going to come, and I didn't want to think about it consciously during the process. I was just going to be open. Associations did come to me, later, but only after I had made the work.

The two blank pieces of paper were like absences, the general sparseness of marks and events suggested a kind of absence and that for me, famously like Barack Obama, my father was more an absence than a presence for most of my life. Although I have very strong memories of him, I was only 11 when he died and lived far away for most of the time growing up even before his death. I wasn't with him that much. That lilac line says something very evocative to me about my girlhood. I had a birthday party the theme colors of which were purple and pink. I thought it was really quite fabulous that all my streamers and balloons and decorations were purple and pink. I remember the pleasure in those colors and the festoonery of that drapery and so on and that's what association that part of the piece has for me. There is also an association with funeral draping, with purple as a funereal color.

MC: I understand that, although people have often been interested in knowing how your work might or might not relate to your father's work, you have resisted talking about it. Is it true that you have just begun to think about the connections and influences? Do you have a sense that now is the time, in your career, to do this?

RS: I was certainly ready to do so in this situation. Yes, I am trying to think about it and talk about it. It has been interesting to think about, but I've come to the conclusion with this project that there's really no kind of planning, no conscious thinking about it that's as helpful as just letting things emerge, as they did in this case in considering the proximity of his work on the same wall. I realized I had braided these three tape lines—I thought of my mother, my father and myself—my mother had died recently, less than a year ago. So I had these three lines, they seemed like life lines, and I had two of the lines end, and one of them not.

MC: I also noted the yellow-and-black caution tape in a couple of places, the kind you might see around a work site or a crime scene. What prompted those references?

RS: It seemed to be a good tape to use because it's about danger and there is a lot of danger in life, and I associate that with my father, too, to a degree. The sculptor Richard Deacon sent me that tape after I had been in a serious car accident. My father died in a car accident. I liked the association with a certain kind of code or directions or uses, so I used a red-and-white and green-and-white striped tape as well.

The aluminum foil tape is kind of an inside joke. I worked on these rising layers of tape quite a long time. These little pieces of tape had to occupy the big wash of white wall in a very particular way. The top one is located almost at the ceiling, but not quite. It's shiny, silver, aluminum foil tape, a little homage to my father, a reference to his stainless steel sculptures, and it's at the very top.[25]

Richard Serra

I had never really looked at Brancusi, and for me, seeing Brancusi for the first time was like a painter seeing Cézanne for the first time: you have to acknowledge the simplicity and the resulting structure of what the guy did. There's no way of getting around it. Also, Brancusi had an added hit in that he got a lot of emotional content into the simplest of forms. I was interested in the fact that the volume seemed to be drawn on the edge, that where he either cut with an axe or where he stopped modeling seemed to be places where the drawing decisions were made. To me, it was interesting to draw from him as from anyone else. I think I really wasn't interested in making sculpture, and I probably didn't understand that Brancusi was going to be a backbone for me, or a core source, until I started just screwing around with different materials. When I really had to start making something by looking at what was relevant and what was not, what was extraneous, silly, trivial, poetic, and what I wanted to do rather than what everybody else wanted to do, to me, Brancusi seemed to be better at making sculpture than anyone else in the century. I think that you pick your heroes and ghosts according to what you want to use or what's useful to you in terms of how you want to grow, and different people haunt your studio at different times. Very early in my career Brancusi was very, very instrumental.[26]

NOTES

1. Arshile Gorky, in Hayden Herrera, *Arshile Gorky: His Life and Work* (New York: Farrar, Straus and Giroux, 2003): 180.

2. Frank O'Hara, "Having a Coke with You," in Donald Allen, ed., *The Selected Poems of Frank O'Hara* (New York: Vintage Books, 1974), 175–176.

3. Brad Cloepfil, in Stuart Horodner, "Brad Cloepfil," *Bomb* (Spring 2005): 45–46.

4. Jørgen Leth, in Anthony Kaufman, "Breaking Von Trier: Jorgen Leth Survives 'The Five Obstructions,'" *Indiewire.com* (May 26, 2004), http://www.indiewire.com/article/breaking_von_trier_jorgen_leth_survives_the_five_obstructions, accessed May 17, 2011.

5. Morton Feldman, "The Future of Local Music," in B. H. Friedman, ed., *Give My Regards to Eighth Street: Collected Writings of Morton Feldman* (Cambridge, MA: Exact Change, 2000), 163.

6. Karyn Olivier, e-mail to author, Apr 10, 2011.

7. Tony Tasset, e-mail to author, Oct 28, 2007.

8. Mike Kelley, in John Miller, *Mike Kelley*, Edited by William S. Bartman and Miyoshi Barosh (New York: A.R.T. Press, 1992), 51.

9. Tom Friedman, in "Interview: Dennis Cooper in Conversation with Tom Friedman," in Bruce Hainley, Dennis Cooper, and Adrian Searle, *Tom Friedman* (London: Phaidon Press, 2001), 24.

10. Matt Bryans, e-mail to author, Mar 20, 2011.

11. Craig Drennen, e-mail to author, Dec 28, 2010.

12. Byron Kim, e-mail to author, Mar 31, 2010.

13. WILL.I.AM, in Steve Marsh, "Black Eyed Peas," *Sky* (Feb 2011): 54.

14. Allan Kaprow, "The Legacy of Jackson Pollock (1958)," *Essays on the Blurring of Art and Life*, Edited by Jeff Kelley (Berkeley and Los Angeles: Univ. of California Press, 1993), 7–9.

15. Jasper Johns, in "Art comes from neither art nor life," in Emile de Antonio and Mitch Tuchman, *Painters Painting: A Candid History of the Modern Art Scene*, 1940–1970 (New York: Abbeville Press, 1984), 87–88.

16. Beck, in Carlo McCormick, "Interview with Beck Hansen," in Beck Hansen and Al Hansen, *Playing with Matches* (Santa Monica, CA: Smart Art Press, 1995), 70.

17. Jennie C. Jones, e-mail to author, Jun 1, 2011.

18. R.B. Kitaj, in Richard Morphet, "The Art of R.B. Kitaj: 'To thine own self be true,'" in Richard Morphet, ed., *R.B. Kitaj: A Retrospective*, Exhibition catalogue (Tate Gallery, Millbank, London, 1994), 22, 34n48, from "A Return to London" (interview with Timothy Hyman), *London Magazine* 19, vol. 11 (Feb 1980), 15–27.

19. Andy Warhol, in Reva Wolf, "Introduction: Through the Looking-Glass," in Kenneth Goldsmith, *I'll Be Your Mirror: The Selected Andy Warhol Interviews*, 1962–1987 (New York: Carroll & Graf, 2004), xvii.

20. Susan Silton, interview with author, Jul 10, 2008.

21. Tom Waits, "Tom Waits' True Confessions," from Robin Hilton, "Tom Waits Interviews Tom Waits," NPR, *All Songs Considered* (May 20, 2008), http://www.npr.org/blogs/allsongs/2008/05/an_interview_with_tom_waits_by.html, accessed Dec 3, 2010.

22. Anya Liftig, Lecture, Atlanta Contemporary Art Center, Jun 6, 2010.

23. Willem de Kooning, "Letter," *Artnews* (Jan 1949): 6.

24. David Smith, "Questions to Art Students," in Karen Wilkin, *David Smith* (New York and London: Abbeville Press, 1984), 110.

25. Rebecca Smith, e-mail to author, Mar 15, 2011.

26. Richard Serra, in "New York City, October 25, 1995," from William Bartman, *The Portraits Speak: Chuck Close in Conversation With 27 of His Subjects*, Edited by Joanne Kesten (New York: A.R.T. Press, 1997), 58–59.

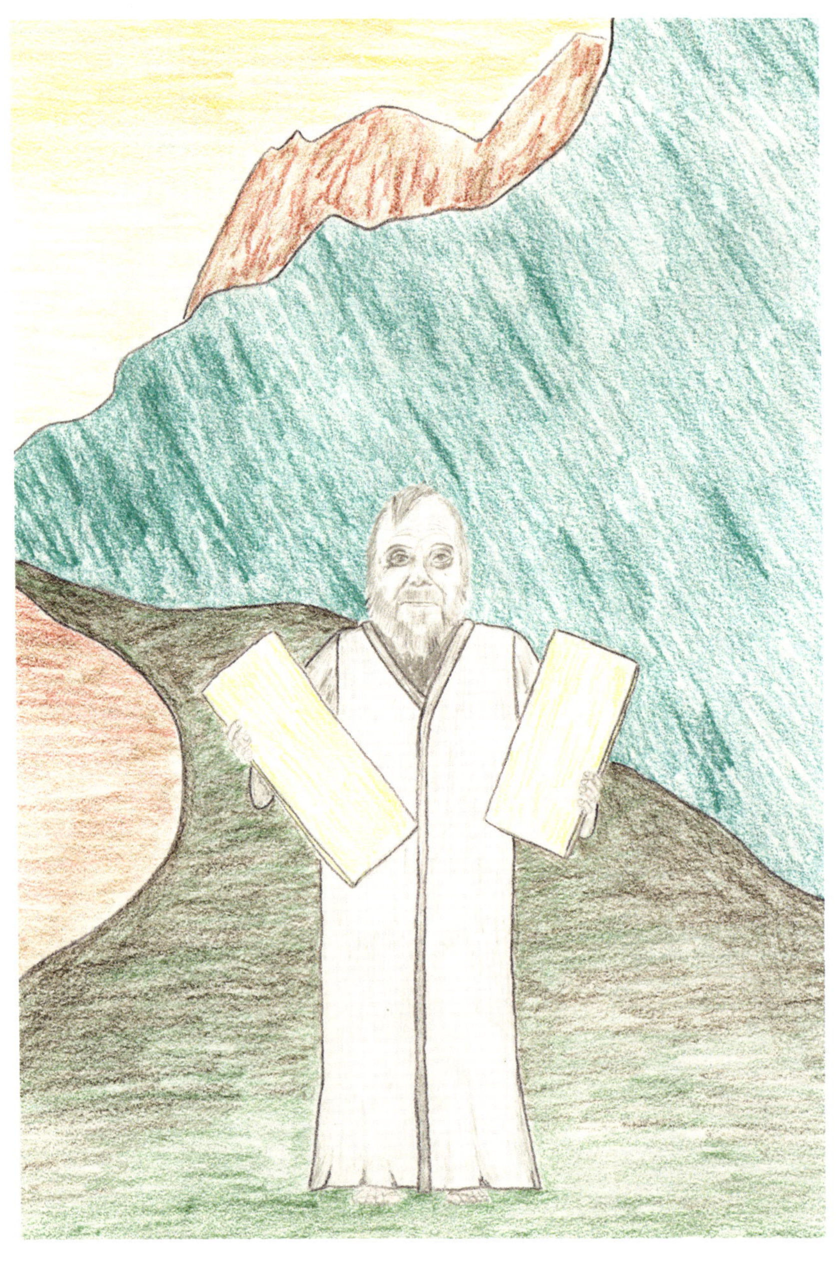

Joe Sola
John Baldessari (detail)
2011

3. ADVICE

An infamous example of advice is the suggestion made to Benjamin Braddock in Mike Nichols's coming-of-age film *The Graduate* (1967):

> Mr. McGuire: I want to say one word to you. Just one word.
> Benjamin: Yes, sir.
> Mr. McGuire: Are you listening?
> Benjamin: Yes, I am.
> Mr. McGuire: Plastics.
> Benjamin: Exactly how do you mean?
> Mr. McGuire: There's a great future in plastics. Think about it. Will you think about it?[1]

Someone starting a conversation with me with the phrase, "You know what you should do," will usually make me tune out before they finish telling me. Unless of course, I asked for their input and then I'm all ears. One of the best pieces of advice I ever received came from Jim Rice, then Vice President for Academic Affairs at Bucknell University. I was about to start my job as Director of the Center Gallery, and had asked for his thoughts on how far I could go in my programming within the university context. He said, "Ask for forgiveness, not permission." I appreciated his strategic encouragement and have used his recommendation ever since.

Parents, teachers, friends, colleagues, and strangers can make thoughtful suggestions about any number of situations. Their counsel may prove to be invaluable as you try to deal with various opportunities or problems. Maybe what they say is not right at the time but is applicable later on. You never know. Sometimes the act of asking for help and being in dialogue is more important than whatever guidance is offered.

Michael Craig-Martin

I sometimes said to students, "You know, I could tell you everything I know, everything I could think of saying to you, in a day or two. But it wouldn't make any difference because you'd understand all the words, you'd write it all down, it would all make sense, and it would be absolutely useless to you. The thing you have to do is *you* have to act it out. I say the things, *you* act the things out. Over two or three, four years you say, "Ah, now I know what you meant."[2]

Willem de Rooij and **Christopher Williams**

WDR: On my first day in art school I was told: you cannot make art about or with shoes, and also not about or with suitcases.

CW: And what was that about?

WDR: It was probably about Christian Boltanski being fashionable with art students at that moment.

CW: On my first day in art school I was taken aside by an older student who said the way to be taken seriously here is to make audio work—those were his words; have the four-track tape recorder ready. And the next older student told me: don't produce objects—collect them and keep them in a warehouse, but just provide inventories. He collected vacuum cleaners. But I was interested in the idea of montage, in the sense of reframing and layering information, and of bringing as much history about specific issues as possible into a single picture that was apparently pretty straightforward. I wanted it to be really disproportional in that regard.[3]

Robert Henri

Don't try to paint *good landscapes*. Try to paint canvases that will show how interesting landscape looks to you—your pleasure in the thing.[4]

Morton Feldman

There is a marvelous story about Duchamp and an art student in San Francisco many years ago. Duchamp goes to this art school and he sees this kind of tough, macho San Francisco painter and Duchamp looks at this picture he doesn't know. He says to the fellow, "What are you doing?" And the painter says, "I don't know what the fuck I'm doing." Duchamp pats him on the back and says, "Keep up the good work."[5]

Dana Friis-Hansen

For every exhibition you should write a text, whether it is a short introductory wall text or a photocopied brochure or a more scholarly catalogue that documents the show. And gallery talks by the curator are vital ways to communicate our ideas and enthusiasm to those who are eager to learn more. Writing and public speaking should be a regular part of the curator's routine, and practice brings improvement. Read and re-read essays by the curators whose ideas most excite you; find colleagues who can read the preliminary drafts of your text or listen as you practice your talk to get candid criticism; invite friends to your talks and get them to provide feedback. Take as much care with your language about art as the artists do with their materials.[6]

Richard Wentworth

My advice to younger artists and exhibition-makers is never to cross the road and read from the Highway Code at the same time.[7]

John Cage

After a long and arduous journey a young Japanese man arrived deep in a forest where the teacher of his choice was living in a small house he had made. When the student arrived, the teacher was sweeping up fallen leaves. Greeting his master, the young man received no greeting in return. And to all his questions, there were no replies. Realizing there was nothing he could do to get the teacher's attention, the student went to another part of the same forest and built himself a house. Years later, when he was sweeping up fallen leaves, he was enlightened. He then dropped everything, ran through the forest to his teacher, and said, "Thank you."[8]

Patti Smith

"I can't do this, I don't know what to say."
"Say anything," he said. "You can't make a mistake when you improvise."
"What if I mess it up? What if I screw up the rhythm?"
"You can't," he said. "It's like drumming. If you miss a beat, you create another."

In this simple exchange, Sam [Shepard] taught me the secret of improvisation, one that I have accessed my whole life.[9]

Henry Flynt

Consider the whole of your life, what you already do, all your doings. Now please *exclude* everything which is naturally physiologically necessary (or harmful) such as breathing and sleeping (or breaking an arm). From what remains *exclude* everything which is *for the satisfaction of a social demand,* a very large area which includes foremost your job, but also care of children, being polite, voting, your haircut, and much else. From what remains *exclude* everything which is an agency, a "*means,*" another very large area which overlaps with others to be excluded. From what remains, *exclude* everything which involves competition. In what remains *concentrate on everything done entirely because you just like it as you do it.*[10]

Anthony Bourdain

If you're twenty-two, physically fit, hungry to learn and be better, I urge you to travel—as far and as widely as possible. Sleep on floors if you have to. Find out how other people live and eat and cook. Learn from them—wherever you go. Use every possible resource you have to work in the very best kitchens that will have you—however little (if anything) they pay—and relentlessly harangue every possible connection, every great chef whose kitchen offers a glimmer of hope of acceptance. Keep at it. A three-star chef friend in Europe reports receiving month after month of faxes from one aspiring apprentice cook—and responding with "no" each time. But finally he broke down, impressed by the kid's unrelenting, never wavering determination. Money borrowed at this point in your life so that you can afford to travel and gain work experience in really good kitchens will arguably be better invested than any student loan. A culinary degree—while enormously helpful—is only helpful to a point. A year working at Mugaritz or L'Arpège or Arzak can transform your life—become a direct route to other great kitchens. All the great chefs know each other. Do right by one and they tend to hook you up with others.

Which is to say: if you're lucky enough to be able to do the above, do not fuck it up.[11]

Frank O'Hara and **Larry Rivers**

How to Proceed in the Arts

1. Empty yourself of everything.
2. Think of faraway things.
3. It is 12:00. Pick up the adult and throw it out of bed. Work should be done at your leisure, you know, only when there is nothing else to do. If anyone is in bed with you, they should be told to leave. You cannot work with someone there.
4. If you're the type of person who thinks in words—paint!
5. Think of a big color—who cares if people call you Rothko. Release your childhood. Release it.

6. Do you hear them say painting is action? We say painting is the timid appraisal of yourself by lions.
7. They say your walls should look no different than your work, but that is only a feeble prediction of the future. We know the ego is the true maker of history, and if it isn't, it should be no concern of yours.
8. They say painting is action. We say remember your enemies and nurse the smallest insult. Introduce yourself as Delacroix. When you leave, give them your wet crayons. Be ready to admit that jealousy moves you more than art. They say action is painting. Well, it isn't, and we all know Expressionism has moved to the suburbs.
9. If you are interested in schools, choose a school that is interested in you. Piero della Francesca agrees with us when he says, "Schools are for fools." We are too embarrassed to decide on the proper approach. However, this much we have observed: good or bad schools are insurance companies. Enter their offices and you are certain of a position. No matter how we despise them, the Pre-Raphaelites are here to stay.
10. Don't just paint. Be a successful all-around man like Baudelaire. [...][12]

Thomas Nozkowski Interview with Francine Prose

FP: Do you give suggestions when you're talking to the art students?

TN: Only in the most general way. You try to follow the logic of what they're doing. I remember teachers telling us all sorts of things. One teacher—I'll leave this person nameless—said, "Never use green, green is the most impossible color!" (*laughter*)

FP: People say the most outrageous shit! A student told me that one of my colleagues had told her, "Never put food in a story!"

TN: There's a kind of homely wisdom you can give to students: Never show in September. Always find a dealer who's hungrier than you are—things like that. But when it comes to practical advice, I genuinely believe one can make a great work of art with any material in any medium to any goal and for any reasons. I don't think there are boundaries.[13]

Amanda Ross-Ho

SURVIVAL IS NOT ENOUGH
DO A GOOD JOB[14]

Tom Waits

Jim Jarmusch once told me, "Fast, Cheap, and Good… pick two. If it's fast and cheap, it won't be good. If it's cheap and good, it won't be fast. If it's fast and good, it won't be cheap." Fast, cheap and good… pick (2) words to live by.[15]

Sister Corita

Immaculate Heart College Art Department Rules

Rule 1: Find a place you trust, and then try trusting it for a while.

Rule 2: General duties of a student: pull everything out of your teacher. Pull everything out of your fellow students.

Rule 3: General duties of a teacher: Pull everything out of your students.

Rule 4: Consider everything an experiment.

Rule 5: Be self-disciplined. This means finding someone wise or smart and choosing to follow them. To be disciplined is to follow in a good way. To be self-disciplined is to follow in a better way.

Rule 6: Nothing is a mistake. There's no win and no fail. There's only make.

Rule 7: The only rule is work. If you work it will lead to something. It's the people who do all of the work all of the time who eventually catch on to things.

Rule 8: Don't try to create and analyze at the same time. They're different processes.

Rule 9: Be happy whenever you can manage it. Enjoy yourself. It's lighter than you think.

Rule 10: "We're breaking all the rules. Even our own rules. And how do we do that? By leaving plenty of room for X quantities." John Cage

Helpful Hints: Always be around. Come or go to everything. Always go to classes. Read anything you can get your hands on. Look at movies carefully, often. Save everything—it might come in handy later.

There should be new rules next week.[16]

Eva Hesse and **Sol LeWitt**

EH: So I sit now after two days of working on a dumb thing which is three-dimensional. Supposed to be continuing with last drawing. All borders on pop at least to the European eye. That is anything not pure or abstract expressionist is pop like the 3-d one now actually looks like breast and penis—but that's ok and I should go on with it maybe…but I don't know where I belong so I give up again. All the time is like that. … Have really been discovering my weird humor and making sick or maybe cool but I can only see things that way—experience them also but I can't feel cool—that is my hopelessness. Like it all is based on fear and cannot be cool when one constantly feels fear. … Everything for me personally is glossed with anxiety. … How do you believe in something deeply? How is it one can pinpoint beliefs into a singular purpose?

SLW: You seem the same as always, and being you, hate every minute of it. Don't! Learn to say "Fuck You" to the world every once in a while. You have every right to. Just stop thinking, worrying, looking over your shoulder, wondering, doubting, fearing, hurting, hoping for some easy way out, struggling, gasping, confusing, itching, scratching, mumbling, bumbling, grumbling, humbling, stumbling, rumbling, rambling, gambling, tumbling, scumbling, scrambling, hitching, hatching, bitching, moaning, groaning, honing, boning, horse-shitting, hair-splitting, nit-picking, piss-trickling, nose-sticking, ass-gouging, eyeball-poking, finger pointing, alleyway-sneaking, long waiting, small stepping, evil-eying, back-scratching, searching, perching, besmirching, grinding grinding grinding away at yourself. Stop it and just DO.

From your description, and from what I know of your previous work and your ability, the work you are doing sounds very good. "Drawings—clean-clear but crazy like machines, larger, bolder, real *nonsense*." That sounds wonderful—real nonsense. Do more. More nonsensical more crazy more machines, more breasts, penises, cunts, whatever—make them abound with nonsense. Try and tickle something inside of you, your "weird humor." You belong in the most secret part of you. Don't worry about cool, make your own uncool. Make your own, your own world. If you fear, make it work for you—draw and paint your fear and anxiety. And stop worrying about big, deep things such as "to decide on a purpose and way of life, a consistent approach to even some impossible end or even an imagined end." You must practice being stupid, dumb, unthinking, empty. Then you will be able to DO! I have much confidence in you and even though you are tormenting yourself, the work you do is very good. Try and do some BAD work. The worst you can think of and see what happens but mainly relax and let everything go to hell. You are not responsible for the world—you are only responsible for your work, so do it. And don't think that your work has to conform to any idea or flavor. It can be anything you want it to be. But if life would be easier for you if you stopped working then stop. Don't punish yourself. However, I think that it is so deeply engrained in you that it would be easier to DO.[17]

Ben Shahn

My capsule recommendation for a course of education is as follows:
Attend a university if you possibly can. There is no content of knowledge that is not pertinent to the work you will want to do. But before you attend a university,

work at something for a while. Do anything. Get a job in a potato field; or work as a grease-monkey in an auto repair shop. But if you do work in a field do not fail to observe the look and feel of earth and of all things that you handle—yes, even potatoes! Or, in the auto shop, the smell of oil and grease and burning rubber. Paint of course, but if you have to lay aside painting for a time, continue to draw. Listen to all conversations and be instructed by them and take all seriousness seriously. Never look down upon anything or anyone as not worthy of notice. In college or out of college, read. And form opinions! Read Sophocles and Euripides and Dante and Proust. Read everything that you can find about art except the reviews. Read the Bible; read Hume; read Pogo. Read all kinds of poetry and know many poets and many artists. Go to an art school, or two, or three, or take courses at night if necessary. And paint and paint and draw and draw. Know all you can, both curricular and non-curricular—mathematics and physics and economics, logic, and particularly history. Know at least two languages besides your own, but anyway, know French. Look at pictures and more pictures. Look at every kind of visual symbol, every kind of emblem; do not spurn sign-boards or furniture drawings or this style of art or that style of art. Do not be afraid to like paintings honestly or to dislike them honestly, but if you do dislike them retain an open mind. Do not dismiss any school of art, not the Pre-Raphaelites nor the Hudson River School nor the German genre painters. Talk and talk and sit at cafés, and listen to everything, to Brahms, to Brubeck, to the Italian hour on the radio. Listen to preachers in small-town churches and in big-city churches. Listen to politicians in New England town meetings and to rabble-rousers in Alabama. Even draw them. And remember that you are trying to learn to think and what you want to think, that you are trying to coordinate mind and hand and eye. Go to all sorts of museums and galleries and to the studios of artists. Go to Paris and Madrid and Rome and Ravenna and Padua. Stand alone in Saint Chapelle, in the Sistine Chapel, in the Church of the Carmine in Florence. Draw and draw, and paint, and learn to work in many media; try lithography and aquatint and silk screen. Know all that you can about art, and by all means have opinions. Never be afraid to become embroiled in art or life or politics; never be afraid to learn to draw or paint better than you already do; and never be afraid to undertake any kind of art at all, however exalted or however common, but do it with distinction.[18]

Joseph Grigely

A lot of the stuff I learned about art and being an artist did not come from visual artists; it came from writers like Keats (in his letters) and composers like Ned Rorem (in his diaries) and outdoorsmen like Ray Bergman (who wrote about fly fishing for trout). So read as much as you can—learn a foreign language, learn things about other people, go places and do things that have nothing to do with art—because it's the stuff that has nothing to do with art that has everything to do with art.[19]

Fischli & Weiss

How to Work Better.

1. Do one thing at a time
2. Know the problem
3. Learn to listen
4. Learn to ask questions
5. Distinguish sense from nonsense
6. Accept change as inevitable
7. Admit mistakes
8. Say it simple
9. Be calm
10. Smile[20]

Preston Sturges

11 Rules for the box office:

1. A pretty girl is better than an ugly one.
2. A leg is better than an arm.
3. A bedroom is better than a living room.
4. An arrival is better than a departure.
5. A birth is better than a death.
6. A chase is better than a chat.
7. A dog is better than a landscape.
8. A kitten is better than a dog.
9. A baby is better than a kitten.
10. A kiss is better than a baby.
11. A pratfall is better than anything.[21]

Julian Schnabel

Never listen to anybody when it comes to being responsible for your own paintings, it's a mistake for young artists to want to please older ones. They're going to make you take out of your paintings the very things that most characterize them as yours. You might think that someone is really smarter than you are, or wiser, or more experienced, and they may be. But you can't listen to them because nobody knows better than you what you need to do. Most older artists are going to try to get you to conform to the standards that you are out to destroy anyway.[22]

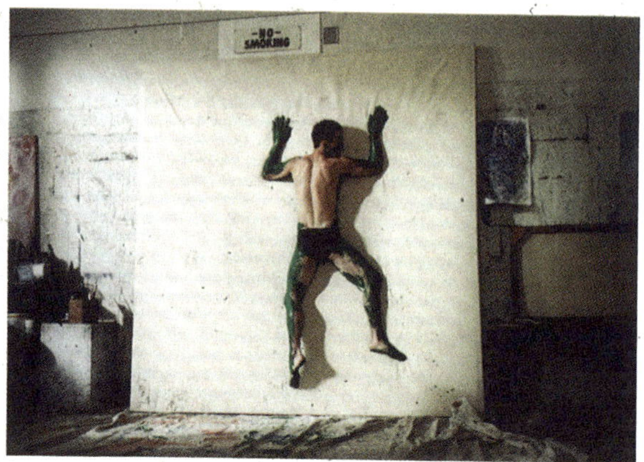

Terry Zwigoff, *Art School Confidential*, 2006, still from a color film in 35 mm, 102 minutes.

"It is well to remember from time to time," said the pedagogue Oscar Wilde, "that nothing worth knowing can be taught." While seduction and self-promotion

once a decade or never at all!" To get ahead, he advises, "you really need to take some lessons in sucking cock and licking ass! Otherwise you might find yourself rotting away in some shithole."

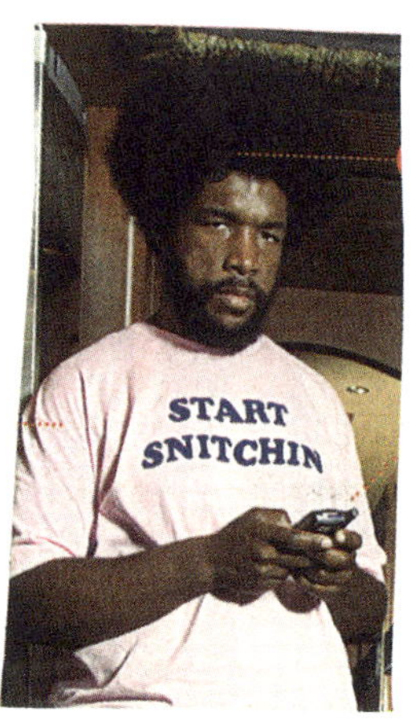

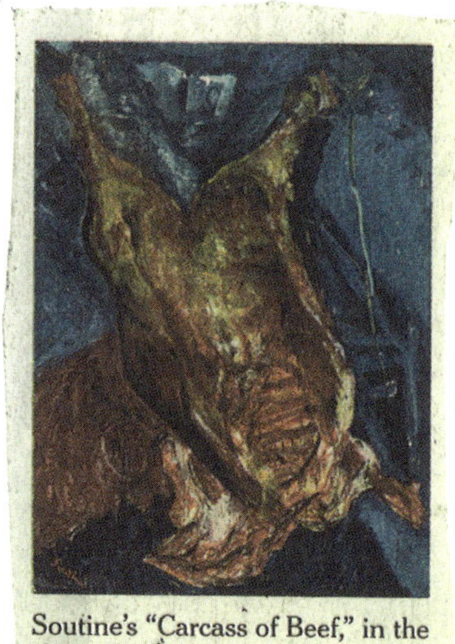
Soutine's "Carcass of Beef," in the

Barbara Pollack

LESSON #4: ENTHUSIASM IS MAGIC

All authors of self-help books from Norman Vincent Peale to last year's bestseller, *Learned Optimism*, talk about enthusiasm—which is probably enough to make most artists run in the opposite direction. However, this is a mistake. In these times, it is essential to value this asset. It does not cost money, requires no education and does not discriminate.

Enthusiasm simply means that you believe that in yourself is the wisdom, courage, strategy, and faith necessary to deal successfully with all difficulties. Popular culture portrays the artist as a morose, manic-depressive overcome by obsessive problems. Few artists can afford to internalize this stereotype anymore. It may take a while for us to turn into cheerleaders but remember—if we don't act enthusiastic about contemporary art, Morley Safer never will.

Here are some simple steps to develop a more enthusiastic self-image:

1. The next time someone asks you if all artists are manic-depressive, ask them what would happen if you locked a lawyer in a room and gave him no money or recognition until he won a Supreme Court case. That should shut them up.
2. Avoid situations that create self-doubts. Artists may have to suffer, but they don't have to suffer humiliation.
3. Keep a file on artists who continued to work against great odds. Art history—especially feminist art history—is filled with them.
4. Develop sympathy for non-artists working in the New York artworld. Dealers, critics, curators, and receptionists have to confront creativity all day. It's a tough job and they don't even have an excuse for being manic-depressive. Try to be kind.
5. Think of ways to help other artists, rather than yourself. If you fill a need, you may eventually get paid to fill that need. Then you will have a way of supporting your art. Even if you don't, you will make friends.
6. Remind yourself that you already made a dream come true, you wanted to be an artist ever since you failed "self-control" on your elementary school report card. Now you are and no one can take that away from you.

<

Stuart Horodner

Notebook

Aug 2006

If you follow these simple steps, you will be a more productive artist. You will also stand out as original and unique—the genuinely happy artist. Few will comprehend your state of mind, so you will seem intriguing and mysterious. Your self-confidence will inspire confidence in your work.

Norman Vincent Peale would say that this is the road to success, fame and fortune. All I know is that it will help you continue making art.

Maybe, I should keep these secrets to myself. It's not supposed to be good to leak information to your competitors. However, I am sincerely concerned that the current economic climate is causing some of our best artists to give up. Many have not yet been recognized, have not yet emerged. I want everyone to continue. I look forward to your new ideas, new images, new art forms. I don't have solutions, just pat answers. That will have to be enough for now.[23]

Samuel Beckett

Ever tried. Ever failed. No matter. Try again. Fail again. Fail better.[24]

NOTES

1. *The Graduate*, Directed by Mike Nichols, Embassy Pictures, 1967.

2. Michael Craig-Martin, in "Conversation: John Baldessari and Michael Craig-Martin," in Steven Henry Madoff, ed., *Art School: (Propositions for the 21st Century)* (Cambridge: MIT Press, 2009), 48–49.

3. Willem de Rooij and Christopher Williams, in Jorg Heiser, Willem de Rooij, and Christopher Williams, "As We Speak," *Frieze* (Oct 2010): 185.

4. Robert Henri, *The Art Spirit*, Compiled by Margery A. Ryerson (Philadelphia and New York: J.B. Lippincott, 1923), 18.

5. Morton Feldman, "The Future of Local Music," in B. H. Friedman, ed., *Give My Regards to Eighth Street: Collected Writings of Morton Feldman* (Cambridge, MA: Exact Change, 2000), 167.

6. Dana Friis-Hansen, "Notes to a Young Curator," in Carin Kuoni, ed., *Words of Wisdom: A Curator's Vade Mecum on Contemporary Art* (New York: Independent Curators International, 2001), 68.

7. Richard Wentworth, "A Highway Code for Art – Not," in Daniel Birnbaum, et al, *Artists at Work: Second Baltic International Seminar*, 26–28 October 2000 (Gateshead, Great Britain: Baltic, 2001), 12.

8. John Cage, "Edgard Varèse," *Silence: Lectures and Writings* (Cambridge and London: MIT Press, 1967, First published 1961 by Wesleyan Univ. Press, Middletown, CT), 85.

9. Patti Smith, "Hotel Chelsea," *Just Kids* (New York: HarperCollins, 2010), 185.

10. Henry Flynt, in Kristine Stiles, "Between Water and Stone: Fluxus Performance: A Metaphysics of Acts," in Elizabeth Armstrong and Joan Rothfuss, *In the Spirit of Fluxus*, Exhibition catalogue (Walker Art Center, Minneapolis, MN, 1993), 72.

11. Anthony Bourdain, "So You Wanna Be a Chef," *Medium Raw: A Bloody Valentine to the World of Food and the People Who Cook* (New York: HarperCollins, 2010), 56.

12. Frank O'Hara and Larry Rivers, "How to Proceed in the Arts," in Frank O'Hara, *Art Chronicles: 1954–1966* (New York: George Braziller, 1975), 92–93.

13. Thomas Nozkowski, in Francine Prose, "Thomas Nozkowski," *Bomb* (Fall 1998), http://bombsite.com/issues/65/articles/2171, accessed Feb 21, 2011.

14. Amanda Ross-Ho, *Absolutely Everything, Volume 1: Invisible Opponent* (Fall 2004–Spring 2005), n.p., text given to author, Aug 23, 2010.

15. Tom Waits, "Tom Waits' True Confessions," from Robin Hilton, "Tom Waits Interviews Tom Waits," NPR, *All Songs Considered* (May 20, 2008), http://www.npr.org/blogs/allsongs/2008/05/an_interview_with_tom_waits_by.html, accessed Dec 3, 2010.

16. Sister Corita, "Immaculate Heart College Art Department Rules," in Julie Ault, *Come Alive! The Spirited Art of Sister Corita* (London: Four Corners Books, 2006), 46.

17. Eva Hesse and Sol LeWitt, in "1959–1965," in Lucy R. Lippard, *Eva Hesse* (New York: New York Univ. Press, 1976), 34–35.

18. Ben Shahn, "The Education of an Artist," in John D. Morse, ed., *Ben Shahn* (New York: Praeger Publishers, 1972), 101–102.

19. Joseph Grigely, in *Letters to a Young Artist*, Peter Nesbett, Shelley Bancroft, and Sarah Andress, eds. (New York: Darte Publishing, 2006), 92.

20. Fischli & Weiss, *How to Work Better*, 1991, in Helen Molesworth, *Work Ethic*, Exhibition catalogue (Baltimore Museum of Art, and Pennsylvania State Univ. Press, University Park, 2003), 6.

21. Preston Sturges, in Manohla Dargis, "Sturges's Travels, A Screwball Tale," *New York Times*, Apr 1, 2005, http://www.nytimes.com/2005/04/01/movies/01stur.html?ref=prestonsturges, accessed Apr 17, 2011.

22. Julian Schnabel, "About Being a Student," *CVJ: Nicknames of Maitre D's & Other Excerpts from Life* (New York: Random House, 1987), 23.

23. Barbara Pollack, in Suzanne Anker, et al, "Forum: On Creativity and Community," *M/E/A/N/I/N/G* (May 1994): 21–22.

24. Samuel Beckett, "Worstward Ho," in *Nohow On: Company, Ill Seen Ill Said, Worstward Ho: Three Novels by Samuel Beckett* (New York: Grove Press, 1995), 89.

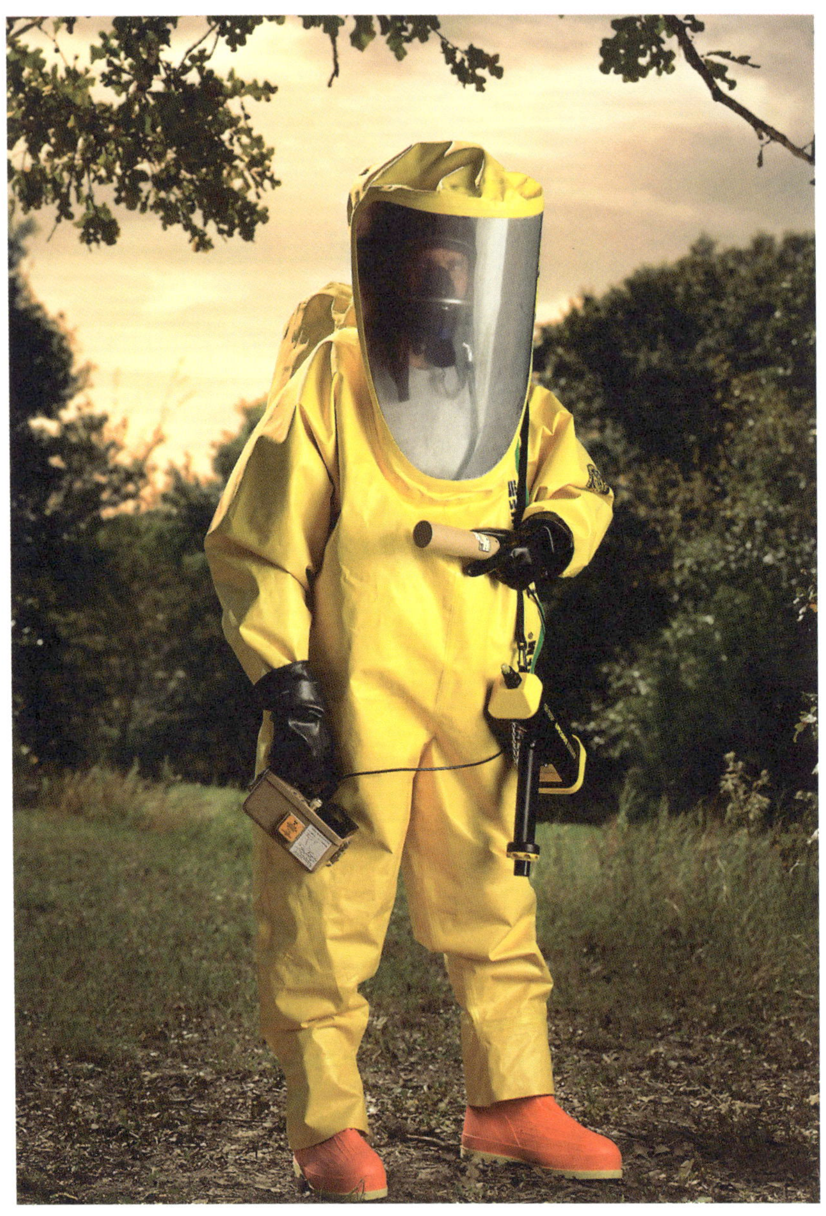

Paul Shambroom
Level A Hazmat suit, yellow ("Disaster City," National Emergency Response and Rescue Training Center, Texas Engineering and Extension Service, College Station Texas)
2004

4. SUBJECTS

Paul Cézanne had Mont Sainte-Victoire and Giorgio Morandi had an assortment of bottles. Each man painted his subject in a way that helped to redefine the acts of looking and representing. Andy Warhol silkscreened images of Campbell's Soup cans and Marilyn and Elvis and Mao, to chronicle popular icons. For decades, William Wegman has immortalized his beloved Weimaraners in photographs and videotapes. Language is Kay Rosen's subject, and she examines how it can perform using typography, color, scale, and space. Louise Lawler documents art as it appears in private homes, institutions, and storage areas. Jack Whitten's abstract memorial paintings honor those elders and colleagues whose creativity and character have inspired him, and commemorate public tragedies and disasters. What are you interested in?

I believe that what is often referred to as "signature style" is less important than an artist's signature subjects—the set of concerns or problems that they repeatedly wrestle with. This is certainly true of Louise Bourgeois, who said, "The subject of pain is the business I am in. To give meaning and shape to frustration and suffering."[1]

Henry Moore

There are three fundamental poses of the human figure. One is standing, the other is seated and the third is lying down... But of the three poses, the reclining figure gives me the most freedom, compositionally and spatially. It is free and stable at the same time. It fits in with my belief that sculpture must be permanent, should last for eternity... The reclining figure is an absolute obsession with me, of course, and at one time the relationship of *Mother and Child* was another. I don't like to repeat an experience that I've once had in my work, but there are some that I can't get away from. I wake up in the morning and there they are, day after day, until I do something about it.[2]

Adrian Piper

Dear Friend,

I am black.

I am sure you did not realize this when you made/laughed at/agreed with that racist remark. In the past, I have attempted to alert white people to my racial identity in advance. Unfortunately, this invariably causes them to react to me as pushy, manipulative, or socially inappropriate. Therefore, my policy is to assume that white people do not make these remarks, even when they believe that there are no black people present, and to distribute this card when they do.

I regret any discomfort my presence is causing you, just as I am sure you regret the discomfort your racism is causing me.

Sincerely yours,

Adrian Margaret Smith Piper[3]

Barnett Newman

I felt the issue in those years was: What can a painter do? The problem of the subject became very clear to me as the crucial thing in painting. Not the technique, not the plasticity, not the look, not the surface: none of these things meant that much. The issue for me—for all the fellows, for Pollock, for Gottlieb—was what are we going to paint?

The best distinction was made by Professor Meyer Shapiro, who was talking about subject in painting. He made the distinction between the subject of a work and the objects in a work. For example, people think that Cézanne's subject was the apples. Well, it's possible to argue that that's what it was, and for a long time I was very antagonistic to those apples, because they were like superapples. They were like cannonballs. I saw them as cannonballs. Even though my painting, as it developed, didn't have any of those objects, that did not necessarily mean therefore that there was no subject there.[4]

Francis Bacon Interview with David Sylvester

DS: What do you think are the essential things that go to make an artist, especially now?

FB: Well, I think there are lots of things. I think that one of the things is that, if you are going to decide to be a painter, you have got to decide that you are not

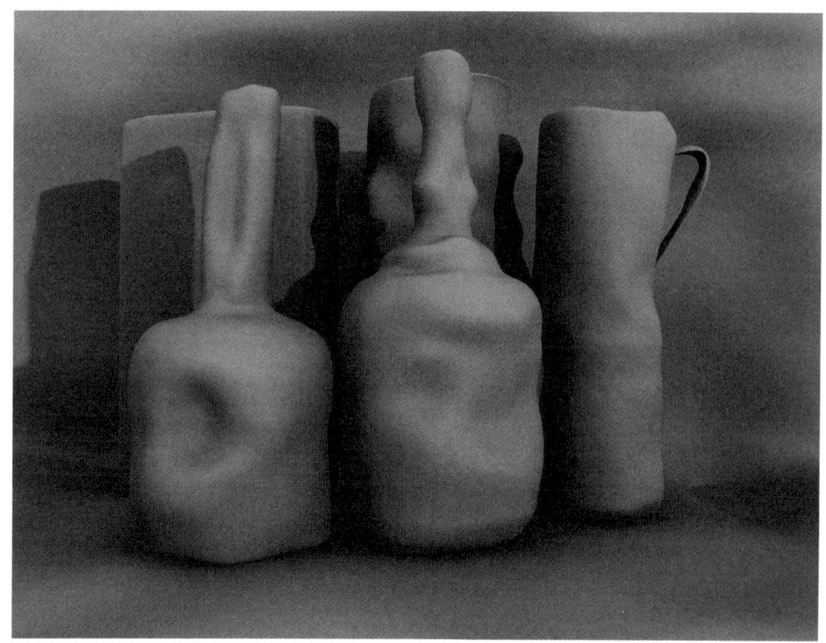

Bill Albertini
Soft Morandi
2008

going to be afraid of making a fool of yourself. I think another thing is to be able to find subjects which really absorb you to try and do. I feel without a subject you automatically go back into decoration because you haven't got the subject which is always eating into you to bring it back—and the greatest art always returns you to the vulnerability of the human situation.[5]

John McCracken Interview with Dike Blair

JM: I realized pretty early that a plank leaning against the wall had to be taller than a human or it just didn't look right. There has always been a kind of figurativeness, in my mind anyway, to my work. The first pieces I did, I felt, were personalities that I was drawing out of the ethers. Even the more abstract geometric things I thought of as personalityish. The planks lend themselves to that kind of thinking. They're vertical and so on. I reasoned that they had to be taller than humans because the energy field of humans, what psychics call an aura, is bigger than a human's physical body. So if you made a piece that was, say, six-feet tall, it wouldn't be big enough because it would only be as big as a physical human being and not as big as an actual human, including their energy field.

DB: You're physically plankish. Are you making yourself?

JM: Yeah, probably. You do something and it tends to be a self-portrait. I suppose if I were chubby I'd tend to do chubbier pieces (*laughs*).

DB: The pieces always look as if they were installed by something other than human hands.

JM: I do try to make things that look like they come from somewhere else—from a UFO or a futuristic environment or another dimension. That things exist in more than one dimension at one time is something that's more than a fascination for me, it's relevant to the human world. I think that humans exist in more than one dimension at once.[6]

Daniel Bozhkov

I'm drawn to subjects that are too large to see. You know how something becomes a cliché—it's been a common truth for a while, until it becomes something that's not true, it becomes a false assumption. I'm interested in the moment where there's an amnesia or opacity. When something is so visible that you stop seeing it—that's the time to pay attention.[7]

David Wojnarowicz

I love mythology, whether it's personal mythology or it's something from a lost civilization. Those are the things that have comforted me in my life. Ever since I was a kid, anything we had no control over—natural events like tornados or floods—signaled other possibilities. That the world wasn't just the family structure or the governmental structure—that there were things in the world that could possibly change the face of what we've come to know and accept as given. These little myths and pieces of information signaled other possibilities.[8]

Dana Schutz Interview with Raphaela Platow

RP: Early on, you began creating paintings—sometimes an entire series of works—based on a set of circumstances that you staked out beforehand. The premises then develop and change while you work. I believe that *Frank from*

Observation is the first series of paintings on which you imposed a hypothetic narrative. Could you talk about Frank, the last man on earth, painted from life but extended into the imaginary according to the parameters you set for him?

DS: Frank was somebody I invented, but I proposed to paint him from observation. He was the last subject and the last audience and I was the last painter. He was a hybrid of information I found in narratives and people I know. In one of the paintings he has my friend Pat's eyes, in another he is part proboscis monkey. He's like a ball of play-dough rolled on the floor, he began to pick up different attributes as the paintings went on. Initially, I was going to commit to making paintings only of him, but then I got restless and wanted to paint other things, so I took him apart and built other people and events out of him.[9]

Luc Tuymans

I find it essential to distance myself from whatever subject matter I'm portraying. Otherwise it is just a personal story. I'm after a broader context. Detachment comes up in the way the figurative is abstracted, in what needs to be done to give something another relevance or purpose, and I'm sure it is why I wasn't able to be an abstract painter—direct mark-making was always too emotive for me.[10]

Robert Motherwell

I take an elegy to be a funeral lamentation or funeral song for something one cared about. "The Spanish Elegies" are not "political," but my private insistence that a terrible death happened that should not be forgot. They are as eloquent as I could make them. But the pictures are general metaphors of the contrast between life and death, and their interrelation.[11]

Kiki Smith

I'm a big Virgin Mary fan. I was raised Catholic. Lots of my work refers to the Virgin Mary and I've made a lot of pieces kind of manipulating her around different ways from my own perverse interests.[12]

Jerry Saltz

I'm not interested so much in subject matter—otherwise all crucifixions, every Virgin Mary holding a baby Jesus, would be the same—but a Piero della Francesca painting of a Pope is very different from a Francis Bacon painting of a Pope. The subject matter may be the same but the content is different. To me, subject matter is the first thing I see in a work of art, and usually it's the first thing I stop seeing.[13]

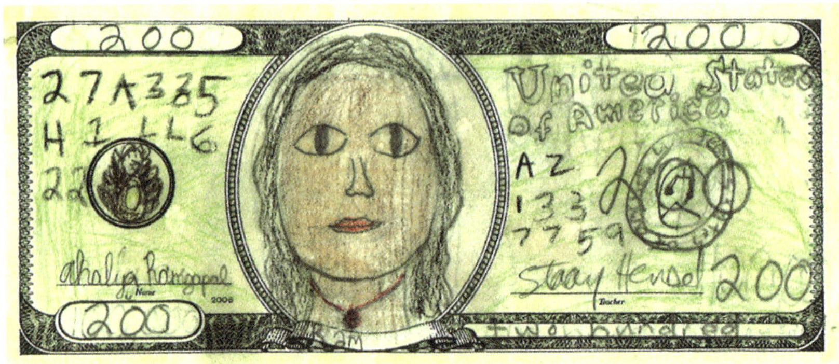

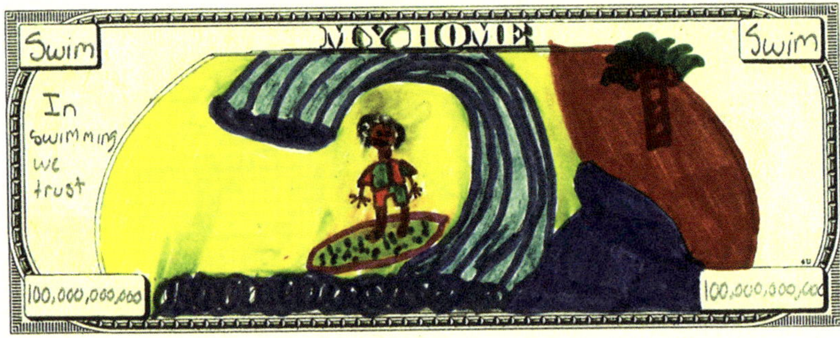

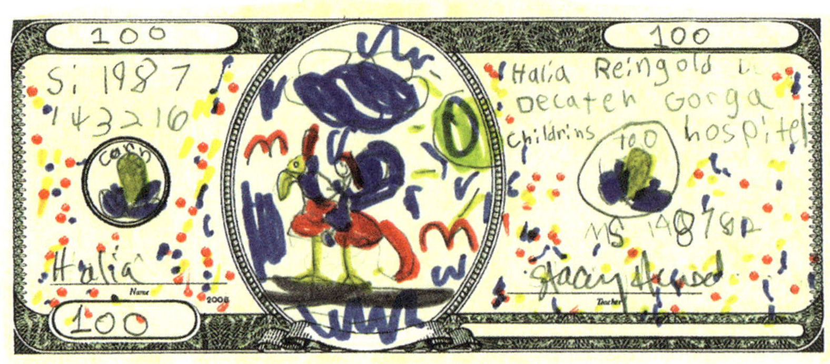

Fundred Dollar Bills
2009

Johnny Cash

Horses, railroads, land, judgment day, family, hard times, whiskey, courtship, marriage, adultery, separation, murder, war, prison, rambling, damnation, home, salvation, death, pride, humor, patriotism, larceny, determination, tragedy, rowdiness, heartbreak, and love. And Mother. And God.[14]

NOTES

1. Louise Bourgeois, in Holland Cotter, "Louise Bourgeois, Sculptor of Psychologically Powerful Works, Dies at 98," *New York Times*, Jun 1, 2010.

2. Henry Moore, "Reclining Figure," in Ionel Jianou, *Henry Moore*, Translated by Geoffrey Skelding (New York: Tudor Publishing, 1968), 172.

3. Adrian Piper, *My Calling (Card) #1*, 1986–1990, in Maurice Berger, *Adrian Piper: A Retrospective*, Exhibition catalogue (Fine Arts Gallery, University of Maryland, Baltimore, 1999), 135.

4. Barnett Newman, in "How can you still be an artist and still be American?" in Emile de Antonio and Mitch Tuchman, *Painters Painting: A Candid History of the Modern Art Scene, 1940–1970* (New York: Abbeville Press, 1984), 42–43.

5. Francis Bacon, in David Sylvester, "Interview 9," *Interviews with Francis Bacon* (New York: Thames and Hudson, 1975), 199.

6. John McCracken, in Dike Blair, "Otherworldly: Interview with John McCracken," *Thing.net* (May 3, 1997), www.thing.net/~lilyvac/writing30.html, accessed Jun 20, 2011.

7. Daniel Bozhkov, in David Coggins, "Stranger Than Fiction: An Interview with Daniel Bozhkov," *Artnet.com* (Mar 31, 2010), http://www.artnet.com/magazineus/features/coggins/daniel-bozhkov3-31-10.asp, accessed Mar 31, 2010.

8. David Wojnarowicz, in Barry Blinderman, "The Compression of Time: An Interview with David Wojnarowicz," in Barry Blinderman, ed., *David Wojnarowicz: Tongues of Flame*, Exhibition catalogue (University Galleries, Illinois State University, Normal, 1990), 58.

9. Dana Schutz, in "Conversation: Raphaela Platow and Dana Schutz, September 2005," in Raphaela Platow, *Dana Schutz: Paintings 2002–2005*, Exhibition catalogue (Rose Art Museum, Brandeis University, Waltham, MA, 2006), 86.

10. Luc Tuymans, in Steel Stillman, "Luc Tuymans," *Art in America* (Feb 2010): 79.

11. Robert Motherwell, in Frank O'Hara, *Robert Motherwell, with Selections from the Artist's Writings* (New York: The Museum of Modern Art, 1965), 54.

12. Kiki Smith, in Art21, "Kiki Smith: Learning by Looking: Witches, Catholicism, and Buddhist Art," *Art21*, http://www.pbs.org/art21/artists/smith/clip1.html, accessed May 17, 2011.

13. Jerry Saltz, in Irving Sandler, "In Conversation: Jerry Saltz with Irving Sandler," *Brooklyn Rail* (Sep 2008), http://www.brooklynrail.org/2008/09/art, accessed May 17, 2011.

14. Johnny Cash, Liner notes, from *Unchained*, Produced by Rick Rubin, Warner Bros., 1996.

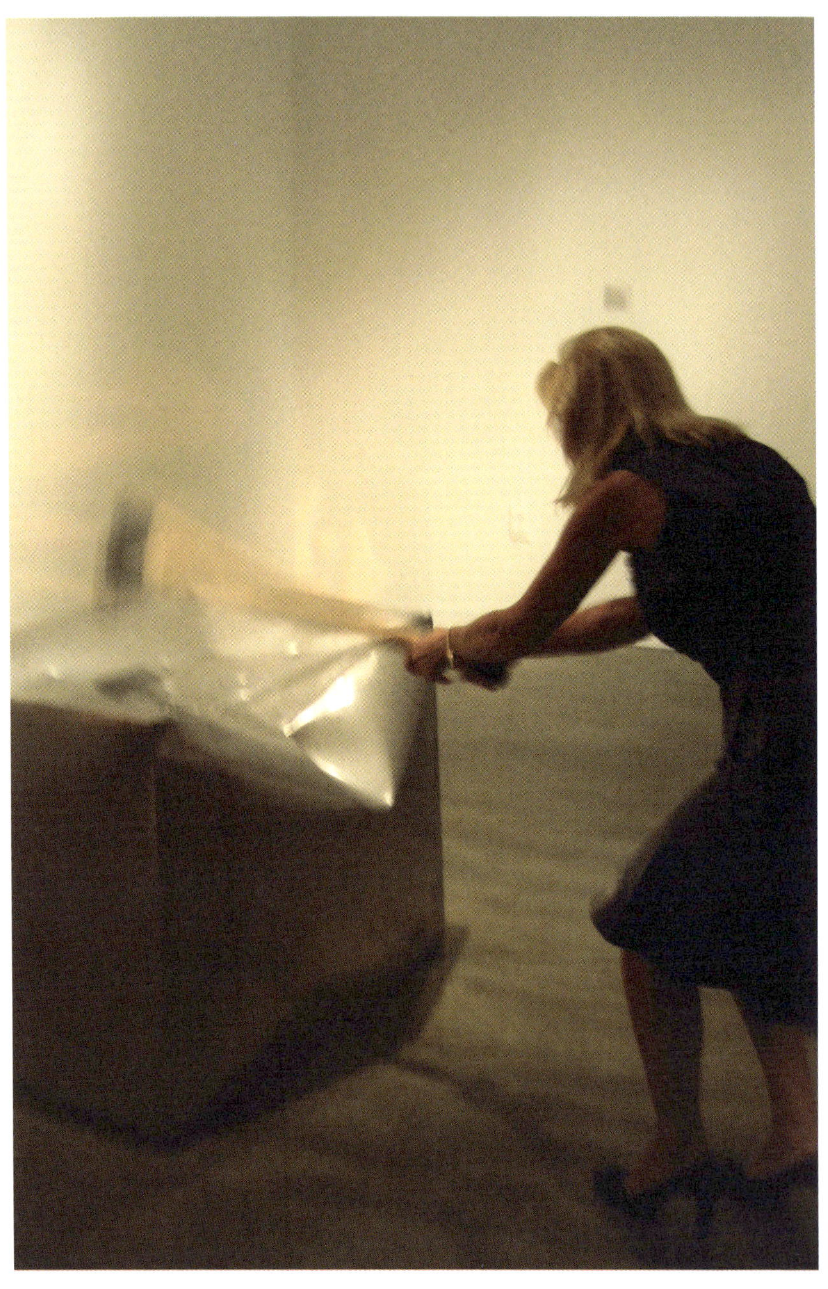

Making *Do Hit Chair*
2007

5. PROCESS

No matter what materials they use or subjects they explore, artists recognize and revel in the flow that can occur during the process of making. In his 1990 book, *Flow: The Psychology of Optimal Experience*, Mihaly Csikszentmihalyi analyzes that state of concentration when the "duration of time is altered; hours pass in minutes, and minutes can stretch out to seem like hours."[1] This being "in the zone" is often one of the most satisfying things about creative activity. I am aware of this as I perform the various activities that are a part of my curatorial projects—reading, traveling, being in studios and galleries, laying out and installing artworks, writing press releases and brochure copy, and giving tours. This is work but it never feels like it. For example, on October 16, 2007, as part of the exhibition *Finding Form*, the staff of the Atlanta Contemporary Art Center, along with board members and invited guests, executed a *Do Hit Chair*. Created by Marijn van der Poll for Droog Design, the chair starts as a hollow cube of steel that is meant to be pounded with a sledgehammer until it takes the ideal shape that satisfies the consumer. We collectively hit that chair until it felt complete and then we drank champagne.

Artists Bruce Nauman and Corin Hewitt have both investigated the nature of "the studio" and the relationship between mundane rituals of daily life and procedures of art-making. In the late 1960s, Nauman recorded himself performing repetitive acts of bouncing balls, walking, and exercising to create one-hour long videos; in *Mapping the Studio 1 (Fat Chance John Cage)*, he documented the nocturnal activity in his rural studio in the summer of 2000. This large-scale installation utilizes seven video projections and audio tracks to capture his own absence plus the presence of scurrying mice, prowling cats, and fluttering moths that occasionally animate the spaces around chairs, tools, and various works in progress. In *Seed Stage* (Oct 3, 2008–Jan 4, 2009), at the Whitney Museum of American Art, Hewitt built a space that combined aspects of science lab, test kitchen, and art studio. During the course of the exhibition he grew vegetables, prepared food and consumed it, read books, built tabletop tableaus with an assortment of organic and commercial materials, took photographs, and printed them out. Images that were deemed exhibition-worthy were displayed on the museum's walls, others were cut, stacked, incorporated into new assemblages and re-photographed, or composted along with fruit rinds and other scraps. *Seed Stage* is an apt title, implying that creative work is developmental, performative, and always in flux.

John Baldessari

Is it silly to say "I am making art" as I make it?[2]

Jake Berthot

I really love the romance of the studio—the oil, the turpentine, the smell of the varnish, the touch and feel of painting, the feeling of the brush as much as seeing what the brush puts down.[3]

Mira Schor

It is customary to send postcards to your friends when you're on vacation.

My "vacation" consists, if I'm lucky, of my working in the studio as intensely as possible in all too short a time frame, like a squirrel madly trying to making sure there are enough nuts to last the long winter during which other aspects of the artist's life prevail and overwhelm.

I always begin by putting up a group of postcards which I then take down at the end of the summer to help preserve their color and because I value the ritual of annual re-installation with gradual changes to the grouping and the order as part of my work process. Once I covered entire walls with hundreds of postcards, with major sequences of thematics interwoven.

Over time I've pared down to a small, metonymic grouping of a few postcards taped to an attic door near my painting table. I hardly look at them once I've put them up yet each one represents something significant to me and each day in passing I may catch the eye of an image, so to speak, and a familiar connection is reignited.[4]

Jørgen Leth Interview with Anthony Kaufman

AK: *The Five Obstructions* is such a great argument for limitations and structure in art.

JL: It's strange, it's a contradiction, but it's true. When I have something to work against, it liberates my imagination. I believe very much in authentic inspiration. I'm not about calculation. I find in Lars' films there is sometimes too much calculation. I like the honesty in this work that we've done together, because that's really the fundamental rule: that there's an extreme degree of honesty between us. He knows I'll never cheat. He says he wants me to make crap, but he knows I'll seek solutions that satisfy myself. And he counts on that.

AK: What do you tell your students about arriving at poetry in the cinema?

JL: To not be too happy with the possibilities at hand. I hate films with a clear message, ones that have their answers already when they start.[5]

Donald Baechler

In 1988 I was painting vegetables, based on illustrations from a children's book that I had bought in India, and was really unhappy with the way I was painting them. I had thought about calling up a commercial sign painter and having him come in and paint on my paintings. Then I met a young artist who said he could paint vegetables. I got the idea from McDermott and McGough, who had hired people for specific painting skills: they had someone to paint dinosaur flesh and a different person to paint flowers. So I hired this artist to help me paint vegetables. I would lay out the outlines and compose the paintings and together we would fill them in. In most paintings I would do some of the cucumbers and okras, and let him do the potatoes and onions.

After a while I ran out of vegetable ideas, and there never really was anything else I needed help painting. I used to delegate a lot more responsibility to assistants. Now I do as much as possible myself. I've realized I want everything to be something I touched; everything that goes on the canvas, goes on by me.[6]

Roger Hilton

As I say, painting is a personal thing, like a shit or a fuck. There is no rationale. [...]

Breaking up or breaking down. Going back or going on. It is all one process. You dredge up bits from the past. Past lives, past women, past children. Above all, past paintings. The trappings is nothing. It is your internal life that counts. The outside things, the ephemeral, are something to be fended off. Like dogs cats chickens and fowls.[7]

Pablo Picasso

There was a time when paintings proceeded towards their final result in successive stages. Each day brought something new. A painting was a sum of additions. For me, a painting is a sum of destructions. First I make a painting, then I destroy it. But in the end nothing is lost, the red taken from one place turns up somewhere else.[8]

Allen Ginsberg

Robert Frank is unable to be anything better than what he is, so he has to settle for what he is out of sheer helplessness. I have to settle for what I did or do in my writing because I can't do any better, mainly because of incompetence, insights, or such genius facility that whatever is done is sufficient in its rhythm or eye. It's like trying to make out as a heterosexual, which I once tried but didn't succeed. So I am stuck with what I am, queer. It's not "sufficient," as it is, but accepting the insufficiency is realizing the humor of the condition. You just relax. You don't have to know everything, to be perfect (the art is in being there)—like Burroughs who allows things to fall their own way. His cut-ups are his way of cutting out of his obsessions. Robert Frank leaves a certain amount to chance, like Burroughs with his cut-ups. This allows the phenomenal world to speak for itself, instead of aggressively dominating it, telling the world what it is too insistently.[9]

Jack Whitten

When I removed my hand and started using my "developers," these tools addressed questions like: How do you make a painting? How is a painting made? What way can I make a painting other than using my hand? The developers were my way of removing my hand. So I went to the floor and started using big rakes as one type of developer. The first paintings were done with Afro combs, which were another type of developer. I took the comb I was combing my hair with and started using it to make paintings, to make a surface of paint. Using the comb gave me a sense of the potential in making a painting that way. Next, I took a standard carpenter's saw and cut the handle off, and I used that carpenter's saw to put the paint down. [...]

The factor of speed was important to me. My mind kept telling me and pushing me to get across that whole picture plane at one shot—not to sit there and make several passes to complete the plane. So I made myself a piece of wood 12 feet wide with a big handle, which made it like a big garden rake, really. And the paint was put down with one sweep with that piece of wood. Next I attached a sheet of neoprene rubber, which made my rake into a giant squeegee. That was the second stage of the developer. What the rubber did was allow me to put down

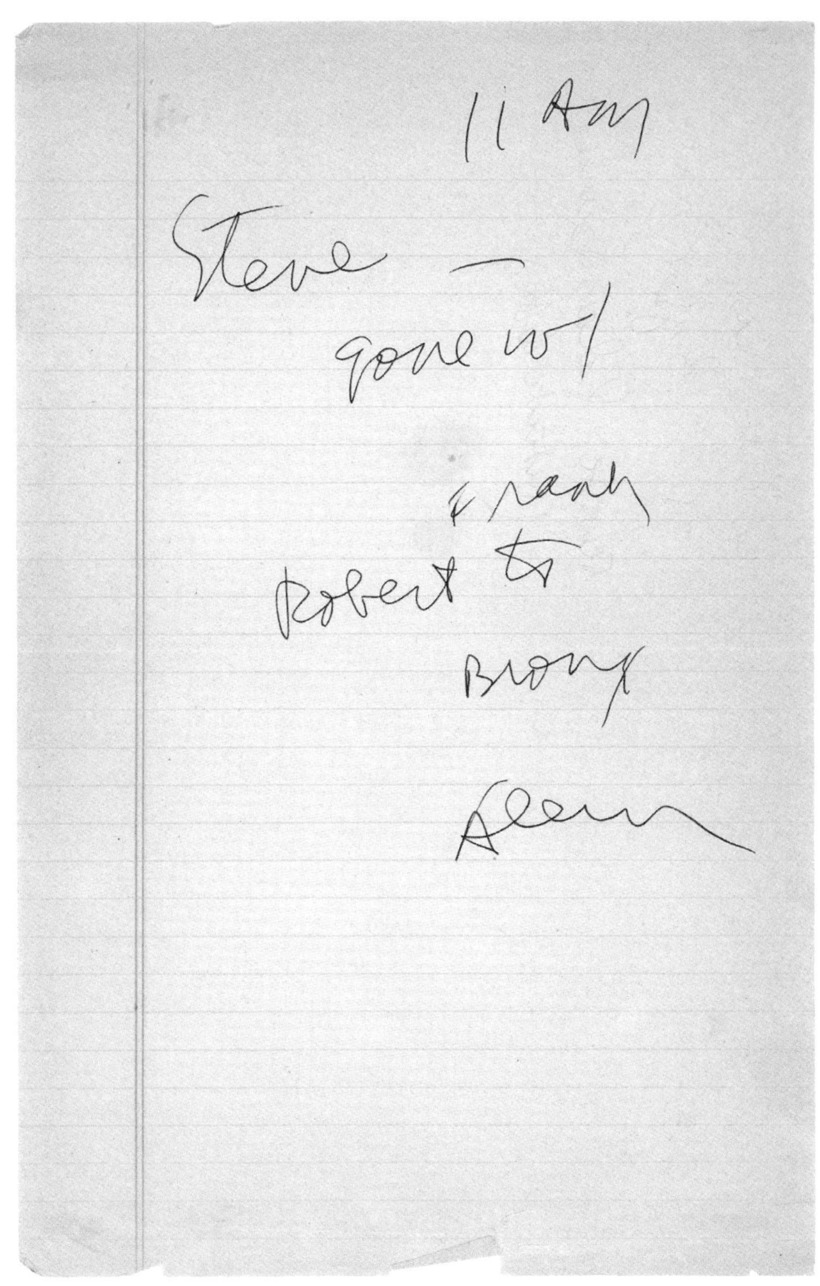

11 AM

Steve —

gone w/

Robert Frank to

Bronx

Allen

Allen Ginsberg
Note to assistant
nd

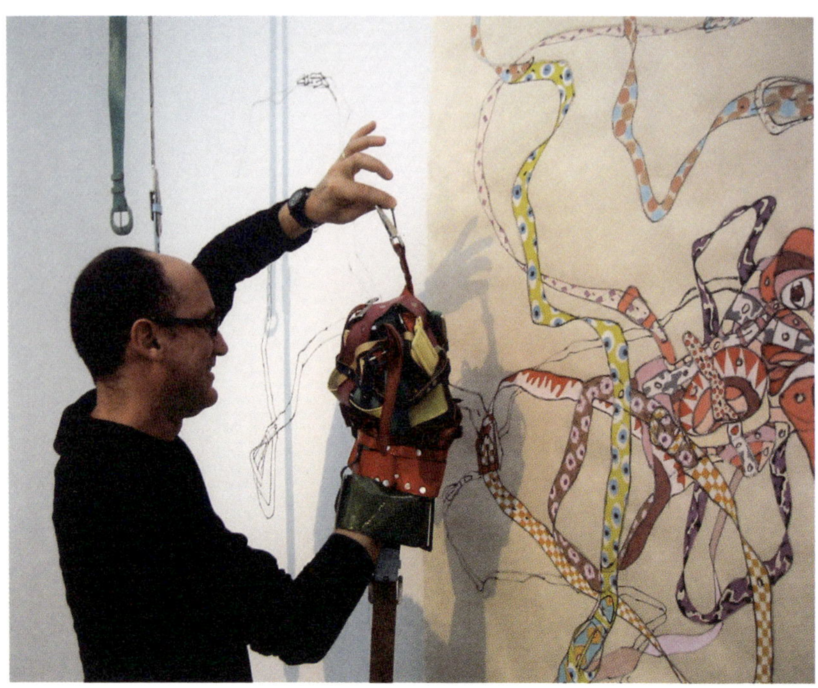

François Morelli
Drawing with *Belt Head*
2007

thin layers of watery acrylic. All these paintings have these fantastic, watery, very thin solutions of paint that I built up in layers. In the third stage of the developer, I removed the rubber and I put on a piece of sheet metal.[10]

François Morelli Interview with Stuart Horodner

SH: What motivated the making of your Belt Heads?

FM: I bought a batch of old belts (raw material) and had them lying around in the studio for over a year until one day I knocked out the first two heads. The initial impetus was head studies no different than my previous works made with metal and cotton strapping (*Body Politic* in the 80's and *Man from Nemsicachingue* in the 90's). I really didn't know what to make of them, their mask-like qualities, S&M overtones, overt fetishistic connotations, and funky expressionism. They stayed under the table for months until I thought of putting a glove inside and began thinking of them as surrogates and myself the artist as a ventriloquist. At which

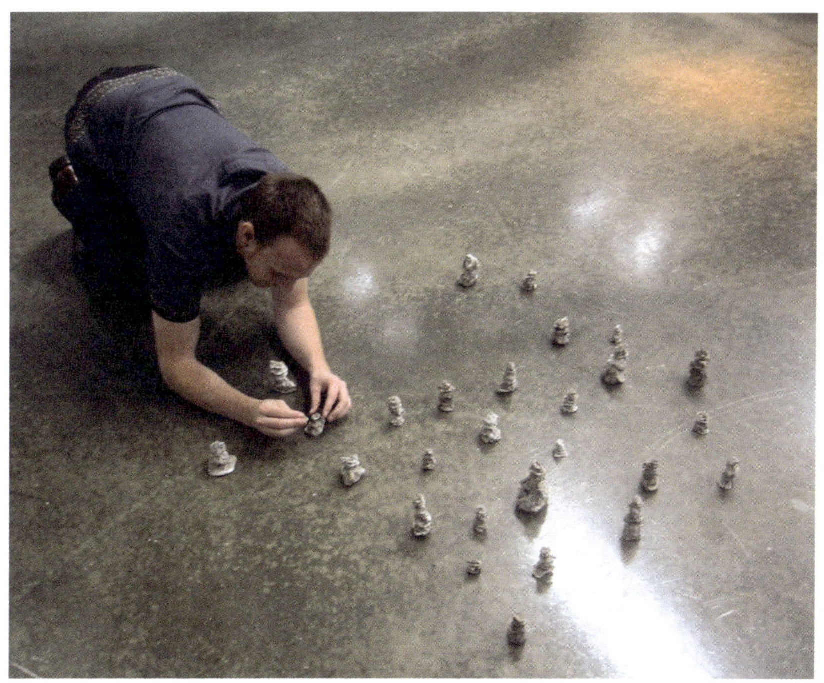

Matt Bryans
Installing *Untitled (Aluminum)*
2006

point I took them with me in my briefcase and had myself photographed in photo booths. All this remained private until I did a first one minute public performance in a gallery—a belt head in each hand hanging by my side slowly raised over my head where they kissed.

SH: And then the using of them as "surrogates" who make drawings?

FM: It wasn't a conscious decision but again one of slippage. I had been doing drawings of the heads throughout this period. They were unsatisfactory. Way too tight and contrived. One day I thought of putting a brush in their mouth. By this point I've got over a dozen of them. I've always been fascinated by armless artists who paint with their mouths. The Belt Heads became an intermediary between me and the paper. I've always said my relationship to drawing is literary. I was raised in between two languages and always felt inadequate in both. Drawing became my non-verbal form of recording. Before the Belt Heads, I always had conversations going on in my head while I was drawing. Sometimes these conversations were about drawing—correcting the gesture, loosening up, critiquing in progress almost as if I had a teacher talking as I was drawing. When the Belt Heads became those who draw, I was able to comment as they drew. I sometimes see them as tools but mostly they are collaborators with personalities and particular attributes and skill sets. I have my favorites. They don't all draw and are never made with the intention of drawing. Besides, I've always wanted a studio with lots of assistants and the Belt Heads are as cheap as they come, giving me the impression of grandeur and power at the same time.[11]

Matt Bryans

Working on newspaper images of faces and heads directly relates to the fact that in real life it is often difficult to look people in the eyes. Doing so can be taken as a sign of aggression. A still image allows you to linger. I was working at an airport seeing thousands of people rushing past me every day, and when I got home my bedroom in a flatshare was covered with these reworked still images of people. The images were all round the room, ceiling, walls, door, cupboards, floor. I actually found it strangely comforting. Can't see why people find the work disturbing, scary, melancholy. It even made the room temperature a lot warmer. In fact one time I had to remove a section because the moisture between the paper and the wall was dripping down so much. These pictures were the first thing I saw in the morning and the last thing at night.

With any of these things, I don't think that you are just doing it endlessly for yourself, because they need to be out in the world somehow so they can leave you. It is an attempt at communication. Talking to yourself is often indicative of the onset of madness after all. For me it is very important, not to mention fun, to get out there and allow a space for something extra to happen. It's sometimes a fine line though. Talking too much about something prior to action kills it for me. It's almost like my imagination is so stunted and under-developed that I need physical experiences to allow me a way into the world. It allows you to forgive yourself and others.[12]

Robert Henri

It is remarkable how many functions one brush can perform.[13]

Willem de Kooning

I have all kind of brushes. A lot of them are house painter's brushes, and when I make those large landscape pictures—so called landscapes—I work with very wet brushes, the kind of brushes you use when you paint a ceiling: it drips all over you. They're made out of a fiber and very little hair. I put them in boiling water until they get kind of rubbery. Then they hold the paint, and it gives me great comfort to paint with them.[14]

Gilbert & George

Gilbert: The making of an art object is not important. Dressing like someone who makes objects is not important. What is important is putting the work in front of people. So we don't want anyone to see how we make our works. The idea that evidence of the hand is good—that's what we dislike. It's all based on order. But we want the order—and our effort—to be invisible.

George: We wouldn't want people to think, My goodness, they must have spent a year on that. The picture should be completely smooth, as if it had been shot out of our brains, onto the paper like magic. In reality, our pieces are extremely handmade, labored objects. But they look the opposite. And that is how we want them to look. That is why we would never exhibit our working drawings.

Gilbert: And that is why no one is allowed in our studio.[15]

Franz Kline

You don't paint the way someone, by observing your life, thinks you *have* to paint, you paint the way you have to in order to *give*, that's life itself, and someone will look and say it is the product of knowing, but it has nothing to do with knowing, it has to do with giving. The question about knowing will naturally be wrong. When you've finished giving, the look surprises you as well as anyone else.[16]

Arnulf Rainer

When I draw I get excited, I talk to myself, I make grimaces, I curse at people, I move about all the time changing bodily as well as character- and personality-wise. [...]

In the years 1968 and 1969 I began to go, at least once a week, to one of the main train stations in Vienna. Located there was a coin-operated photo-booth in which both passport- and postcard-size photos could be made. During the day people either waiting impatiently in front of the booth or peeking curiously between the curtains would disturb me; worse, some even wanted to see the pictures when I took them, some ten or fifteen postcards, out of the slot and often destroyed many of them because I felt they did not correspond to my expectations.

So I decided to arrive late, when the last trains had left and it was almost time for the station to be closed. After a quick glass of wine at the buffet-counter under suspicious glances of policemen I would go to work. A certain amount of excitement was necessary; an abundance of expression of the facial muscles and nerves. I would talk myself into such a state all day, especially while driving the car through the city. I still use this method combined with more or less harmless drugs. Intoxicating drugs do not work because while they intensify the imagination they weaken the muscular reflexes.[17]

Mary Shelley

With an anxiety that almost amounted to agony, I collected the instruments of life around me, that I might infuse a spark of being into the lifeless thing that lay at my feet. It was already one in the morning, the rain pattered dismally against the panes, and my candle was nearly burned out, when, by the glimmer of the half-extinguished light, I saw the dull yellow eye of the creature open; it breathed hard, and a convulsive motion agitated its limbs.[18]

Vito Acconci

In everything you do, you see something wrong with what you've done before, or something that maybe made sense once, but doesn't make much sense now, so you try to bring something else in. [...] I always wish I can get to the point where I can include everything, but I don't know if that's necessarily possible.[19]

Yoko Ono

REVALUE PIECE II

Use all existing art work as pieces of
furniture and household appliances.
i. e. Use sculpture such as Henry Moore's
as diaper hangers, or chairs, bookshelves,
tables and beds. Use paintings such as
Monet and Picasso as heavy curtains, sofa
covers, etc.

Use all existing armaments as decorative objects and
accessories. i. e. Use cannons and fighters for garden
sculptures, bullets and earrings, etc.

1968 winter [20]

Robert Watts

In looking over the things I've done over the past few years I cannot find any special continuity or even any specific interest. I suspect it is a good thing that everything is up in the air, although I must admit I am not always comfortable with that feeling. I've been making a point recently not to shut out so many things as I used to. Some years ago I had to keep out anything that did not seem appropriate to what I was doing at the moment. All those other things were somehow distractions. Now when a distraction comes along I may take out time to think about it, or write it down, or photograph it, record it, film it, cast it or eat it, or something else; as a matter of fact, it seems more and more that distractions are more interesting than anything else. ... One day I tore up a letter by mistake and later on it seemed that it was the only important thing that happened all week.[21]

Anthony Bourdain

You either can—or can't—make an omelet. You either can—or can't—chop an onion, shake a pan, keep up with the other cooks, replicate again and again, perfectly, the dishes that need to be done. No credential, no amount of bullshit, no well-formed sentences or pleas for mercy will change the basic facts. The kitchen is the last meritocracy—a world of absolutes; one knows without ambiguity at the end of each day how one did.[22]

Brad Cloepfil **Interview with Stuart Horodner**

SH: What's the difference between amending an existing building and making one from scratch? You're working now on additions that change existing buildings that are quite notorious: the Seattle Art Museum and Two Columbus Circle.

BC: There are different acts of architecture. You're always operating in an existing context, whether that context is a beautiful wheat field or a block in a city or a building in a city. To me it's all the same. There are restrictions given and opportunities granted. And a preexisting dialogue. I mean, agriculture is building.

SH: So no difference working with a Robert Venturi building or at the Maryhill Museum in the Columbia Gorge?

BC: No question they are different opportunities, but frankly the scale and vastness of the unbuilt space at Maryhill was just as daunting and as restrictive as a historically significant piece of architecture. Finding out what one is capable of doing in that landscape is not that different from understanding what would communicate in the landscape of Two Columbus Circle, on that existing building.

It's the same challenge of trying, as an architect, to find out what is possible in all of these things. It's not like I enter these projects filled with what I want to do or even what I should do. A lot of times what you want to do isn't what you should do.

SH: When do you know that?

BC: After a lot of really confusing bad work. Self doubt and self reflection.[23]

Allan Kaprow

What if I had only a vague idea about "art" but didn't know the conventions that told me when I was in its presence or was making it? What if I were digging a hole—would that be art? What if I didn't know about audiences and publicity? What if I were to just go shopping? Would that not be art? What if I didn't realize that art happened at certain times and in certain places? What if I were to lie awake imagining things in bed at 4 A.M.?

Would that be the wrong place and the wrong time for art? What if I weren't aware that art was considered more marvelous than life? What if I didn't know that an artist was meant to "create" art? What if I were to think art was just paying attention? What if I were to forget to think about art constantly? Could I still make, do, engage in art? Would I be doing something else? Would that be okay?[24]

Jay-Z

Everywhere I went I'd write. If I was crossing a street with my friends and a rhyme came to me, I'd break out my binder, spread it on a mailbox or lamppost and write the rhyme before I crossed the street.[25]

WILL.I.AM Interview with Steve Marsh

SM: *The Beginning* is such a brazenly direct record. Every song has a phrase that's repeated so many times, it's hypnotic.

W: That's how I write songs. I listen to people talking. Or my girl sends me a text: XOXOXO. Oh s***! I'm turning that into a [bleepin'] song! I listen to the world. I listen to conversations. I listen to the room. And then I mark down things that I want to turn into records. And I listen to how people say things. And then I write a melody to how they said it naturally. Like, "That's crazy." Whoa! I'm making a song called "That's Crazy." And the melody has to go, "Bewwmp/Bewwwmn." Then it's going to flow out your mouth naturally, because that's how you would say it in a sentence.[26]

Joe Sola

Eleven reasons why I work with myself:

I am easy to work with
I show up on time
I usually give good feedback about the project
I am very critical of the project
I take good direction
I work on a sliding scale
I will work for beer
I am extremely sensitive to others when working in public spaces
I don't have to do much paperwork for image release, personal liability, etc.
I won't sue myself, if something goes wrong
I never complain about the food during the project[27]

Daniel Day-Lewis Interview with Eileen Myles

EM: In some weird way, the spaces between the work are what's really interesting.

DDL: Definitely. That part is obscured when you're young because your drive is always leading you from one place to another. It's the resting places or the periods of lying fallow where you do the real work.

EM: The thing that's scary about not doing anything, or not doing what people are inviting you to do, is you feel like you are facing death in a way.

DDL: Yeah, I think you're right. It's a little death and you have lots of little practices. How do you work?

EM: I started writing poems in my twenties, and it got to be how I made a map of the world. That's always happening, though it does stop sometimes. I started writing fiction slowly in my thirties, then that became novels. Making a living as a poet is a huge trick, so I stumbled into being a performance artist, teaching journalism, reviewing art. I'll be very, very busy, but at the end of the year, I'll think, "What did I do this year?"[28]

Hokusai

From the age of six, I had a passion for drawing the form of objects. By the age of about fifty, I had published an infinity of drawings, but nothing I produced before the age of seventy is worth counting. It was at the age of seventy-three that I more or less understood the structure of true nature, of animals, grasses, birds, fish, and insects.

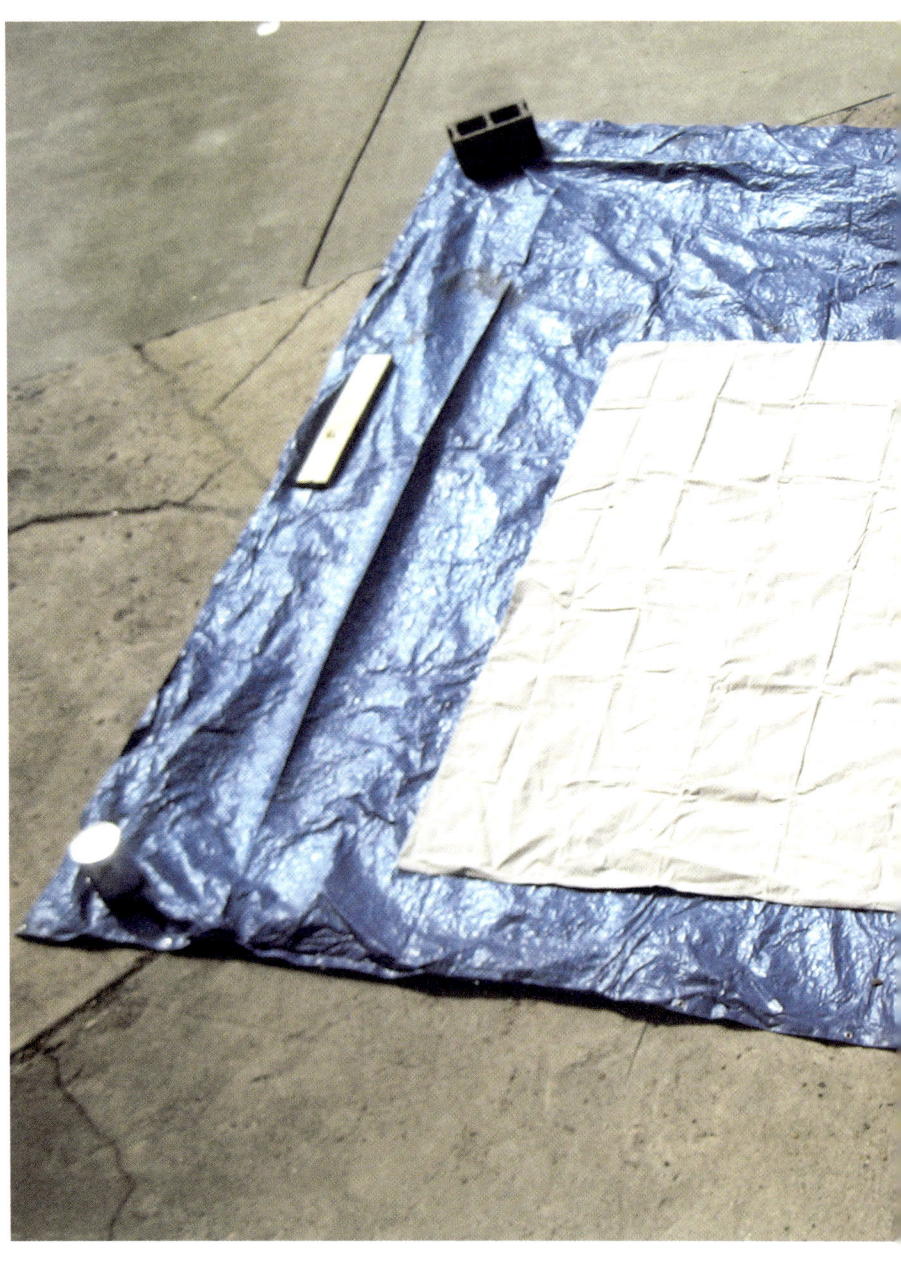

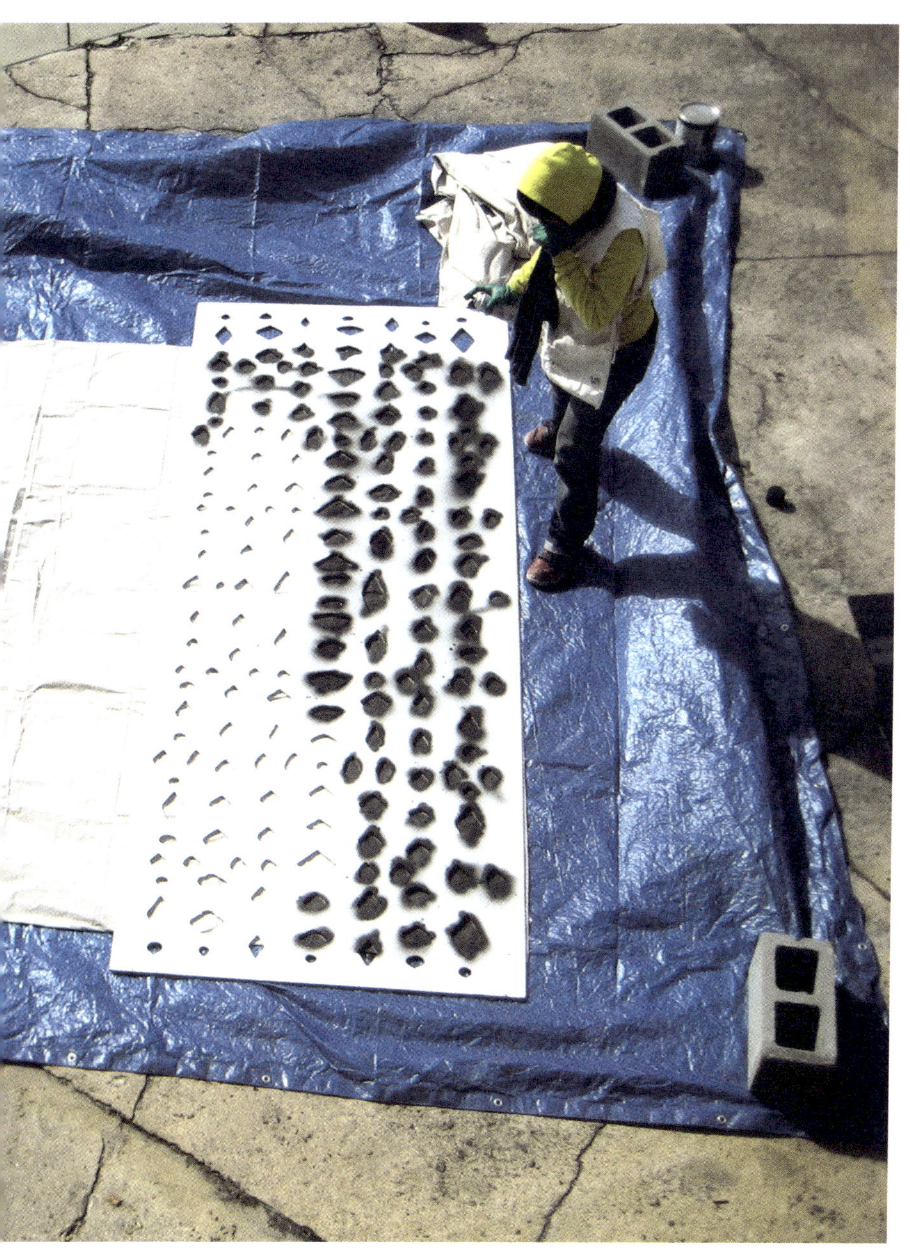

Amanda Ross-Ho
Making *Untitled Home and Gift Showroom (Negative Reinforcement)*
2009

Consequently, by the age of eighty, I will have made even more progress; at ninety I will penetrate the mystery of things; at a hundred I will definitely have reached a degree of wonder, and when I am a hundred and ten, for my part, be it a dot, be it a line, everything will be alive.

I ask those who will live as long as I do to see if I keep my word.

Written at the age of seventy-five by myself, formerly Hokusai, today Gwakio Rojin, the old man crazy about drawing.[29]

Vija Celmins

I think one of the things I've noticed in doing the drawings is that I tend to take very small increments and steps in changing. An example was that I had been working with the pencil and I began to see that the graphite itself had a certain life to it. So I did a series of images of oceans and deserts using different grades of graphite and pushing each to its limit. I learned a lot about the possibilities of expressiveness in graphite by doing this. Then I moved into the galaxy drawings. Even though you may think they came from lying under the stars, for me, they came out of loving the blackness of the pencil. It's almost as if I was exploring the blackness of the pencil along with the image that went with it.[30]

Morton Feldman

I work every day, more in terms of feeling that I have done a good day's work. Now, it could be two hours, it could be sixteen hours, it could be two days going into each other without sleep. Unless I feel that the day's work is completed, I'm not counting how much work I do, I just psychologically feel that I have to do a day's work. By day's work I don't mean, you know, seven hours, it could be any time. Sometimes a day's work is waiting.[31]

Frank Stella

There are two problems in painting. One is to find out what painting is and the other is to find out how to make a painting. The first is learning something and the second is making something.[32]

Brian Grazer

When I started out in the entertainment business, I made a list of people who I thought it would be good to meet. Not people who could give me a job or a deal. But people who could shake me up, teach me something, challenge my ideas about myself and the world.

So I started calling up experts in all kinds of fields: trial lawyers, neurosurgeons, CIA agents, embryologists, firewalkers, police chiefs, hypnotists, forensic anthropologists, and even presidents.[33]

Amanda Ross-Ho

THINGS I MIGHT DO TODAY

PUT MY COAT ON
TAKE MY COAT OFF
PLUG SOMETHING IN
BECOME TOO WARM
BECOME TOO COLD
USE THE BATHROOM
CHECK MY EMAIL
MAKE SOME PHONE CALLS
GET SOME COFFEE
MAKE A LIST
SHUFFLE SOME PAPERS AROUND
RE-ARRANGE SOME STACKS
TURN ON CLIP LAMPS
TURN OFF CLIP LAMPS
TAKE SOMETHING OUT OF A BAG
PUT SOMETHING INTO A BAG
WRITE THINGS DOWN
TYPE SOMETHING
DRAG SOMETHING INTO THE TRASH
RINSE MY HANDS
CROSS THINGS OFF A LIST
PIN SOMETHING TO THE WALL
GLANCE AT A CALENDAR
GLANCE AT A CLOCK
FILL A WATER BOTTLE
DRINK SOME MORE WATER
CHARGE THINGS
DOWNLOAD SOMETHING
LISTEN TO MP3'S[34]

Werner Herzog

Shooting a film itself is nothing but banalities. However, there's very rare moments where I get the feeling sometimes I'm like the little girl in the fairy tale

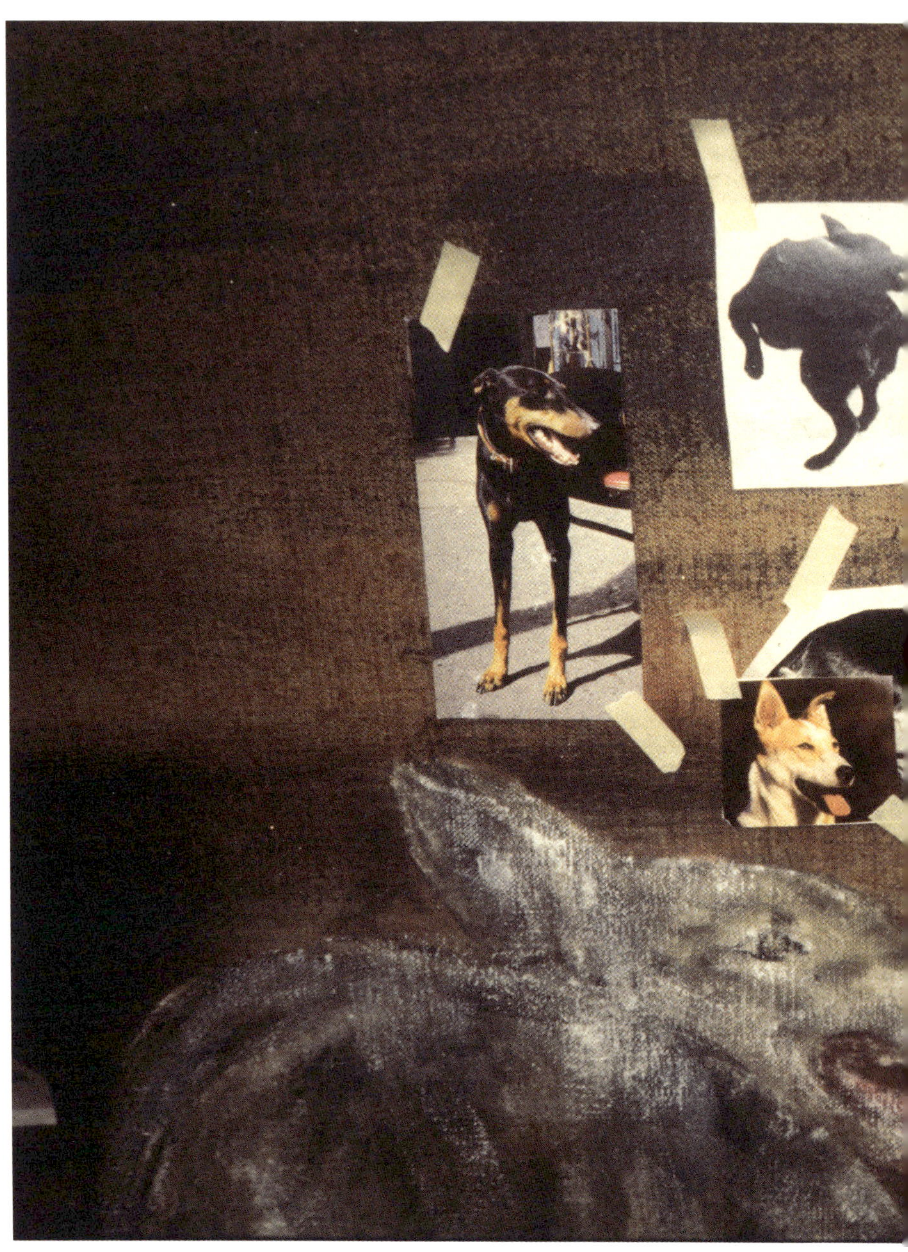

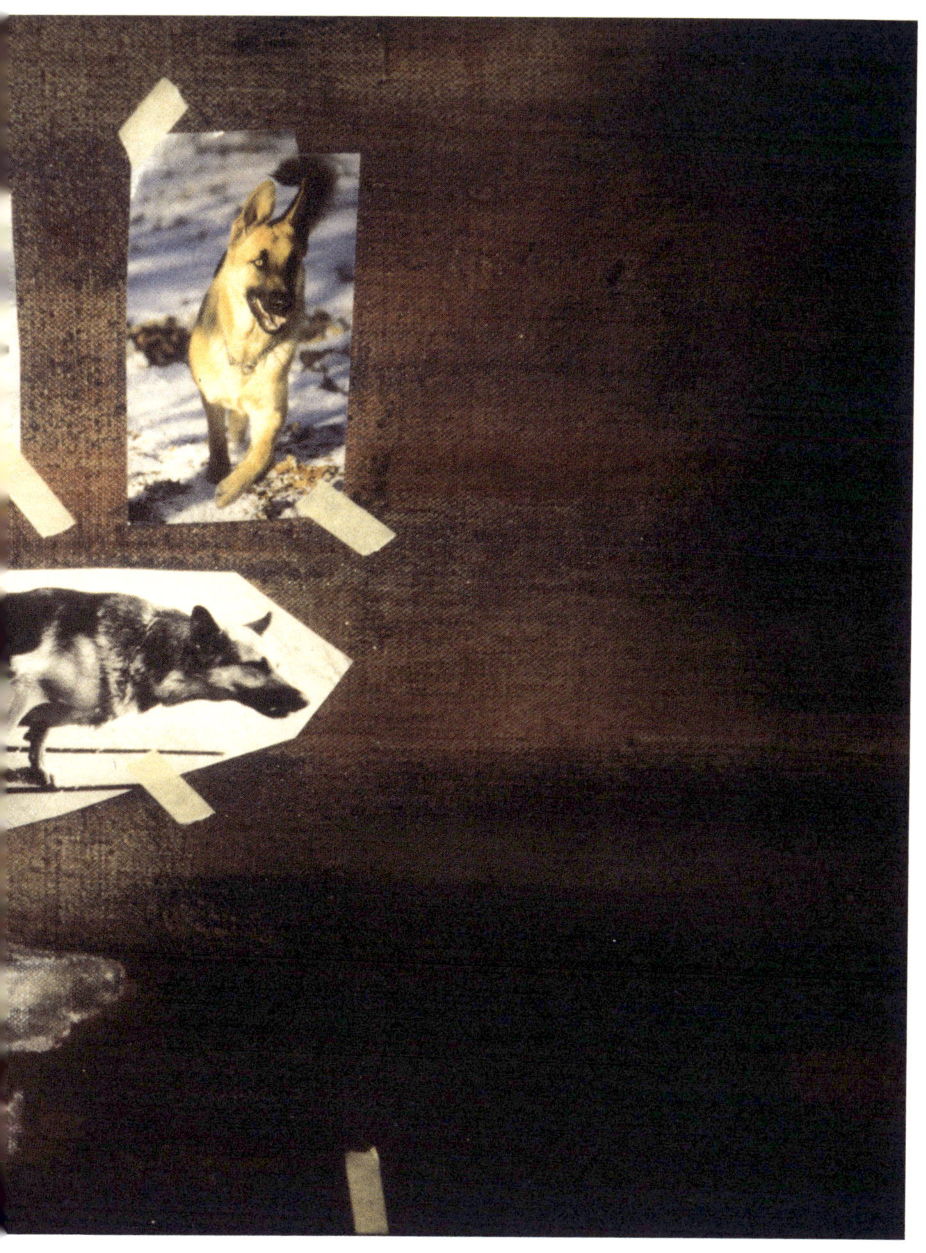

Leon Golub
Scratch, In progress
1999

who steps out into the night, in the stars, and she holds her apron open, and the stars are raining into her apron. Those moments I have seen and I have had. But they are very rare.[35]

John Berger

The first thing painters ask about a studio-space usually concerns the light. And so one might think of a studio as a kind of conservatory or observatory or even a lighthouse. And of course light is important. But it seems to me that a studio, when being used, is much more like a stomach. A place of digestion, transformation and excretion. Where images change form. Where everything is both regular and unpredictable.[36]

Thomas Nozkowski Interview with Francine Prose

FP: So what about your process? What is it?

TN: I assume that if something interests me enough to get my hand moving on the canvas, that's a good enough reason. I finish ten, twenty paintings a year. I start about thirty. I operate on the premise that every battle can be won, every idea can be completed somehow. I keep these extra ten to twenty paintings a year that don't get finished. I've got maybe three hundred unfinished paintings in racks in my studio, and every so often I go back and try to complete one. Sometimes you wake up one morning and realize you've found a way to finish a painting.

FP: How do you know when it's finished?

TN: To put it as simply as possible—and this is a simple answer, not a total answer—I know when a painting's finished when I understand why I wanted to do it in the first place.[37]

Agnes Martin

[…] To feel confident and successful is not natural to the artist.
To feel insufficient,
to experience disappointment and defeat in waiting for
inspiration
is the natural state of mind of an artist.
As a result praise to most artists is a little embarrassing.
They cannot take credit for inspiration,
for what we can see perfectly, but we cannot do perfectly. […][38]

Bob Dylan

I wrote these songs in not a meditative state at all, but more like in a trancelike, hypnotic state. *This* is how I feel? Why do I *feel* like that? And who's the *me* that feels this way? I couldn't tell you that, either. But I know that those songs are just in my genes and I couldn't stop them comin' out.[39]

Alberto Giacometti

I know that it is utterly impossible for me to model, paint or draw a head, for instance, as I see it and, still, this is the only thing I am attempting to do. All that I will be able to make will be only a pale image of what I see and my success will always be less than my failure or, perhaps, the success will be equal to my failure. I do not know whether I work in order to make something or in order to know why I cannot make what I would like to make.[40]

Leon Golub

Working on something, I ask, "Am I getting too soft? Is the thing easing up too much? Am I just smoothing out the edges of what I've done?" So I say "Watch it." Another part of me says, "For Christ's sake man, do you really have to be so fucking ugly? Do you really have to be? Can't you just take it from another angle?" Then I think, "Well, maybe I can't, you see. Being who I am, you know, I can't. Or if I can, I don't want to."[41]

Charles Simic

My entire practice consists of submitting to chance only to cheat on it. I agree with Vincent Huidobro, who said long ago, "Chance is fine when you're dealt five aces or at least four queens. Otherwise, forget it."[42]

It was Octavio Paz, I believe, who told me the story about going to visit André Breton in Paris after World War II, being admitted and told to wait because the poet was engaged. Indeed he could see, from the living room where he was seated, Breton furiously writing in his study. After a while he came out, they greeted each other, and set out to have lunch in a nearby restaurant.

"What were you working on, *maître*?" Paz inquired as they were strolling to their destination.

"I was doing some automatic writing," Breton replied.

"But," Paz exclaimed in astonishment, "I saw you erase repeatedly!"

"It wasn't automatic enough," Breton assured the young poet.[43]

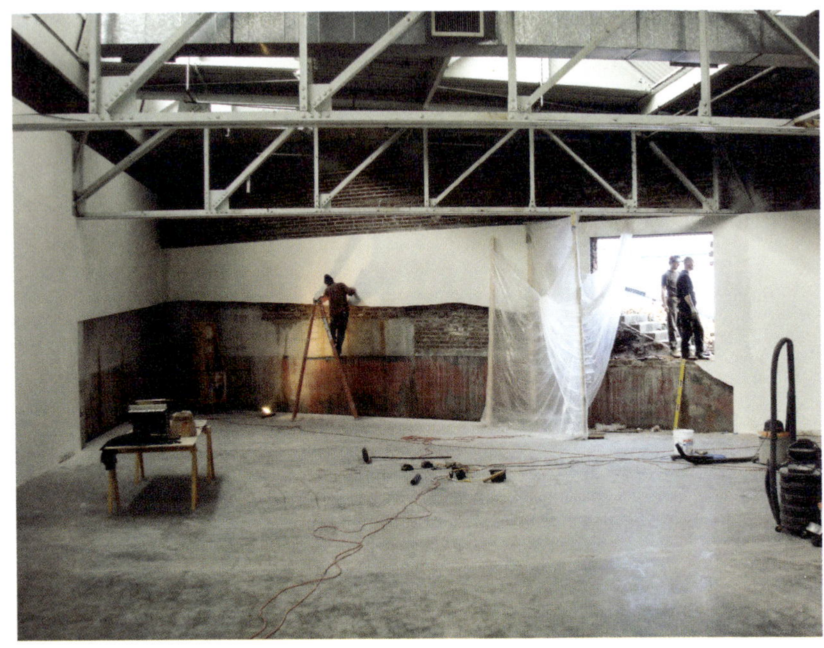

bldgs
Installing *Boundary Issues*
2008

Philip Guston

What measure is there, other than the fact that at *one* point in your life you trusted a feeling? You have to trust that feeling and then continue, trusting yourself. And it works in a reverse way. I know that I started similar things in the past, 20 to 25 years ago, and would scrape them out. I remember the pictures I scraped out very well, in fact some of them are sharper in my mind than the ones that remained. Well then, I would subsequently ask myself, "Why did I scrape them out?" Well, I wasn't ready to accept it, that's the only answer. This leads me to another point: it doesn't occur to many viewers that the artist often has difficulty accepting the painting himself. You can't assume that I gloried in it, or celebrated it. I didn't. I'm a night painter, so when I come into the studio the next morning the delirium is over. I know I won't remember detail, but I will remember the feeling of the whole thing. I come into the studio very fearfully, I creep in to see what happened the night before. And the feeling is one of, "My God, did *I* do that?" That is the about the only measure I have. The kind of shaking, trembling of..."That's me? I did that?"[44]

Woody Allen Interview with Dave Itzkoff

DI: Has getting older changed your work in any way? Do you see a certain wistfulness emerging in your later films?

WA: No, it's too hit or miss. There's no rhyme or reason to anything that I do. It's whatever seems right at the time. I've never once in my life seen any film of mine after I put it out. Ever. I haven't seen *Take the Money and Run* since 1968. I haven't seen *Annie Hall* or *Manhattan* or any film I've made afterward. If I'm on the treadmill and I'm scooting through the channels, and I come across one of them, I go right past it instantly, because I feel it could only depress me. I would only feel, "Oh God, this is so awful, if I could only do that again."[45]

Malcolm Gladwell

The Beatles ended up traveling to Hamburg five times between 1960 and the end of 1962. On the first trip, they played 106 nights, five or more hours a night. On their second trip, they played 92 times. On their third trip, they played 48 times, for a total of 172 hours on stage. The last two Hamburg gigs, in November and December of 1962, involved another 90 hours of performing. All told, they performed for 270 nights in just over a year and a half. By the time they had their first burst of success in 1964, in fact, they had performed live an estimated twelve hundred times. Do you know how extraordinary that is? Most bands today don't perform twelve hundred times in their entire careers. The Hamburg crucible is one of the things that set the Beatles apart.[46]

Jonathan Adler

When I am making a piece of pottery, I know that it is finished—and that it's good—if it looks like it's supposed to be that way, like it's been uncovered rather than created.[47]

David Smith

How do you spend your time? More talking about art than making it? How do you spend your money? On art materials first—or do you start to pinch here?[48]

Jonathan Borofsky

I began to write the numbers small on 8½-by-11-inch sheets of paper, usually both sides. I thought if I kept this up for a while it might teach me something or give me the answer I was searching for. After a few months it got to be a kick. I'd do it for several hours each day, and then I thought I'd at least take it to a million.

After counting for a few hours at a time, I often found myself making little scribbles on the page—stick figures, heads attached to trees—but I let them go by. Then one day I looked at one of the past scribbles and thought, I'd like to make a painting of that. So I went out and got a little canvas board and some oil paints—like I was eight years old again and beginning my first painting lesson. It took me about two hours to finish it. Then I took the number I had been on in my counting and put it in the corner of the painting.

Something connected there. I had both a recognizable image and a conceptual ordering in time.[49]

Luc Tuymans

The source images may go through many stages, over many months, before being painted. A clear, sharp photograph is never a point of departure for me. I have to degrade the image, to make holes in it, "leap holes" you might say, because what stimulates me most in an image is inconsistency.[50]

Henry Wessel

Most musicians I know don't just play music on Saturday night. They play music every day. They are always fiddling around, letting the notes lead them from one place to another. Taking photographs is like that. It is a generative process. It pulls you along.[51]

Jerry Saltz

I don't even really think of myself as a writer; I think I'm more of a folk-critic, a raw nerve, or a loudmouth. I agree with the sportswriter Red Smith who wrote, "Writing is easy: You sit down at a typewriter, put a piece of paper in ... and open a vein." For me there is no such thing as writing. There is only re-writing. Before I write I don't hate anything more than writing. Once I'm writing, I don't love anything more. When I'm done I often think I've written a bullet-proof review. Then when I read it in print, I cringe at the kinks and flaws. Each week I try to learn from my mistakes and not make them again and again. Other than the love of looking at art, what keeps me going is the desire to write better.[52]

Janine Antoni Interview with Stuart Horodner

SH: Can you talk about two quotes from past interviews? One, the idea that you "give yourself an experience." That you structure a project around the desire to go through something, to give yourself that which you can't think through entirely to satisfaction. And two, your comment that "if the object doesn't change me, then it's not finished."

JA: If I don't have an experience with the object, how can I hope that the viewer will have an experience with the object? I start from that place. Making something is like a fight. I start out with an idea of what I want the object to be, and I try to impose it on the material. Usually the material resists me all the way. If I can stay open and have the courage not to hang on to my original idea, the material starts to speak back and tell me what it wants to be. A lot of meaning comes out in the fight that I couldn't have known before starting. It becomes this back-and-forth relationship. When my work takes my body to a physical and sometimes psychological extreme, it becomes a complex relationship. It makes me face certain things about myself which are hard to deal with; I find something incredibly valuable about bringing the body to that edge. Something happens physically in the work, but also psychologically that I believe in and count on. There is a point where I'm actually feeling the repercussions of the object on my body. My hope is to have that happen psychologically as well. Then it's almost like the ideal relationship—not only in art. (*laughter*) So that's what I'm looking for. Because a lot of my work is repetitive and accumulative, many people ask me, "When do you know something is done?" It has nothing to do with the way it looks or formal composition. It's done when the work embodies this complex relationship.[53]

Stephen Schofield

Notes for taking down *Dibutade*

Tools

Wire cutters to cut cable
Electric screwdriver for removing the sconces
Water sprayer
Plastic drop cloth enough to protect the floor during the take down plus enough to wrap the pieces for transportation
Plastic containers for transportation
Scissors
Utility knife

- Place plastic on the floor below the pieces.
- To soften the pieces you need to go over them several times with the water sprayer. You don't need to soak the pieces but to soften them. Several

light passes rather than one heavy one is more efficient and less messy. Concentrate on the "feeding tubes" to soften them so you can introduce the sprayer on the inside of the bodies in order to soften supporting walls. This is important because the sugar has made the cloth so still that it can crack under pressure. The walls are situated in the head, bridge of the nose, the mouth and the temples along the vertebrae and across the waist line. The horizontal piece and the floor supported piece both also have a tube running up the leg as a sheath for the PVC tube.

- It is better to start humidifying all the pieces at once, this way you let the water do its work. As you proceed, you can start to flatten gently the pieces. Concentrate on the parts that are hard i.e., those that are still dry.
- In terms of *Dibutade III*, which is hung from the wall, you need to soften the fabric enough to be able to soften the zipper and get your hand and sprayer in to soften the inside. Then cut the cable near the PVC tube and undo the eyelet so you can pull the wire out the foot hole. The PVC tube should separate easily from the cloth as you spray where they meet close to the wall.
- *Dibutade II* is supported only by the PVC tube that runs through his leg, again move slowly wetting all the way to reach any dry parts.
- *Dibutade II* can be first softened at the top, then lift it off the PVC tube and put horizontally on the floor to be able to wet the leg sleeve from the bottom of the foot.
- For *Dibutade III*, try to avoid over soaking it as the black fabric still bleeds when wet and can stain the white tuxedo fabric.
- Once the cables are cut and the PVC tubes removed, you can cut another sheet of plastic and start to flatten the pieces on the clean plastic. At times, an air bubble will just keep moving around as the air cannot escape, in that case I roll the piece between two sheets of plastic to get rid of the air.
- The pieces need to be folded for transportation but they also need to dry out. In order to do both, I establish my fold lines first, let the pieces dry a bit in one position, unfold gently and let them dry out in another, this way you can expose each surface to the air for drying. It usually takes two days for the pieces to dry out properly.[54]

Richard Wentworth

By having things in the studio, and if there's enough of them, it raises the level to which they might tap me on the shoulder and go, "Psst. Did you notice that I've been sitting next to so and so? And when you were out of the room, I spoke to so and so." I need that.[55]

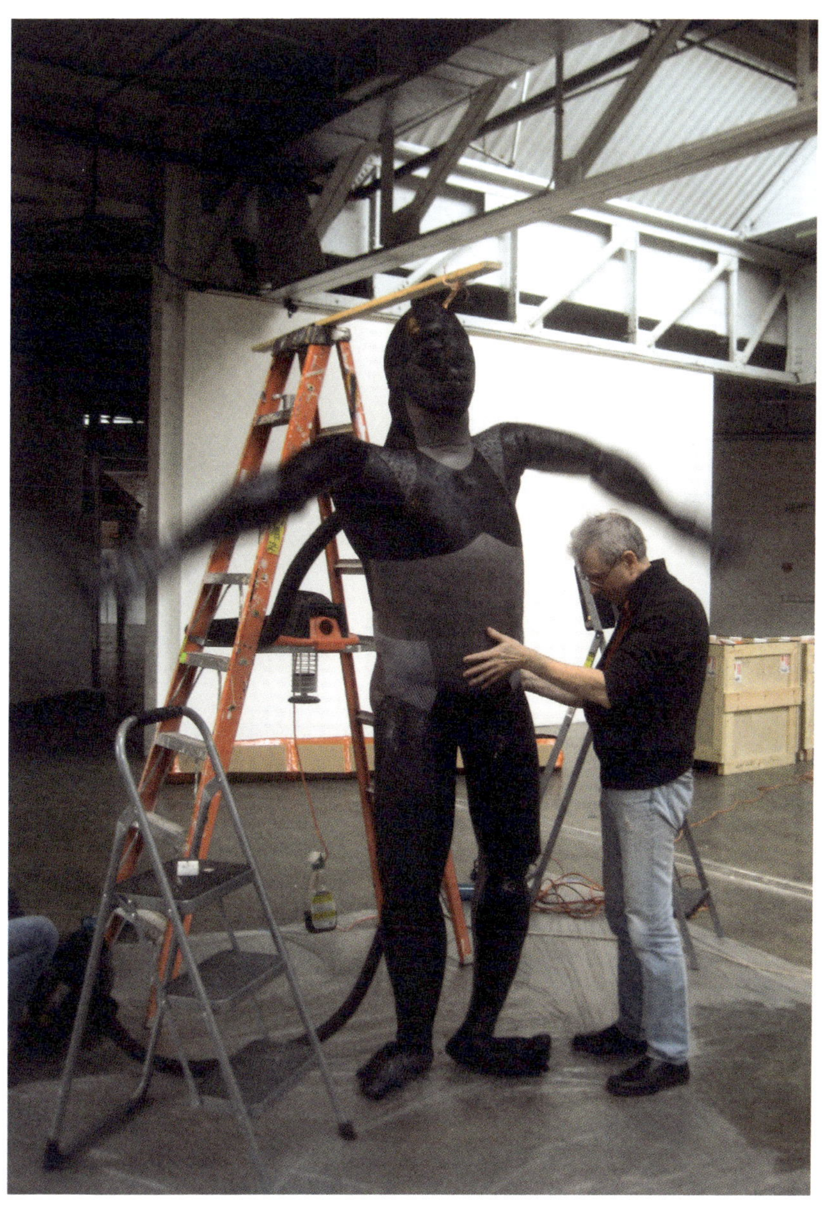

Stephen Schofield
Installing *Dibutade II*
2011

Tony Bennett

The first day you don't do the scales, you know. The second day, the musicians know. The third day, the audience knows.[56]

Matthew Higgs

In my own work as an artist, curator, writer, gallery director, and educator, I'm interested in the points of intersection and the points of departure inherent to these disciplines. Negotiating these different roles is what I enjoy the most. In all cases it's about making decisions and thinking about the context for the decision making process.[57]

David Wojnarowicz

[...] every painting or photograph or film I make I make with the sense that it may be the last thing I do and so I try and pull everything in to the surface of that action. I work quickly now and feel there is no time for bullshit; cut straight to the heart of the senses and map it out as clearly as tools and growth allow. And in the better moments I can see my friends; vague transparencies of their faces maybe over my shoulder or superimposed on the surfaces of my eyes; thus I'm more aware of myself—seeing myself from a distance; seeing myself see others I can almost see my own breath see my internal organs functioning pump pumping; these days I see the edge of mortality; the edge of death and dying around everything like a warm halo of light sometimes dim sometimes irradiated—I see myself seeing death; it's like a transparent celluloid image of myself is accompanying myself everywhere I go. I see my friends and I see myself and I see breath coming from my lips and the plants are drinking it and I see breath coming from my chest and everything is fading; becoming a shadow that may disappear as the sun goes down.[58]

Paul Ramírez Jonas

What role does chance play in your work?
What is not in your work, but you wish it were?
What parts of your work are medieval?
Do you still believe in "truth to materials"?[59]

NOTES

1. Mihaly Csikszentmihalyi, "Enjoyment and the Quality of Life," *Flow: The Psychology of Optimal Experience* (New York: Harper Perennial Modern Classics, 1990), 49.

2. John Baldessari, in Coosje van Bruggen, "But This is Not the Moral of the Story..." *John Baldessari*, Exhibition catalogue (Museum of Contemporary Art, Los Angeles, 1990), 76.

3. Jake Berthot, in *Jake Berthot*, Exhibition catalogue (Rose Art Museum, Brandeis University, Waltham, MA, 1988), 2.

4. Mira Schor, "Postcard Post," *A Year of Positive Thinking* (Aug 8, 2010), http://ayearofpositivethinking.com/2010/08/08/postcard-post, accessed Aug 8, 2010.

5. Jørgen Leth, in Anthony Kaufman, "Breaking Von Trier: Jorgen Leth Survives 'The Five Obstructions,'" *Indiewire.com* (May 26, 2004), http://www.indiewire.com/article/breaking_von_trier_jorgen_leth_survives_the_five_obstructions, accessed May 17, 2011.

6. Donald Baechler, in Wade Saunders, "Making Art, Making Artists," *Art in America* (Jan 1993): 80.

7. Roger Hilton, in "La Vie de Bohème," in Martin Gayford and Karen Wright, eds., *The Grove Book of Art Writing* (New York: Grove Press, 1998), 178.

8. Pablo Picasso, "Picasso on Picasso," in Domenico Porzio and Marco Valsecchi, *Pablo Picasso: Man and his Work* (Secaucus, NJ: Chartwell Books, 1973), 79.

9. Allen Ginsberg, in Mark Holborn, "Allen Ginsberg's Sacramental Snapshots," *Aperture* (Winter 1985): 14.

10. Jack Whitten, in Beryl J. Wright, "Interview," *Jack Whitten*, Exhibition catalogue (Newark Museum, Newark, NJ, 1990), 9.

11. François Morelli, e-mail to author, Mar 24, 2011.

12. Matt Bryans, e-mail to author, Mar 20, 2011.

13. Robert Henri, *The Art Spirit*, Compiled by Margery A. Ryerson (Philadelphia and New York: J.B. Lippincott, 1923), 75.

14. Willem de Kooning, in "There was no audience in the beginning," in Emile de Antonio and Mitch Tuchman, *Painters Painting: A Candid History of the Modern Art Scene, 1940–1970* (New York: Abbeville Press, 1984), 54.

15. Gilbert & George, in Carter Ratcliffe, "Gilbert & George: The Fabric of Their World," in Gilbert & George, *Gilbert & George: The Complete Pictures, 1971–1985* (New York: Rizzoli, 1986), XIV.

16. Franz Kline, in *The New American Painting*, Exhibition catalogue (The Museum of Modern Art, New York, 1959), 48.

17. Arnulf Rainer, "Face Farces," in *Arnulf Rainer Self-Portraits*, Exhibition catalogue (Galerie Ulysses, Vienna, Austria, and Ritter Art Gallery, Florida Atlantic University, Boca Raton, 1986), n.p.

18. Mary Shelley, *Frankenstein; or, The Modern Prometheus* (New York: Bantam Books, 1967, First published 1818), 42.

19. Vito Acconci, Lecture (transcript), Skowhegan School of Painting & Sculpture, Madison, ME, Jul 19, 1998.

20. Yoko Ono, "Revalue Piece II," *Grapefruit* (New York: Simon & Schuster, 2000; first published 1964 by Wunternaum Press, Tokyo): n.p.

21. Robert Watts, "In the Event," *Times Literary Supplement*, London (Aug 6, 1964), in Benjamin H. D. Buchloh and Judith F. Rodenbeck, *Experiments in the Everyday: Allan Kaprow and Robert Watts – Events, Objects, Documents*, Exhibition catalogue (Miriam and Ira D. Wallach Art Gallery, Columbia University, NY, 1999), 88–89.

22. Anthony Bourdain, "The Fury," *Medium Raw: A Bloody Valentine to the World of Food and the People Who Cook* (New York: HarperCollins, 2010), 209.

23. Brad Cloepfil, in Stuart Horodner, "Brad Cloepfil," *Bomb* (Spring 2005): 44.

24. Allan Kaprow, "The Real Experiment (1983)," *Essays on the Blurring of Art and Life*, Edited by Jeff Kelley (Berkeley and Los Angeles: Univ. of California Press, 1993), 201–202.

25. Jay-Z, in Michiko Kakutani, "Street Poet, Explores His Life," *New York Times*, Nov 23, 2010.

26. WILL.I.AM, in Steve Marsh, "Black Eyed Peas," *Sky* (Feb 2011): 54.

27. Joe Sola, e-mail to author, Dec 7, 2010.

28. Daniel Day-Lewis, in Eileen Myles, *The Importance of Being Iceland: Travel Essays in Art* (Los Angeles: Semiotext(e), 2009), 122.

29. Hokusai, in Hélène Cixous, "The Last Painting or the Portrait of God," in Hélène Cixous, *"Coming to Writing" and Other Essays,* Edited by Deborah Jenson (Cambridge, MA: Harvard Univ. Press, 1991), 128.

30. Vija Celmins, in Chuck Close, "Vija Celmins Interviewed by Chuck Close," in William S. Bartman, ed., *Vija Celmins* (New York: A.R.T. Press, 1992), 36.

31. Morton Feldman, "The Future of Local Music," in B. H. Friedman, ed., *Give My Regards to Eighth Street: Collected Writings of Morton Feldman* (Cambridge, MA: Exact Change, 2000), 163.

32. Frank Stella, "The Pratt Lecture," in Kristine Stiles, "Geometric Abstraction," in Kristine Stiles and Peter Selz, eds., *Theories and Documents of Contemporary Art: A Sourcebook of Artists' Writings* (Berkeley and Los Angeles: Univ. of California Press, 1996), 113, from Frank Stella, "The Pratt Lecture," *Frank Stella: The Black Paintings* (Baltimore: Baltimore Museum of Art, 1976), 78.

33. Brian Grazer, "Disrupting My Comfort Zone," in Jay Allison and Dan Gediman, eds., *This I Believe: The Personal Philosophies of Remarkable Men and Women* (New York: Henry Holt, 2007), 91.

34. Amanda Ross-Ho, *Absolutely Everything, Volume 1: Invisible Opponent* (Fall 2004–Spring 2005), n.p., text given to author, Aug 23, 2010.

35. Werner Herzog, in Chris Heath, "Mad German Auteur, Now in 3-D!," *GQ* (May 2011): 88.

36. John Berger, "Drawing: Correspondence with Leon Kossoff," *The Shape of a Pocket* (New York: Vintage Books, 2003), 71.

37. Thomas Nozkowski, in Francine Prose, "Thomas Nozkowski," *Bomb* (Fall 1998), http://bombsite.com/issues/65/articles/2171, accessed Feb 21, 2011.

38. Agnes Martin, "Reflections," in Dieter Schwarz, ed., *Agnes Martin: Writings* (Verlag, Germany: Hatje Cantz, 1992), 32.

39. Bob Dylan, in Jonathan Lethem, "The Genius of Bob Dylan," *Rolling Stone* (Sep 7, 2006), 75.

40. Alberto Giacometti, Paris, May 17, 1959, Statement included in *New Images of Man* (The Museum of Modern Art, New York, 1959), 68, from Stuart Horodner, "The F Word," *New Observations* (Spring 1997): 4.

41. Leon Golub, New York, Jun 13, 1996, from Horodner, "The F Word," 4.

42. Charles Simic, "The Little Venus of Eskimos," in *The Return of the Cadavre Exquis*, Exhibition catalogue (The Drawing Center, New York, 1993), 27.

43. Ibid., 26.

44. Philip Guston, in *Philip Guston: Paintings 1969–1980*, Exhibition catalogue (Whitechapel Art Gallery, London, 1982), 55.

45. Woody Allen, in Dave Itzkoff, "Woody Allen on Faith, Fortune Tellers and New York," *New York Times*, Sep 15, 2010.

46. Malcolm Gladwell, "The 10,000–Hour Rule," *Outliers: The Story of Success* (New York: Back Bay Books, 2008), 49–50.

47. Jonathan Adler, "Timeless: Stoked," *New York Times Style Magazine* (Winter 2010): 82.

48. David Smith, "Questions to Art Students," in Karen Wilkin, *David Smith* (New York and London: Abbeville Press, 1984), 110.

49. Jonathan Borofsky, in Joan Simon, "An Interview with Jonathan Borofosky," *Art in America* (Nov 1981): 158.

50. Luc Tuymans, in Steel Stillman, "Luc Tuymans," *Art in America* (Feb 2010): 81.

51. Henry Wessel, in Philip Gefter, "Henry Wessel: Capturing the Image, Transcending the Subject," *New York Times*, May 21, 2006, http://www.nytimes.com/2006/05/21/arts/design/21geft.html?pagewanted=all, accessed May 17, 2011.

52. Jerry Saltz, in Irving Sandler, "In Conversation: Jerry Saltz with Irving Sandler," *Brooklyn Rail* (Sep 2008), http://www.brooklynrail.org/2008/09/art, accessed May 17, 2011.

53. Janine Antoni, in Stuart Horodner, "Janine Antoni," *Bomb* (Winter 1999): 50-51.

54. Stephen Schofield, e-mail to author, Jan 7, 2011.

55. Richard Wentworth, in Stuart Horodner, "The Language of Stuff: An Interview with Richard Wentworth," *Sculpture* (Apr 2001): 21.

56. Tony Bennett, in Gay Talese, "Onward and Upward with the Arts: High Notes: Tony Bennett Sings with Lady Gaga," *The New Yorker* (Sep 19, 2011): 64.

57. Matthew Higgs, in Stephanie Bailey, "Catching up with Matthew Higgs," *Aesthetica* (Sep 9, 2010), http://aestheticamagazine.blogspot.com/2010/09/catching-up-with-matthew-higgs.html, accessed May 17, 2011.

58. David Wojnarowicz, "Living Close to the Knives," in Barry Blinderman, ed., *David Wojnarowicz: Tongues of Flame*, Exhibition catalogue (University Galleries, Illinois State University, Normal, 1990), 103.

59. Paul Ramírez Jonas, "220 Questions I Ask Myself and Others," e-mail to author, Nov 4, 2010.

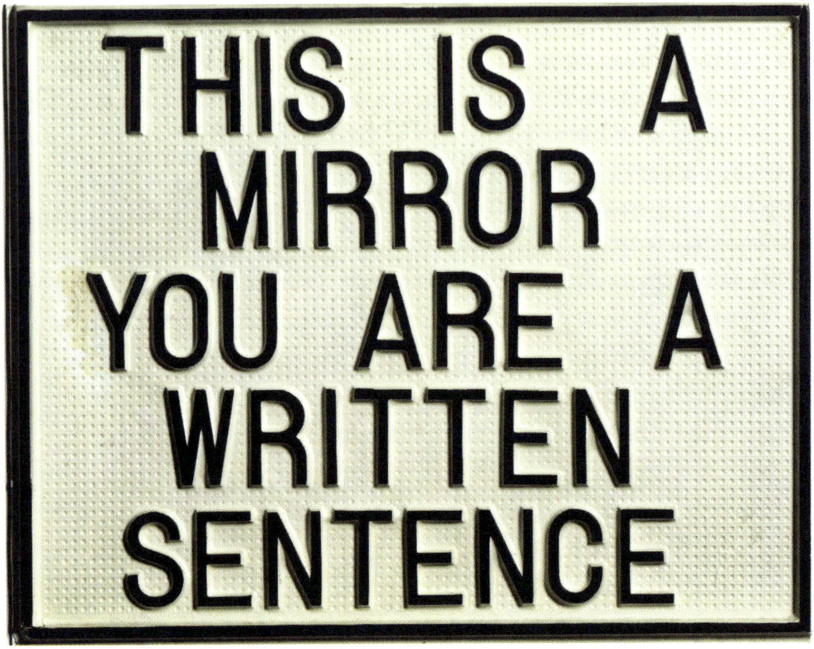

Luis Camnitzer
This Is a Mirror, You Are a Written Sentence
1966–1968

6. WRITING

Artists have always assessed, described, or defended what they do in different modes of writing. This includes everything from the titling of their works, to composing statements and theses to satisfy the requirements of art schools and universities. Some issue manifestos that declare philosophical or procedural imperatives for themselves and like-minded comrades. In applying for jobs, grants, juried exhibitions, and residency programs, artists answer questions about their interests, goals, and abilities, building arguments to try and distinguish themselves from other talented and earnest individuals.

Writing can be an anathema or a pleasurable part of one's creative activities. Like anything else, the more you do it, the better you get. The challenge is to find the appropriate tone or format that gets your ideas across. Tom Wesselman once wrote a monograph about his work under the pseudonym Slim Stealingworth. Consider this provocative pitch for membership used on a poster from Blue Sky Gallery:

> Size does count! We can make your watch bigger. We are a Nigerian photo gallery that needs your check to cash in on our big new gallery. Get in on the ground floor of a major contribution opportunity. This is a real blue sky property that is going nowhere but straight up like a rocket. See your donation investment pay huge programming dividends. Let's be frank. Your fellow arts patrons have been whispering behind your back but they will scream with shock and delight when they experience the unbelievably increased volume of your charitable output. We've got some very exciting photographs just for you to look at on our free website, but for the ultimate satisfaction you'll want to become a member. A really big member. Our Executive Director is ready to take your call right now and we guarantee total donation satisfaction

with discreet check or credit card billing. Transfer your stock holdings to a can't miss gallery that has a 33 year record of unmatched results, then sit back and watch the fireworks. We proudly feature an assortment of powerful long-acting Canadian ph0t09rafs specially imported for you (along with ph0t09rafs from 30 other countries).[1]

Titles can be an important way to reveal intentions and references, or merely a way to keep track of inventory. Some artists dread coming up with them, others feel that a title completes their work. Particularly effective ones can be straightforward descriptions of what can be seen in the work (or not seen, as the case may be), including Willem de Kooning's *Self Portrait with Imaginary Brother*, Jasper Johns's *Painting with Two Balls*, Tom Friedman's *1000 Hours of Staring* (it's important to know that the artist lists his medium as "stare on paper"), Chris Burden's *You'll Never See My Face In Kansas City*, Douglas Gordon's *24 Hour Psycho*, and Sarah Lucas's *Chicken Knickers*. Evocative titles with lively word combinations include Joseph Cornell's *Medici Slot Machine* and *Keepsake Parakeet*, Hans Hoffman's *In Sober Ecstacy*, Peter Schuyff's *Son of Random Checkerboard*, and Jessica Stockholder's *Recording Forever Pickled*.

There are many artists who excel at using language to explain their own work or that of others. A short list includes Leon Golub, Donald Judd, Sol LeWitt, Barnett Newman, Adrian Piper, Gerhard Richter, Mira Schor, Robert Smithson, and Andy Warhol. Some artists offer such clear conceptual or ethical frameworks that their texts become essential reading for future generations. One of my favorites is Claes Oldenburg's "I Am for an Art" (1961), a rhythmic manifesto packed with urban imagery and energy. I like to think of it as Pop Art's answer to Allen Ginsberg's infamous 1956 poem *Howl*. Here are its opening lines:

> I am for an art that is political-erotical-mystical, that does something other than sit on its ass in a museum.
> I am for an art that grows up not knowing it is art at all, an art given the chance of having a starting point of zero.
> I am for an art that embroils itself with the everyday crap & still comes out on top.
> I am for an art that imitates the human, that is comic, if necessary, or violent, or whatever is necessary.
> I am for an art that takes its form from the lines of life itself, that twists and extends and accumulates and spits and drips, and is heavy and coarse and blunt and sweet and stupid as life itself.[2]

Richard Serra's *Verb List* (1962–1968) compilation offers an inventory of sculptural gestures for consideration, including: to roll, to crease, to fold, to impress, to scatter, to enclose, and to splash.[3] We can recognize many of these being put into practice by Serra over the years, with materials including lead, vulcanized rubber, paintstick, and COR-TEN steel.

In 1971, John Baldessari generated an important act of art writing. Invited by the Nova Scotia College of Art and Design to create an on-site work, he sent a piece of paper printed with the words, "I will not make any more boring art."[4] He instructed the school to recruit students to write the sentence repeatedly on the gallery walls. I can think of no other phrase that is more essential for artists to internalize as a promise to themselves and to audiences.

Judy Linn

SOMEONE ASKED

Words and pictures by nature don't agree. There is no good fit. I can't say what I do or have done, but I know what I want, what I try to do. I can tell how I aim. I can't say how I land.

When I began, I hated what I couldn't control—all the annoying things I couldn't see in the moment of taking a photograph, the crazy stuff that jumps into the edges of pictures. Now I like that part the best. But I do want to be accurate, although "accurate" is a slippery word. I don't mean a quality of photography. I think Cézanne, Ingres, and de Kooning are all accurate. I don't think Ansel Adams is accurate. If you look at a Hiroshige woodcut of a whirlpool, you figure it is a fanciful rendition because how accurate can a woodcut be? But if you go to see the whirlpool, you see that he is telling you exactly what it looks like.

I think when someone first looks at a photograph they automatically wonder, "What is it?" I want a photograph that easily answers that question. I want to be extremely obvious; obfuscation is bad grammar. Hopefully, the two-dimensional arrangements of shapes on the paper will be as lively and interesting as the three-dimensional world trapped inside the photograph. There should also be something there you haven't seen before. Something should happen in the act of looking.

I want a photograph that makes me aware of what is physically in front of me, a photograph that gives me the pleasure of getting lost. It is like asking yourself a joke: not really knowing what the answer is, giving up, and then seeing the punch line and really laughing.[5]

John Heward

Intention, accident, acceptance.[6]

Christopher Williams **Interview with Jörg Heiser**

JH: Your last show at Galerie Gisela Capitan in Cologne had a very distinctive press release, which in a good way didn't match the show; it seemed like a different layer.

CW: At a certain point I became frustrated by the necessarily reductive nature of the standard press release, so instead I adopted a collage style, allowing me to lay down facts or information in the hope that it could spark more complex associations. So it's not about telling people how to read it, but just about providing more information. For example, the knowledge that a certain percentage of the rubber in the Michelin tires of 1968 was produced in Vietnam. The idea of riding around in Paris in '68 on Vietnamese rubber has a kind of resonance, but it speaks in a very different way than the picture itself, which is more related to industrial photography.[7]

Marcel Duchamp **Interview with Pierre Cabanne**

PC: You called "The Bride" a "delay in glass."

MD: Yes. It was the poetic aspect of the words that I liked. I wanted to give "delay" a poetic sense that I couldn't even explain. It was to avoid saying, "a glass painting," "a glass drawing," "a thing drawn on glass," you understand? The word "delay" pleased me at that point, like a phrase one discovers. It was really poetic, in the most Mallarméan sense of the word, so to speak.

PC: In *The Bride Stripped Bare By Her Bachelors, Even*, what does the word "even" mean?

MD: Titles in general interest me a lot. At that time, I was becoming literary. Words interested me; and the brining together of words to which I added a comma and "even," an adverb which makes no sense, since it relates to nothing in the picture or title. Thus it was an adverb in the most beautiful demonstration of adverbness. It has no meaning.[8]

Thomas Nozkowski

I would like future writers to create new compound words and acronyms. They should also use long and complex words in short and simple sentences.

Misspelling some words—either by doubling and tripling letters or by omitting them—could be especially meaningful as well.[9]

Jackson Pollock

I intend to paint large movable pictures which will function between the easel and mural. I have set a precedent in this genre in a large painting for Miss Peggy Guggenheim which was installed in her house and was later shown in the "Large Scale Painting" show at the Museum of Modern Art. It is at present at Yale University.

I believe the easel picture to be a dying form, and the tendency of modern feeling is toward the wall picture or mural. I believe the time is not yet ripe for a full transition from easel to mural. The pictures I contemplate painting would constitute a halfway state, an attempt to point out the direction of the future, without arriving there completely.[10]

Jasper Johns

Find ways to apply/make paint
with simple movements
of objects—the hand
a board, feather, string,
sponge, rag, shaped tools, comb
(and move the canvas against paint-smeared objects).
How
(What) can this be used to mean if it
were language? In what ways can one
intend to use them.[11]

An invisible drawing
made in the air.
Make a drawing
behind your back.
Make a stolen painting.[12]

Peter Halley

Notes on the Paintings

1. These are paintings of prisons, cells, and walls.
2. Here, the idealist square becomes the prison. Geometry is revealed as confinement.

3. The cell is a reminder of the apartment house, the hospital bed, the school desk—the isolated endpoints of industrial structure.
4. The paintings are a critique of idealist modernism. In the "colour field" is placed a jail. The misty space of Rothko is walled up.
5. Underground conduits connect the units. "Vital fluids" flow in and out.
6. The "stucco" texture is a reminiscence of motel ceilings.
7. The Day-Glo paint is a signifier of "low budget mysticism." It is the afterglow of radiation.[13]

Harrell Fletcher

IDEAS

Video that I shoot of the sunset every day for six months of a year, show them one after another sped up really fast.

I dig up a pile of dirt in one area and then take it to another area and water it over time and see what weeds come up.

I produce a free newspaper that is all just quotes from local people about good things that have happened to them lately.

I go to a Laundromat and get the people there to help write a film script, then videotape the people acting out the script.

A video of me talking very awkwardly and for a long time about cats.

Show about the "natural environment" around the art institution. Videos, photographs, drawings and writings based on animals, insects, plants, etc. found around the museum.

Go back to the grade school, Junior High and high school that I went to and do projects with the kids there.

Make an ongoing video of close up shots of peoples' scars with them telling the story of how they got the scar.[14]

Luc Tuymans Interview with Steel Stillman

SS: Often with your work, we wouldn't know what we are looking at unless we had the title. Are the titles as much constructions as the paintings themselves are?

LT: A title like *Secretary of State* is just what it is, but with *Bend Over* or *Gas Chamber* the title suggests other readings. Titles just don't superimpose meaning—they also serve to mark the differences between language and the visual. Each in its own way is inadequate, leaving the viewer in a twilight zone, in the gap in between.[15]

Robert Motherwell

The painting *The Homely Protestant* (1948) was the result of all kinds of revisions. It's what's left over after revising and revising and revising. There was always meant to be a figure in it. There has been such interest in my Elegies to the Spanish Republic and collages and some of the abstract pictures that it tends to be forgotten that I was involved in a very abstract, but nevertheless really figurative painting. I was very puzzled by this figure, and it was then to be in an exhibition, and I was given the form to fill out with a place for the title, and I thought, "What shall I call it?" And because I was puzzled by the picture, I couldn't think of a title. (I usually title pictures after the fact.) In my difficulty in finding a title for the picture, in my despair of finding the title ... because I think titles are important; I like titles that lead into the picture and in that sense try to make them either very accurate or, if I can't, make them not misleading. In this particular picture, which puzzled me, I wanted an accurate title, could not find one, and then I remembered the Surrealist device, which I'd never used before, of taking a book—and it had to be a favorite book, so I took Joyce—and opening it at random. Without looking at it, I put my finger on a page, and where my finger rested, it said, "The homely Protestant," and I thought, "Of course. The picture is *The Homely Protestant,*" which is to say, it is myself. And I called it that.[16]

Luis Camnitzer

Manifesto, 1982

I presume to be a revolutionary artist, with a vision for the world and with the mission of implementing it: to eradicate the exploitation of man by man, to implement the equitable distribution of goods and tasks, to achieve a free, just and classless society.

In order for my mission to succeed, I have to try to communicate with the highest possible percentage of the public, something only possible with a great amount of production and a good system of distribution for my products.

The production needed to reach the public who might be converted to my ideas cannot be realized through a limited, craftsman approach. I need means of production that are as efficient as possible and assistants who can perform those tasks that do not require my creative effort, but can be executed under my instructions.

Having limited funds to acquire equipment, I have to extend my ingenuity to find good buys, to profit from errors by the sellers, to bargain to my advantage; that is, to act with more intelligence than those who would exploit me if I weren't careful.

Having limited funds to employ assistants with the salaries they deserve, I have to try to pay as little as possible, prolong working hours for the same money, try to achieve a maximum of productivity with a minimum of expense. If this operation should leave some money left over, it should be invested in more equipment or in employing more people under the same conditions.

The biggest problem for the distribution of my work is competition. Other artists, sharing as well as opposing my ideas, interfere with my potential contact with the public. The public spends money on works that are not mine, money that would be useful to improve and increase my means of production, works that distract their attention from my revolutionary aims. I have to be able to establish my work over those obstacles.

I cannot physically eliminate the artists competing with me, but I can try to harm their image, spread rumors, create rifts between them and their dealers, and generally, try to sabotage their distribution systems.

With some luck and some manipulation I can then add these distribution networks to mine and ensure my preeminence in the public's view. Thus I will increase my sales which will allow me to acquire more and better means of production. I will be able to consider gaining access to other audiences, an international public.

The day when my revolutionary ideals will become a reality therefore could be near.[17]

NOTES

1. Blue Sky Gallery, Membership solicitation poster (Blue Sky Gallery, Portland, OR, 2009).

2. Claes Oldenburg, "I Am for an Art," in Kristine Stiles, "Material Culture and Everyday Life," in Kristine Stiles and Peter Selz, eds., *Theories and Documents of Contemporary Art: A Sourcebook of Artists' Writings* (Berkeley and Los Angeles: Univ. of California Press, 1996), 335, from Claes Oldenburg, "I Am for an Art..." in *Environments, Situations, Spaces* (New York: Martha Jackson Gallery, 1961); reprinted in an expanded version in Oldenburg and Emmett Williams, eds., *Store Days: Documents from The Store (1961) and Ray Gun Theater (1962)* (New York: Something Else Press, 1967), 39–42.

3. Richard Serra, *Verb List*, 1962–1968, in Richard Serra, "Rigging," in Kristine Stiles, "Process," in Kristine Stiles and Peter Selz, eds., *Theories and Documents of Contemporary Art: A Sourcebook of Artists' Writings* (Berkeley and Los Angeles: Univ. of California Press, 1996), 602, from Richard Serra, "Rigging," in Richard Serra and Clara Weyergraf, *Richard Serra: Interviews, Etc. 1970–1980* (New York: Hudson River Museum, 1980), 119–131.

4. John Baldessari, in Coosje van Bruggen, "Interlude: Between Questions and Answers," *John Baldessari*, Exhibition catalogue (Museum of Contemporary Art, Los Angeles, 1990), 58.

5. Judy Linn, "Someone Asked," Artist Statement, Feature Inc., New York, Jun 8, 2005, http://www.featureinc.com/artist_bios-texts/linn-text.html, accessed on Feb 21, 2011.

6. John Heward, Artist statement, in Sylvia Safdie, *John Heward: A Portrait*, Video, 2008.

7. Christopher Williams, in Jörg Heiser, Willem de Rooij, and Christopher Williams, "As We Speak," *Frieze* (Oct 2010): 185.

8. Marcel Duchamp, in Pierre Cabanne, "A Window onto Something Else," *Dialogues with Marcel Duchamp*, Translated by Ron Padgett (New York: Da Capo Press, 1979), 40.

9. Thomas Nozkowski, in Sam Sherman, "Interview with Thomas Nozkowski," *KultureFlash*, 2003, http://www.kultureflash.net/archive/67/priview.html, accessed Aug 8, 2010.

10. Jackson Pollock, "Guggenheim Application," in Peter Selz, "Gestural Abstraction," in Kristine Stiles and Peter Selz, eds., *Theories and Documents of Contemporary Art: A Sourcebook of Artists' Writings* (Berkeley and Los Angeles: Univ. of California Press, 1996), 22, from Francis V. O'Connor and Eugene Victor Thaw, eds., *Pollock: A Catalogue Raisonné 4* (New Haven: Yale Univ. Press, 1978), 238.

11. Jasper Johns, "S-11. Book A, p. 32, c. 1963," in "Sketchbook Notes," in *Jasper Johns: Writings, Sketchbook Notes, Interviews*, Edited by Kirk Varnedoe, compiled by Christel Hollevoet (New York: The Museum of Modern Art, 1996), 52–53.

12. Jasper Johns, "S-14. Book A, p. 40, c. 1963–1964," ibid., 53.

13. Peter Halley, "Notes on the Paintings," in Kristine Stiles, "Geometric Abstraction," in Kristine Stiles and Peter Selz, eds., *Theories and Documents of Contemporary Art: A Sourcebook of Artists' Writings* (Berkeley and Los Angeles: Univ. of California Press, 1996), 165; from Peter Halley, "Notes on the Paintings" (1982), in *Effects* (Winter 1986), reprinted in *Collected Essays: 1981–1987* (Zurich and New York: Bruno Bischofberger Gallery and Sonnabend Gallery, 1989), 23.

14. Harrell Fletcher, "Ideas from Notebooks," *Harrell Fletcher* website (2001–2003), http://www.harrellfletcher.com, accessed Aug 8, 2010.

15. Luc Tuymans, in Steel Stillman, "Luc Tuymans," *Art in America* (Feb 2010): 83.

16. Robert Motherwell, in "There was no audience in the beginning," in Emile de Antonio and Mitch Tuchman, *Painters Painting: A Candid History of the Modern Art Scene, 1940–1970* (New York: Abbeville Press, 1984), 63.

17. Luis Camnitzer, "Manifesto, 1982," in Jane Farver, *Luis Camnitzer: Retrospective Exhibition 1966–1990*, Exhibition catalogue (Lehman College Art Gallery, City University of New York, Bronx, 1991), 38.

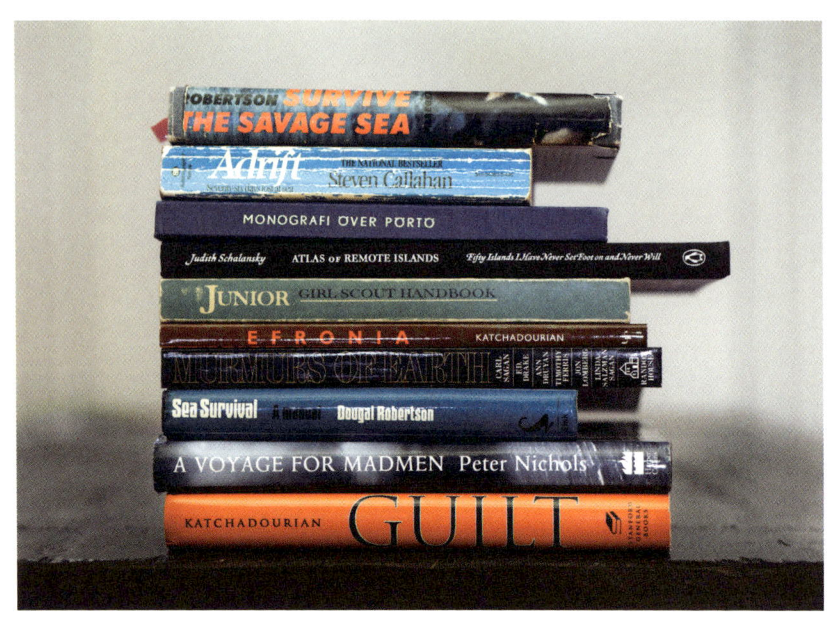

Nina Katchadourian
Ten Books I'd Save in a Fire
2011

7. READING

I'm interested in the literature that artists have found helpful in expanding their knowledge or clarifying their thinking. Certain essays and books have come up repeatedly in discussions over the years. A short list includes: Walter Benjamin's "The Work of Art in the Age of Mechanical Reproduction" (1936), Clement Greenberg's "Avant Garde and Kitsch" (1939), Susan Sontag's "Notes on Camp" (1964), Robert Smithson's "A Tour of the Monuments of Passaic" (1967), Leo Steinberg's *Other Criteria* (1972), Hal Foster's *The Anti-Aesthetic: Essays on Postmodern Culture* (1983), and Dave Hickey's *The Invisible Dragon: Four Essays on Beauty* (1993).

I don't know many artists who don't read regularly and, in my experience, the most interesting artists read the most. But each person's need for and taste in reading materials is their own business. In 2005, e-flux presented the Martha Rosler Library at their space on the Lower East Side of New York, and it has been on tour around the world since then. The project was conceived as a temporary solution to the artist's storage problems and a public reading room featuring over 7000 books whose content ranges from political theory to children's books. Asked how she uses her library, Rosler replied:

> Well I don't use it to make work. I use it to learn things, to be inspired, to follow trains of thought. It is true that it would not be unusual for me to be reading something and to "have an idea"—but an idea about the same thing I was picking up the books for. That is, if I am interested in finding out about torture, it is because I am wondering how to communicate something about torture that is within my grasp. So I am looking for a kind of underpinning of

knowledge to help me think about what I could produce, even when there is nothing visibly translated into the work. Being able to read rational, or poetic discussions of things opens a pathway, seeing how words define, encircle or layout a field I am interested in helps me to then insert myself and "make something."[1]

I love having and holding books and seeing them stacked up around me. I'm a junkie for the pleasures that words provide, and I would not be me (the person and the arts professional) without Joe Brainard's *I Remember* (1970), Tom Phillips's *A Humument* (1973), and the writings of John Berger, Richard Brautigan, Allen Ginsberg, Lucy Grealy, Franz Kafka, and Phillip Roth, to name a few.

In this chapter, I've invited artists, curators and critics to answer the following question: If your house was burning and you had to grab ten books to save, which would they be?

Wayne Koestenbaum

Here are ten books I'd grab. I've chosen biggies.

1. *The Poems of Emily Dickinson*
2. *The Book of Disquiet* by Fernando Pessoa
3. *The Collected Poems of Frank O'Hara*
4. *The Arcades Project* by Walter Benjamin
5. *The Complete Poems of John Keats*
6. *In Search of Lost Time* by Marcel Proust
7. *The Making of Americans* by Gertrude Stein
8. *The I Ching*
9. *The 120 Days of Sodom* by Marquis de Sade
10. *The Idiot* by Fyodor Dostoevsky[2]

David Humphrey

1. *Habitations of the Word* by William H. Gass
2. *65 Poems* by Paul Celan
3. *Aesthetic Theory* by Theodor Adorno
4. *Essays* by Michel de Montaigne
5. *Jokes and Their Relation to the Unconscious* by Sigmund Freud
6. *On the Genealogy of Morals* by Friedrich Nietzsche
7. *The Castle* by Franz Kafka
8. *A Lover's Discourse* by Roland Barthes

9. *The Loser* by Thomas Bernhard
10. *Collected Poems* by Wallace Stevens[3]

Michael David Murphy

1. *Letters to Wendy's* by Joe Wenderoth
2. *Poems of Gerard Manley Hopkins*
3. *Collected Poetry and Prose* by Wallace Stevens
4. *The Complete Poems* of Emily Dickenson
5. *A Fan's Notes* by Fred Exley
6. *Camera Lucida* by Roland Barthes
7. *Remote* by David Shields
8. *The Mooring of Starting Out* by John Ashbery
9. *The World of Ten Thousand Things* by Charles Wright
10. *Safe Area Gorazde* by Joe Sacco[4]

Nancy Princenthal

1. *Against Interpretation* by Susan Sontag
2. *The Fall of Public Man: On the Social Psychology of Capitalism* by Richard Sennett
3. *Lord Jim* by Joseph Conrad
4. *Jacob's Room & The Waves: Two Complete Novels* by Virginia Woolf
5. *The Rustle of Language* by Roland Barthes
6. *On the Future of Art* by Arnold J. Toynbee, Louis I. Kahn, Annette Michelson, B.F. Skinner, James Seawright, J.W. Burnham, Herbert Marcuse
7. *Autobiography of Red* by Anne Carson
8. *Twilight of the Superheroes: Stories* by Deborah Eisenberg
9. *The Collected Stories of Amy Hempel*
10. *Infinite Jest* by David Foster Wallace[5]

Jennifer Coates

1. *Leaves of Grass* by Walt Whitman
2. *Walden* by Henry David Thoreau
3. *The Planets* by Dava Sobel
4. *Imaginary Landscape: Making Worlds of Myth and Science* by William Irwin Thompson
5. *Food of the Gods* by Terence McKenna
6. *Dune* by Frank Herbert

7. *Zipper Mouth* by Laurie Weeks
8. *Scented Gardens for the Blind* by Janet Frame
9. *Frost* by Thomas Bernhard
10. *60 Stories* by Donald Barthelme[6]

Michael Rooks

1. *Ulysses* by James Joyce
2. *Moby Dick* by Herman Melville
3. *The Confidence-Man: His Masquerade* by Herman Melville
4. *April Morning* by Howard Fast
5. *The Sexuality of Christ in Renaissance Art* by Leo Steinberg
6. *Against the Grain (À Rebours)* by Joris-Karl Huysmans
7. *The Cantos* by Ezra Pound
8. *On the Museum's Ruins* by Douglas Crimp
9. *The History of Love* by Nicole Krauss
10. *Varieties of Religious Experience* by William James[7]

Craig Drennen

1. *The Inhuman* by Jean-François Lyotard

I put this book at the top of any reading list for artists. It was Lyotard's last published work, and it lays out a way of being in the world that legitimizes artistic practice within world culture in a manner that—to my mind—has not been surpassed.

2. *Painting at the Edge of the World*, edited by Douglas Fogle

In the beginning of the millennium it was noted that painting was behaving oddly, and that maybe it had been for some time. The problem wasn't that painting had changed, it was that all other pictorial media had radically recalibrated to mimic the creative template that painting epitomized—that if you can imagine it, you can make it visible. This book is the catalog essay for the show at the Walker Art Center that tries to address this new condition. Fogle's lead essay is worth the price of admission.

3. *A Dictionary of the Avant-Gardes* by Richard Kostelanetz

I consider this book to be a true gift from its author. First you have to believe in the possibility that creativity resides in individuals, and that individuals can create new things. Then you have to trust the encyclopedic knowledge of one human being who's seen it all, and all first hand. Where else will you see an alternative artistic universe where Joseph Beuys and Jenny Holzer are considered lesser talents, and an Appalachian mystic named Aethelred Eldridge or the Russian Vkhutemas studio program receives praise. This book will dislodge the standards by which quality is determined.

4. *Culture & Value* by Ludwig Wittgenstein
The small episodic nuggets are worth reading—in English and German.
5. *Edward Ruscha: Romance with Liquids* by Yves-Alain Bois and Walter Hopps
The images are very good, and the surprising essay by Bois shows that he is capable of enjoying a good picture now and then.
6. *Cabinet* magazine issue 18, "Fictional States"
Again, this writes a history that no one else has cared to write. Like Cotton Mather's *The Wonders of the Invisible World*, this issue of *Cabinet* reveals that there are phantom states in our midst.
7. *The Essays of Montaigne*
At some point I plan to print and wear t-shirts that say "Everything I Needed to Know in Life I Learned from Michel de Montaigne."
8. *Hotel Lautréamont* by John Ashbery
A title poem about a teen poet who committed suicide as a result of his failures. The recurring end line haunts me: "The people know what they want and they know how to get it."
9. *Ramon's Brownie Calendar* of the current year
These circulate in rural towns like the one I grew up in. They maintain the typographical conventions of the 19th century and reading weather forecasts and planting advice in the black+white+red layout provides just the mix of formalism and fatalism that my aesthetic seems to require. On the first day of January, this calendar tells you that on a Thursday in October it will rain. Some days have complex advice, such as "Most fruitful day for planting root crops & excellent for seedbeds and flower gardens." Other days will contain only grim, one-word advice: "Wean."
10. *Directions to Servants* by Jonathan Swift
It begins as satire then quietly becomes real, then reverses itself. It was true of haberdashers and char women then, and it's true of caterers and museum interns today.[8]

Regine Basha

1. *The Shape of Time: Remarks on the History of Things* by George Kubler
2. *The Gift* by Lewis Hyde
3. *Illuminations* by Walter Benjamin
4. *Mythologies* by Roland Barthes
5. *Writings* by Agnes Martin
6. *Labyrinths* by Jorge Luis Borges
7. *Someday This Will Be Funny* by Lynne Tillman
8. *The Poetics of Space* by Gaston Bachelard

9. *The Dignity of Difference* by Jonathan Sacks
10. *Tell Me What You Want, What You Really, Really Want* by Jan Verwoert[9]

Nubar Alexanian

1. *Landscape* by Paul Caponigro
2. *Psyche Speaks: A Jungian Approach to Self and World* by Russell Arthur Lockhart
3. *Rilke on Love and Other Difficulties: Translations and Considerations* by Rainer Maria Rilke
4. *The Founding Fish* by John McPhee
5. *Parzival* by Wolfram von Eschenbach
6. *Striped Bass on the Fly* by Russell D. Chatham
7. *Memories, Dreams, Reflections* by C.G. Jung
8. *My Name Is Asher Lev* by Chaim Potok
9. *All And Everything: Meetings With Remarkable Men 2nd Series* by George Gurdjieff and A.R. Orage
10. *The Selected Poetry of Rainer Maria Rilke*[10]

Daniel Duford

1. *Landscape and Power* by Simon Schama
2. *Moby Dick* by Herman Melville
3. *The Sacred Paw* by Paul Shepard and Barry Sanders
4. *The Back Country* by Gary Snyder
5. *Primitive Pottery* by Hal Riegger
6. *Painter of Darkness* by Gerald Marzorati
7. *Jack Kirby's Fourth World Omnibus (Vols. 1–4)*
8. *The Saga of the Swamp Thing* by Alan Moore and Stephen Bissette
9. *Robert Smithson: The Collected Writings*
10. *The Collected Poems of Walt Whitman* (I still have the same copy I did in high school)[11]

Richard Torchia

1. *Water Towers* by Bernd and Hilla Becher
2. *Heaven and Hell* by Aldous Huxley
3. *Hollis Frampton, Recollections/Recreations* edited by Bruce Jenkins and Susan Krane

4. *Essays in Idleness, the Tsurezuregusa of Kenko,* translated by Donald Keene
5. *The Nature of Light and Colour in the Open Air* by M. Minnaert
6. *Conversing With Cage* by Richard Kostelanetz
7. *The Journals of Henry David Thoreau*
8. *The Stories of Denton Welch*
9. *The Mysterious Island* by Jules Verne
10. *The Golden Book Encyclopedia,* 1960[12]

NOTES

1. Martha Rosler, in Stephen Wright, "Deinstrumentalizing Knowledge: Interview with Martha Rosler," in *Martha Rosler Library*, Edited by Paul Domela and John Byrne, Exhibition catalogue (Liverpool School of Art and Design, Liverpool, UK, 2008), 10.

2. Wayne Koestenbaum, e-mail to author, Feb 13, 2011.

3. David Humphrey, e-mail to author, Sep 12, 2011.

4. Michael David Murphy, e-mail to author, Feb 2, 2011.

5. Nancy Princenthal, e-mail to author, Feb 6, 2011.

6. Jennifer Coates, e-mail to author, Sep 21, 2011.

7. Michael Rooks, e-mail to author, Aug 30, 2011.

8. Craig Drennen, e-mail to author, Feb 7, 2011.

9. Regine Basha, e-mail to author, Aug 24, 2011.

10. Nubar Alexanian, e-mail to author, Jan 9, 2011.

11. Daniel Duford, e-mail to author, Feb 4, 2011.

12. Richard Torchia, e-mail to author, Feb 11, 2011.

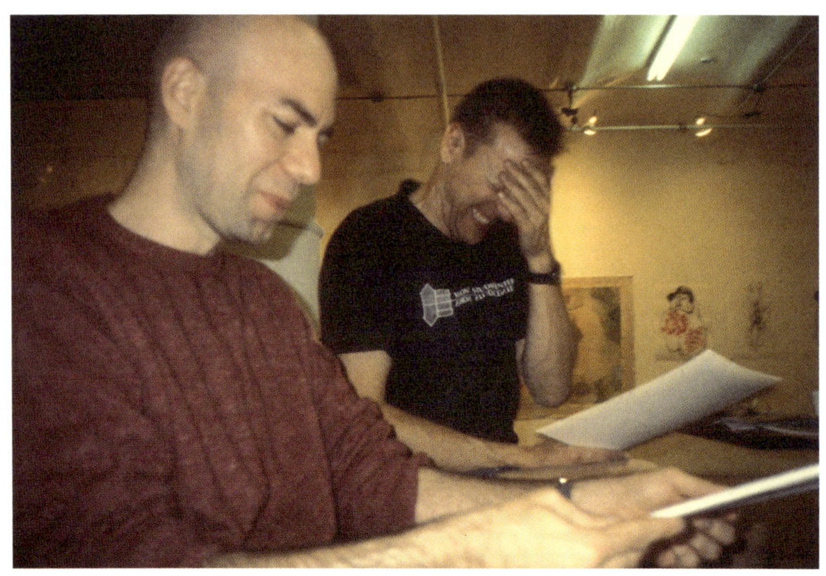

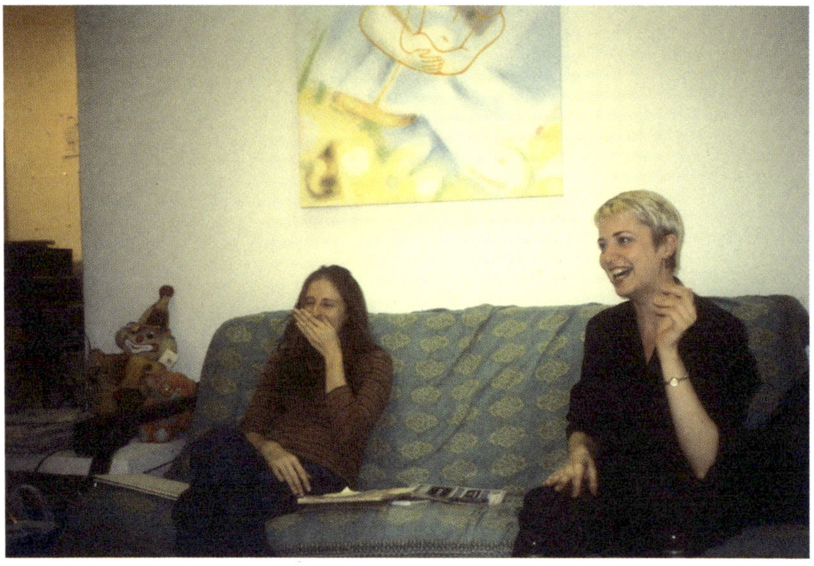

Collaborative drawing session with
David Borchart, David Humphrey,
Jennifer Coates, Sharon Mesmer
2001

8. COMMUNITY

Most artists cannot survive or succeed without the recognition of their peers and consistent dialogue. Schools are one place where this happens, offering a readymade group of fellow makers and mentors, a space to work, and a structured system of feedback. After graduation there is none of this and it can get very quiet, very quickly. It is up to each artist to find out about lectures and workshops to attend, gain access to the equipment that they need, and discover who to talk to about what they're making.

In order to understand the art ecology of your town or city, you have to show up and participate in it. You need to see and be seen. How else will you meet potential supporters and learn about exhibition opportunities or studios to rent or grants to apply for? And how can the vitality of galleries, art centers, and museums in your community be assured without your attendance and involvement?

When art-making gets particularly difficult, either because the work in your studio isn't going well or no one seems to be interested, it is those members of your inner circle who will provide solidarity and encouragement. Tom Marioni's *The Act of Drinking Beer with Friends Is the Highest Form of Art*, an action and installation in 1970, is a reminder of just how important the social aspect of art can be.

Joe Zucker

All we did was work and talk.[1]

Xu Bing

My viewpoint is that wherever you live, you will face that place's problems. If you have problems then you have art.[2]

Dave Hickey

I think art is for people who like art, who like to talk about physical things in the world. I don't think there is any difference, say, between talking about the Lakers and talking about Terry Winters. Maybe that the Lakers are better, and you talk about them with different people. They are both occasions for discourse.[3]

Lisa Sigal

Our weekly dinner parties began about 17 years ago when we first moved into our house in Brooklyn. Our son was a year old. It started for practical reasons, we wanted to have contact with friends and not leave the baby. My husband Byron and I realized that we both enjoyed cooking together, planning the menu and endlessly deliberating on the next combination of people to invite. The majority of our guests over the years have been artists, educators, writers, musicians, composers and curators. We have worked to perfect a good chemistry of people and food. Friendships have started at our dinner parties, though they have not started any romances we are aware of. We have a core group, we call "regulars" that we invite often. These are our closest friends. The "regulars," are also mixed in to take the edge off a dinner with first time guests, to ease any shyness or social tension. We have it down to a science by now. For example, if we want to ensure one conversation at the table we invite no more than four people. A larger crowd and there are splinter groups (which is not necessarily bad). Baking an apple pie is always a charm. Our dinners are relaxed, intimate and often chaotic. I love that the "regulars" are artists that I have been involved with for over a decade. These friends are my most treasured "viewers," listening and commenting on ideas yet to be realized. We have had meals that have spontaneously become working dinners where one person's art project will be discussed. We brainstorm for titles, make suggestions or solve problems for each other. I remember a dinner party when Janine Antoni was making a rope, an artwork from recycled personal objects. That night the guests at the dinner had brought bags of personal items to give to Janine. We spent the evening sharing stories about the objects that were to become her rope, a metaphor for the connection between people. I cherish these dinners and the friendships that have grown from them. The dinner party has shown me the importance of having a strong community of artists, merging art and life. Every Saturday I bake a pie and look forward to getting to know new people whose work is interesting and might become "regulars" to our dinners. Our kids, three of them now, are nearly grown up and often join the dinners and the conversation around the table.[4]

John Baldessari

Artists are human; art isn't something esoteric that's in books and magazines and museums, it's done by real people, and sometimes they're real jerks, and sometimes they're very articulate, sometimes they can barely get two words out. Sometimes they do a lot of garbage, sometimes they do a lot of good work.[5]

Norman Bluhm

At the Cedar one night—"the cathedral of Abstract Expressionism" as I call it—a big collector or dealer or museum person, whatever he was, came in. We had been drinking quite a bit and he went up to Franz (Kline) and he said, "Franz, I will be at your studio tomorrow morning at 10." And Franz says, "Oh yes? Well, I'll tell you what we'll do. You can come to my studio at 10, and then at 11 we'll go to Norman's and at 12 we'll go to Bill's." The man said, "I don't have time for all that." Franz says, "Then you don't have time to come to my studio!"

At that moment in my life I certainly was not at the level of Bill (de Kooning) and Franz, but still there was a kind of friendship and respect among us because of the mere fact that we were all in the same boat.[6]

Mira Schor

My hope is that I can continue to create communities for myself throughout my life. This hope is framed by my concerns about how to find commonality with younger artists who form actual and ideological communities of their own—community is often generationally coded—and my sad awareness that communities ultimately are eroded by the illness and death of their members, as I see in the lives of older artists. Thus my hope is that I can identify, create, and maintain cross-generational communities that will enrich my life and sustain my existence in a wider world. It is as important to me as the life of my mind and the life of the studio, and that is saying a lot, given that, of course, I'm one of those individualistic driven loners![7]

Amanda Ross-Ho

VOICEMAIL: EMAIL ME
EMAIL: CALL ME[8]

Douglas Gordon and **Jan Debbaut**

JD: I heard you say once, or perhaps I read it somewhere, that "Art is only an excuse for a conversation." What do you mean by that? [...] What do you mean by an "excuse?"

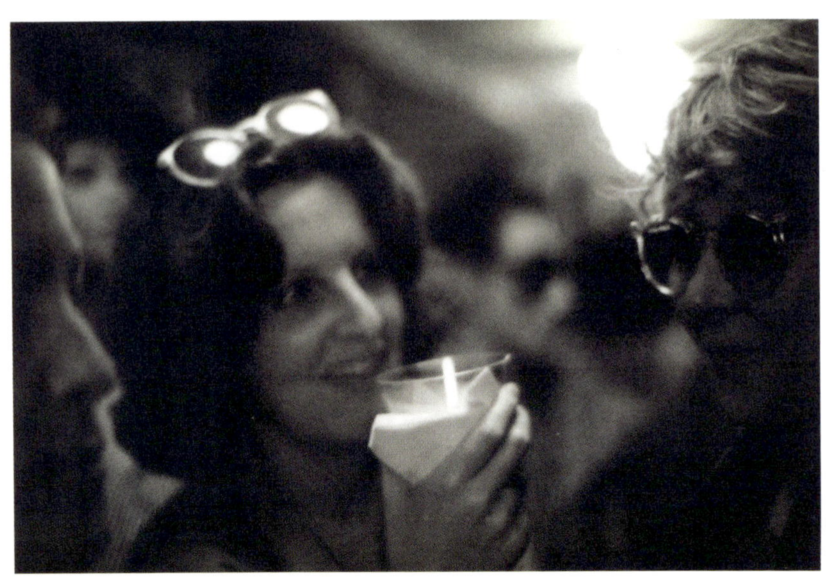

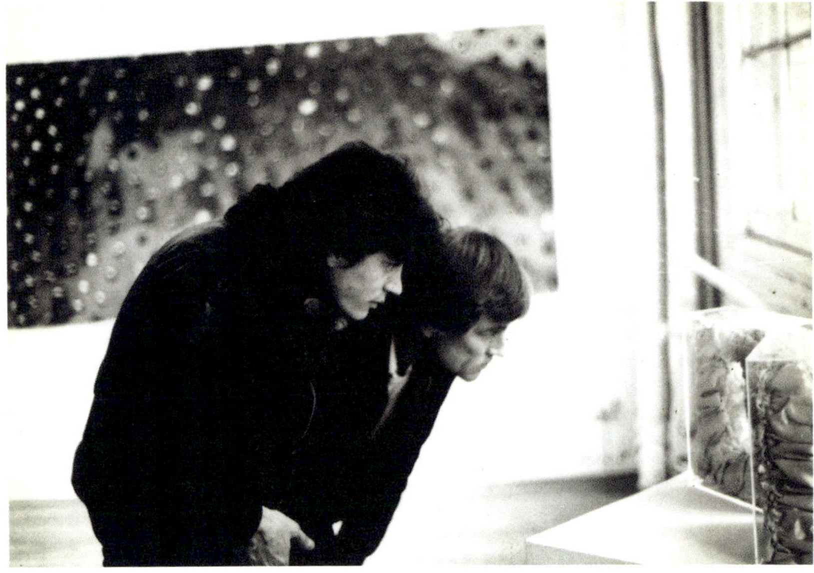

Jerald Ordover
Roberta Smith
Robert Mapplethorpe, Sam Wagstaff
c. 1979

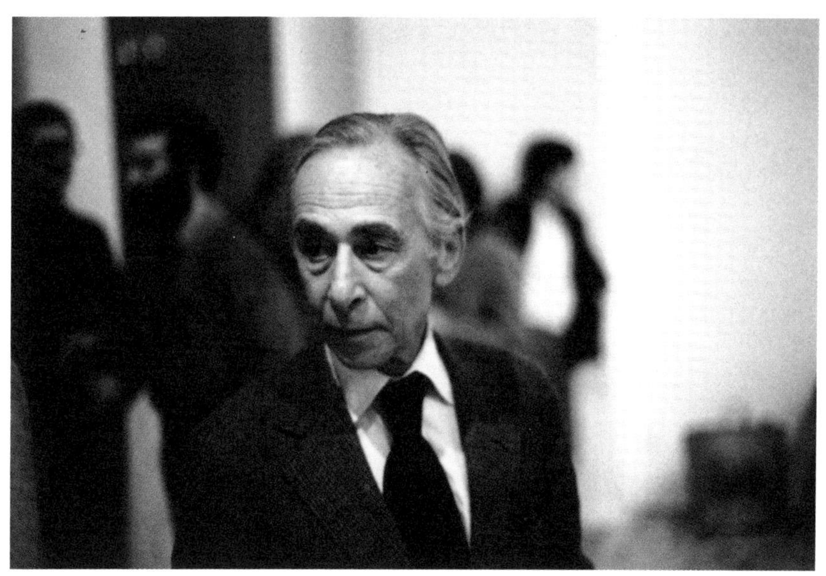

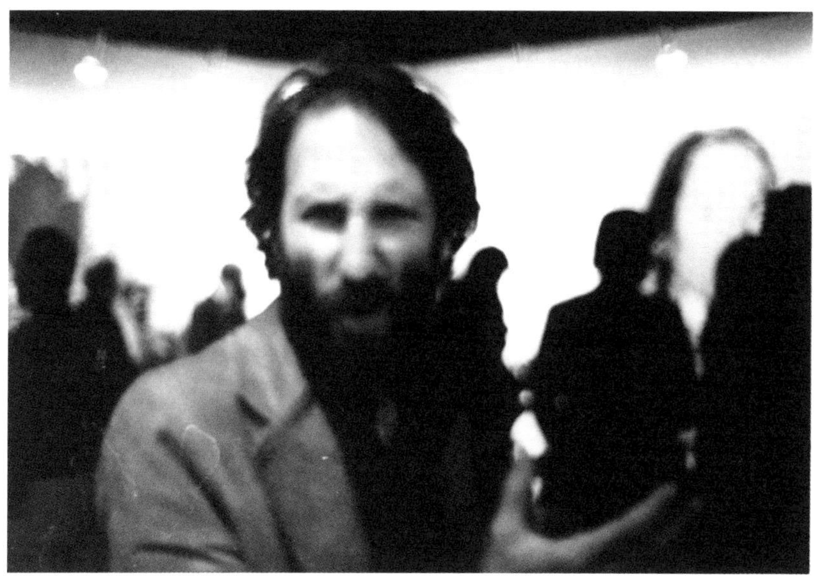

Jerald Ordover
Leo Castelli
Bruce Nauman
c. 1979

DG: Well, it's like when you ask someone to go for a drink, which is just an excuse to ask them to go to dinner, which is just an excuse to ask them to go to bed with you. And things can move on from there... Sometimes.[9]

Matthew Higgs

In the summer of 2009 at the 25th Street flea market in New York I purchased a group of approx. 100 black and white, 5" x 3 ½" photographs taken at openings, events and parties in the New York art world. The first image I saw was of Philip Glass performing solo in what looked like White Columns former gallery space on Spring Street. The man selling the photographs didn't know anything about the images or who took them. (There were maybe 300 photographs in total—many of the others were images of road trips and other family occasions.) A handful of the images were stamped with the name "Jerald Ordover" on the reverse, and a number were dated, all from 1979. Only a few were inscribed—in ink—with the names of the subjects. I recognized perhaps fifteen or twenty people depicted in other images, including Roberta Smith, RoseLee Goldberg, Robert Mapplethorpe, Lawrence Weiner, Leo Castelli, Marian Goodman, Holly Solomon, Richard Serra, and Louise Bourgeois. The rest I knew little or nothing about, nor who Ordover was. However a "Google" search revealed that Jerald Ordover died in 2008, and that he had been a prominent lawyer in the New York art world, with strong connections to Leo Castelli's gallery and his artists, amongst many others. I subsequently showed the photographs to Artnet's Walter Robinson and to Tony Shafrazi, who helped me identify more of the subjects. Roberta Smith told me that she remembered seeing Jerald at openings, always taking photographs. I would imagine these photographs are fairly unusual, in that it seems unlikely that many other people were documenting the social milieu of the art world at this time. (By comparison with today's digital photography and social networking sites the proliferation of such images has become ubiquitous.)[10]

NOTES

1. Joe Zucker, in "New York City, February 21, 1994," from William Bartman, *The Portraits Speak: Chuck Close in Conversation With 27 of His Subjects*, Edited by Joanne Kesten (New York: A.R.T. Press, 1997), 120.

2. Xu Bing, in *Letters to a Young Artist*, Peter Nesbett, Shelley Bancroft, and Sarah Andress, eds. (New York: Darte Publishing, 2006), 15.

3. Dave Hickey, in Sari Carel, "Dave Hickey with Sari Carel," *Zingmagazine* (2000): 179.

4. Lisa Sigal, e-mail to author, May 20, 2011.

5. John Baldessari, in Daniel Birnbaum, "Teaching Art: Adorno and the Devil," in Steven Henry Madoff, ed., *Art School: (Propositions for the 21st Century)* (Cambridge: MIT Press, 2009), 233.

6. Norman Bluhm, in Frank O'Hara and Norman Bluhm, "The Scene," in "Poem Paintings," *Lingo* (1997), 18.

7. Mira Schor, in Suzanne Anker, et al, "Forum: On Creativity and Community," *M/E/A/N/I/N/G* (May 1994): 27–28.

8. Amanda Ross-Ho, *Absolutely Everything, Volume 1: Invisible Opponent* (Fall 2004–Spring 2005), n.p., text given to author, Aug 23, 2010.

9. Douglas Gordon and Jan Debbaut, "In Conversation: Jan Debbaut and Douglas Gordon," in Jan Debbaut, Douglas Gordon, and Francis McKee, *Douglas Gordon: Kidnapping*, Edited by Marente Bloemheuvel (Stedelijk Van Abbemuseum, Eindhoven, Netherlands, 1998), 30.

10. Matthew Higgs, e-mail to author, Aug 3, 2011.

Terry R. Myers.

Joan Goldberg

Judith Linhares

Irving Sandler

ROSS NEHER

MAURICE COLTON III

C. REID

Jan Frank

Raphael Rubinstein

MORF-/94

C SCHWARTZ
1 IRVING PL [illegible] NY

Horodner Romley Gallery
Guest book
1994

9. AUDIENCE

Part of my duty as a curator is to be an active member of the art audience, one of many enthusiastic viewers who follow artists, institutions, critics, and the ebb and flow of the marketplace. My ongoing desire is to be surprised and shaken up by ideas, objects, and venues that I don't know, as well as those that I think I know. I write my name in the various sign-in books that galleries put out on their front desks because I want to let others know that I was there, and I usually glance through the preceding pages to see who came before me. The signatures of those who visit exhibitions is the clearest registry of who is paying attention to whom, for any number of reasons including the obligations of friendship, competitiveness between peers, professional responsibilities, and monthly keeping up with the scene.

Entries in this chapter reveal that some artists have a specific idea of who their audience is and what they want. Others cannot create for anyone other than themselves and while they are happy to have enthusiastic followers, they do not think of them while working. The relationship between producers and receivers can be understood as enabling, sympathetic, antagonistic, and filled with expectations from both sides. One's doubts about connecting to an audience are often alleviated by a thoughtful response from one viewer or listener, as in a story Tom Waits tells of "a little midwestern girl who wrote him a letter saying that his voice reminded her of a cherry bomb and a clown, to which he replied, 'You got it, babe. Thanks for listening.'"[1]

Marcel Duchamp Interview with Pierre Cabanne

PC: You have also said that the artist is unaware of the real significance of his work and that the spectator should always participate in supplementing the creation by interpreting it.

MD: Exactly. Because I consider, in effect, that if someone, any genius, were living in the heart of Africa and doing extraordinary paintings every day, without anyone's seeing them, he wouldn't exist. To put it another way, the artist exists only if he is known. Consequently, one can envisage the existence of a hundred thousand geniuses who are suicides, who kill themselves, who disappear, because they didn't know what to do to make themselves known, to push themselves, and to become known.

I believe very strongly in the "medium" aspect of the artist. The artist makes something, then one day, he is recognized by the intervention of the public, of the spectator; so later he goes on to posterity. You can't stop that, because, in brief, it's a product of two poles—there's the pole of the one who makes the work, and the pole of the one who looks at it. I give the latter as much importance as the one who makes it.[2]

Byron Kim

I am constantly thinking about (sometimes despairing over) who my audience is.[3]

Ivan Albright

I hope to control the observer, to make him move and think the way I want him to ... I'm trying to lead the observer back, sideways, up or down into the picture, to make him feel tossed around in every direction, to make him realize that objects are at war, that between them is a constant movement, tension, and conflict.[4]

Nato Thompson

I was an undergraduate in a first year writing class and we were writing poems. I had become convinced that the best poems would reference myself and would have words that only I understood. I said to my professor, "Mr. Budd, what if I write poetry only for myself?" He turned to me, smiled and said, "Those are the best poems of them all. The only catch is, you have to keep them to yourself."

And so goes the problem of art. If you want to communicate, then communication is absolutely a plural experience. If you don't, well then you can't expect anyone to understand you. That is just the nature of things.[5]

Lady Gaga Interview with Neil Strauss

NS: Your fans seem to really like what you stand for because some people need to be reminded that it's OK to be different.

LG: I love what they stand for. I love who they are. They inspire me to be more confident everyday. When I wake up in the morning, I feel just like any other insecure 24-year-old girl. But I say, "Bitch, you're Lady Gaga, you better fucking get up and walk the walk today," because they need that from me. And they inspire me to keep going.

I love writing on the road, because I go out there every night, and while I'm on-stage performing the old songs, I literally imagine them singing the lyrics to my new songs. If I can't imagine them singing the lyrics in the audience, why even write the song? What? To fulfill some fucking therapy in my soul?[6]

Claude Chabrol

I like using the thriller genre because when people go see a thriller—unless it's really worthless—they never say, "We've wasted our time." It's a good way to make people feel like going and not complain too much. Because you don't make a film to express your ideas. You make a film to distract people, to interest them, perhaps to make them think, perhaps to help them be a little less naïve, a little better than they were.[7]

Buster Keaton Interview with Christopher Bishop

CB: Was it your father who persuaded you never to smile?

BK: No. Nobody did that. I just simply worked that way, because I learned as a kid growing up with an audience that I just had to be that type of comedian—if I laughed at what I did, the audience didn't.

CB: So you stopped laughing?

BK: Sure. The more serious I turned the bigger laugh I could get. So at the time I went into pictures, that was automatic—I didn't even know I was doing it.

CB: Have you ever smiled on screen?

BK: I did it for somebody once—just to prove a point—that an audience wouldn't like it—and they didn't. We actually went into the projecting room when I started to get a reputation from film magazines and critics of being a frozen face, blank pan. We ran our first few pictures to see if I had smiled—I was unconscious of it and didn't know it. I hadn't, so everything was fine.[8]

Vito Acconci

A two-level space: street level and basement. As people come in on street level, next to the door leading down to the basement, there's a video monitor. So the monitor acts as a kind of announcement to viewers, maybe a kind of warning to viewers. Seeing and hearing what's going on by means of the video monitor, a person decides whether or not to open the door, come downstairs. The piece is a three-hour piece called *Claim*. I'm seated on a chair, at the foot of the stairs in the basement. I'm blindfolded, I have with me, 2 lead pipes and a crow bar. For the three hours, I'm constantly talking, talking aloud, but talking directly to myself. Saying things like, "I'm alone here in the basement, I want to stay alone here in the basement, I don't want anybody to come down in the basement with me. I'll stop anybody from coming down in the basement with me, I'm alone here in the basement, I want to stay alone." In other words, using talk as a sort of hypnotizing device. Using talk as a device to convince myself that this basement is mine, so whenever I hear someone coming down the stairs, I swing in front of me, with the lead pipe, with the crow bar, as the title of the piece says, "Claiming this space."

OK, so what interested me in these pieces was that it started me thinking of art as a kind of exchange system. An exchange between person in the role of artist, and person in the role of viewer. I started to think of art as a kind of meeting of person in the role of artist, with person in the role of viewer. When I think of these pieces in retrospect, I think what I really wanted at this time, was to get to a piece that would give me a chance to say a very simple hello to viewers. But I didn't seem to know how to make the "Hello" make sense, I used the opposite approach. If I couldn't say "Hello," maybe I could say "Good-bye" as often as possible, as hard as possible, and maybe eventually a kind of hello kind of oozes its way out. In other words, in this piece, for example. If a person is constantly saying, "I'm alone in the basement, I don't want anybody to come down with me," eventually somebody says, "We're going to get him." The claim to be alone invites others.[9]

William Pope.L Interview with Lowery Stokes Sims

LSS: How would you describe your approach to your audience?

WP.L: I like audience. I like giving good audience. I like people. My appreciation comes more from my background in theater and rock bands than from being in the art world. A lot of artists say they don't care about audience; they claim they only make art for themselves. If that's true, why do they display it? I don't get it. But let's imagine a situation. For the sake of argument, let's imagine an artist who is paid tremendous sums to make art, let's say by the King. Anything the artist

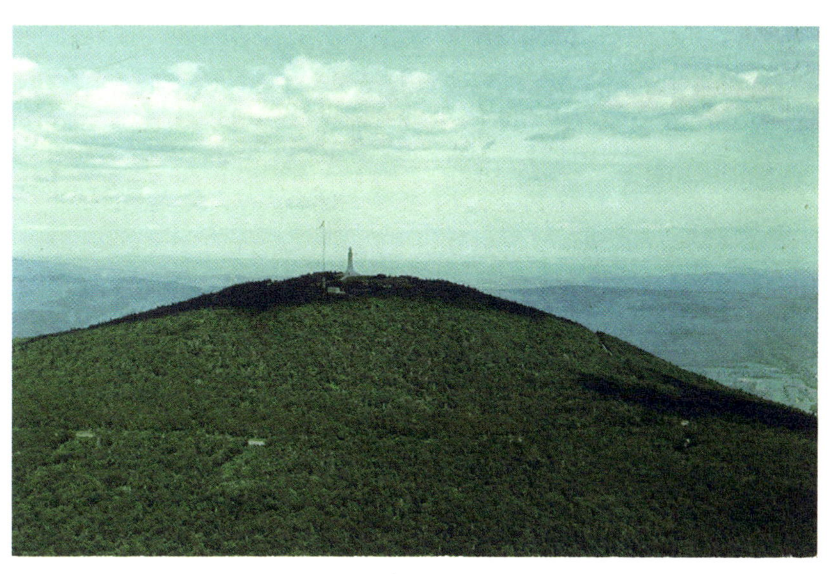

William Pope.L
My Penis Is Fine How Are You?
1995

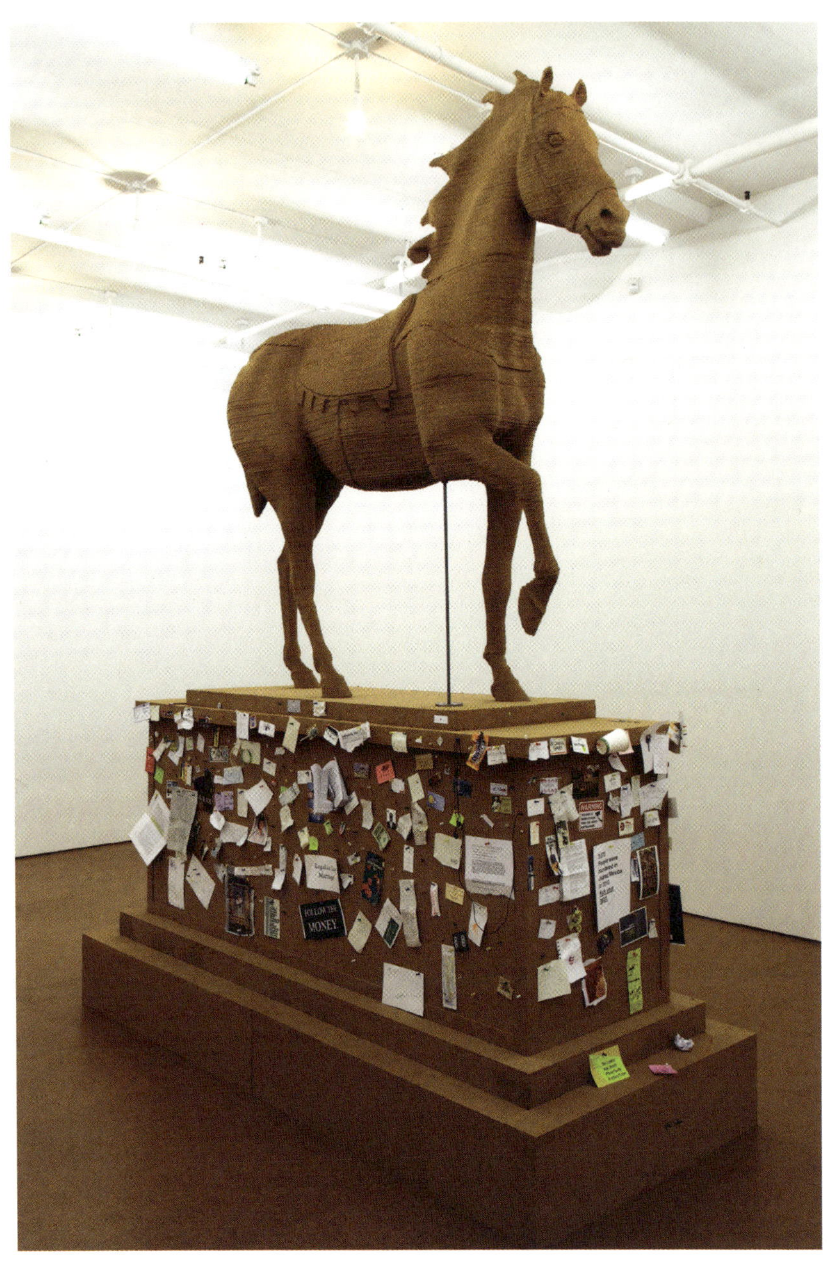

Paul Ramírez Jonas
The Commons
2011

wants, the artist gets. No boundaries. Even the artist's thoughts and behavior; even that goes in the pot. But no one ever sees what the artist makes. And every six months, the King's Minister of Culture loads all the product into a very powerful eraser and it is turned into absence. I wonder how many artists would choose this situation. The situation would turn the artist, him or herself, into an absence. And if the artist chose this situation, how long would he or she do it? I could not do it. At least not like that. And if not like that, then how? I'd fuck it up on purpose. Start talking in my sleep to my favorite concubine. She'd leak it to the guys on the parapets. Next thing it's in the hands of the enemy: the people. Bottom line, artists don't make art, they make conversation. They make things happen. They change the world.

I also respect and fear the audience. Like my family, the audience is also bigger than me. I see my relation to audience as a kind of dance in which I must be sensitive to the ebb and flow of the choreography. This choreography is a collaboration. No one owns it. Its nature is mutually influencing. Bridges must be built and burnt viscerally.[10]

Paul Ramírez Jonas

How many viewers are enough?[11]

Jules Olitski

I remember hearing Adolph Gottlieb on a panel once at NYU, and Adolph said, in effect—I'm not quoting him exactly—"I don't paint for the masses. I paint for the elite. The masses are not interested in what I do. They won't understand this kind of painting that I do, and it wouldn't come through to them."

I understood perfectly what he meant, and I was totally sympathetic. But the audience, which was not quite an audience of proletariat workers but an audience of school of education, art teachers, or art teachers to be, were going out of their heads with rage just at the mention of the elite.

I think there is an elite, and there always was an elite for painting or for good music or for good literature. For a long time there has been, and I don't see anything wrong with it. What it means to a lot of people, the elite is the wealthy or something like that. Adolph, I don't think, was referring to an elite of the wealthy, where the people run the government or something like that, but to those people who are concerned and interested in the most sophisticated, meaningful painting there is.[12]

Edward Ruscha

I never think of an audience or never did think about communicating a particular idea or trying to twist some kind of logic into what I'm doing. It's inexplicable, from one point to another, how I do something. I never really understood my audience or knew who my audience was. I thankfully am happy about that.[13]

Andrea Fraser

When you produce a piece that goes out into the world, it exists and circulates as a representation that may have very little to do with your experience of making it or your intentions. It becomes a screen for people to project things onto, or an opportunity to produce or reproduce certain stereotypes.[14]

Walead Beshty

I started writing and teaching because it was a way to participate when just making work didn't allow me to do so to the extent I wanted. It was simply another way to enter into the dialogue. On a personal level, it often clarifies my own intentions and my own lazy preconceptions. I do like the fact that both teaching and writing circulate in a very specific way that is distinct from the movement of art objects. They both highlight that art traffics in more than just objects—in ideas, concepts, and communities.[15]

Dana Friis-Hansen

One's audience might be considered as a series of concentric circles, the innermost circle consisting of those people most connected to the organization (such as colleagues and trustees), and, radiating outward, artists and regular art aficionados, then occasional visitors, and finally those who have never entered the gallery before. Each must be welcomed, but served in different ways by the various (visible and invisible) aspects of the exhibition's organization and presentation.[16]

John Currin

I am definitely not in love with the viewer. There is this assumption that the artist is supposed to put their arm around the viewer and both step back to admire this thing that you've made. I always thought it should be the opposite, it should be an antagonistic relationship.[17]

Philip Guston

My work must be demanding for a spectator, but what can I do? I think there's some law at work—an invisible law—that means you can only accept certain

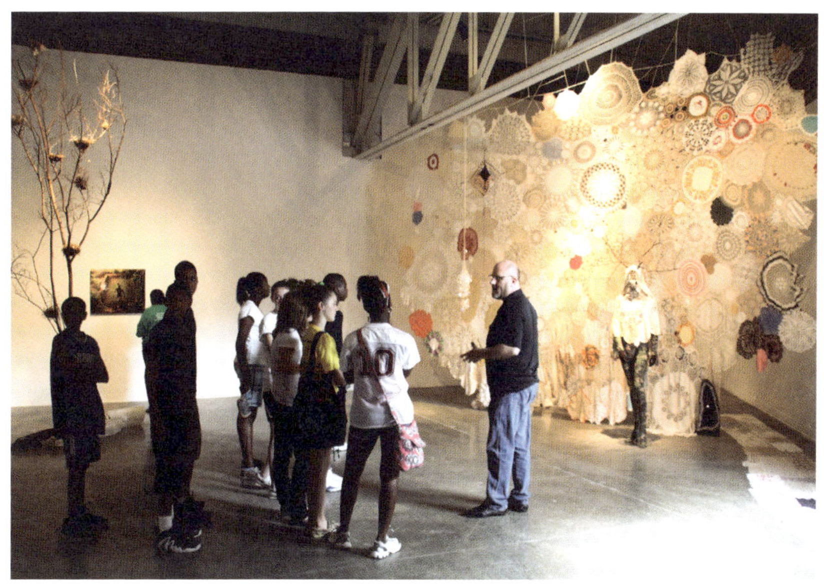

Group tour of
Shana Robbins
Supernatural Conductor
2010

things at a certain time—so that if you're working to please yourself or catering to yourself, why should you cater to a looker or art critic? Why should you meet their expectations? If I destroy my own expectations, why should I worry about other's expectations?[18]

Chris Burden

I purchased 24 thirty-second commercial spots on two New York television channels, Channel 4 and Channel 9, and 21 spots on three Los Angeles channels, Channel 5, Channel 11 and Channel 13.

My "ad" consisted of a series of names: "Leonardo da Vinci, Michelangelo, Rembrandt, Vincent van Gogh, Pablo Picasso, Chris Burden." The series was repeated twice and followed by the disclaimer "paid for by Chris Burden—artist." The names were written in bold graphics—yellow letters on a blue ground. The individual names zoomed forward, starting very small and increasing in size until they filled the entire screen. As the names became readable, I spoke them aloud. The first five names were chosen from the results of a nationwide survey which showed them to be the most well-known artists to the general public.[19]

Harry Shearer

The information we get is packaged with an eye, I think, more now than ever before, to here's what you should think about this, or here's the judgement you should take from this, or here's what you should conclude about this. So I want to present a series of images with as little framing, as little context, as little of what I think, or think I know, or know I think, as possible, and trust you to come to your conclusion about it. That, I think, is a futile little gesture of rebellion on my part against all the great media forces in our lives. [...] When I work with Christopher Guest on the improv movies, the feeling that suffuses that enterprise is trust. We are trusted for some magical reason by a company to do these things. He trusts us to come up with the dialogue, we trust each other, therefore, and overall we trust the audience to not have to be hammered into the ground with a punchline.[20]

Francis Bacon Interview with David Sylvester

DS: You really are not working with any thought of an audience?

FB: I'm working for myself; what else have I got to work for? How can I work for an audience? What do you imagine that an audience would want? I have got nobody to excite except myself, so I am always surprised if anybody else likes my work sometimes. I suppose I'm very lucky, of course, to be able to earn my living by something that really absorbs me to try and do, if that is what you call luck.[21]

NOTES

1. Tom Waits, in Elizabeth Gilbert, "Play It Like Your Hair's On Fire: Tom Waits Would Be America's Springsteen – If America Were A Strange Dispossessed Land Of Circus Freaks," *GQ* (Jun 2002), http://www.tomwaitslibrary.com/interviews/02-june-gq.html, accessed Feb 21, 2011.

2. Marcel Duchamp, in Pierre Cabanne, "I Like Breathing Better than Working," *Dialogues with Marcel Duchamp*, Translated by Ron Padgett (New York: Da Capo Press, 1979), 69–70.

3. Byron Kim, e-mail to author, Mar 31, 2010.

4. Ivan Albright, in Michael Croydon, "The Paintings (1931-1963)," *Ivan Albright* (New York: Abbeville Press, 1978), 83.

5. Nato Thompson, e-mail to author, Mar 28, 2011.

6. Lady Gaga, in Neil Strauss, "The Broken Heart & Violent Fantasies of Lady Gaga," *Rolling Stone* (Jul 8–22, 2010): 71.

7. Claude Chabrol, in Dave Kehr, "Claude Chabrol, Pioneer French Filmmaker, Dies at 80," *New York Times*, Sep 13, 2010.

8. Buster Keaton, in Christopher Bishop, "An Interview with Buster Keaton," in Kevin W. Sweeny, ed., *Buster Keaton: Interviews* (Jackson: Univ. Press of Mississippi, 2007), 57.

9. Vito Acconci, Lecture (transcript), Skowhegan School of Painting & Sculpture, Madison, ME, Jul 19, 1998.

10. William Pope.L, in Lowery Stokes Sims, "Dialogue: Interview with William Pope.L," in Mark H.C. Bessire, ed., *William Pope.L: The Friendliest Black Artist in America*, Exhibition catalogue (Institute of Contemporary Art at Maine College of Art, Portland, and Massachusetts Institute of Technology, Cambridge, 2002), 64–65.

11. Paul Ramírez Jonas, "220 Questions I Ask Myself and Others," e-mail to author, Nov 4, 2010.

12. Jules Olitski, in "Everybody talks about the art establishment," in Emile de Antonio and Mitch Tuchman, *Painters Painting: A Candid History of the Modern Art Scene, 1940–1970* (New York: Abbeville Press, 1984), 104.

13. Ed Ruscha, in Mark Rappolt, "Ed Ruscha," *Art Review* (Oct 2009): 77.

14. Andrea Fraser, in Praxis, "Andrea Fraser in Conversation with Praxis," *Brooklyn Rail* (Oct 2004): 12.

15. Walead Beshty, in Noah Simblist, "Concreteness and Circumstance: In Conversation with Walead Beshty," *Art Papers* (Mar/Apr 2010): 36.

16. Dana Friis-Hansen, "Notes to a Young Curator," in Carin Kuoni, ed., *Words of Wisdom: A Curator's Vade Mecum on Contemporary Art* (New York: Independent Curators International, 2001), 69.

17. John Currin, in Alison M. Gingeras, "John Currin: The Backdoor Man," *Flash Art* (Oct 2002): 73.

18. Philip Guston, "Artist's Statements," in Robert Storr, *Philip Guston* (New York: Cross River Press, 1983), 108.

19. Chris Burden, *Chris Burden Promo*, in *Chris Burden: A Twenty-Year Survey*, Exhibition catalogue (Newport Harbor Art Museum, Newport Beach, CA, 1988), 160.

20. Harry Shearer, from *The Silent Echo Chamber* panel discussion, High Museum of Art, Nov 20, 2009, http://forum-network.org/lecture/harry-shearers-silent-echo-chamber, accessed May 17, 2011.

21. Francis Bacon, in David Sylvester, "Interview 9," *Interviews with Francis Bacon* (New York: Thames and Hudson, 1975), 198.

big world

HI ANYA!

Thanks so much for sending your material. Wonderful stuff but it just isn't What we need Right now.

Sorry!

All the best

Jim

P.O. Box 7656
Lancaster, PA 17604-7656

Phone: 717/569-0217
US fax: 810/277-8376
UK fax: (44) 0870 063 5896

e-mail: bigworld@bigworld.com
web: http://www.bigworld.com

Anya Liftig
Rejection note
c. 2000

10. CRITICISM

Criticism comes in many forms—individuals assessing your work at school, studio visits by dealers and curators, letters of acceptance or rejection, reviews in print and on websites. In the course of your art life, both knowledgeable and uninformed people will tell you what they think. What do you do with their opinions?

Imagine being Richard Tuttle when Hilton Kramer's review of his 1975 exhibition, curated by Marcia Tucker at the Whitney Museum of American Art, begins with these lines:

> To Mies van der Rohe's famous dictum that less is more, the art of Richard Tuttle offers definitive refutation. For in Mr. Tuttle's work, less is unmistakably less. It is, indeed, remorselessly and irredeemably less. It establishes new standards of lessness, and fairly basks in the void of lessness. One is tempted to say that, so far as art is concerned, less has never been as less as this.[1]

Conversely, imagine being Lee Bontecou opening up *Arts Magazine* and reading that Donald Judd's review of her 1963 exhibition at Leo Castelli contains this assessment:

> This exhibition is even better than the last one. Bontecou is one of the best artists working anywhere. [...] The work has a primitive, oppressive and unmitigated individuality. It is credible and awesome.[2]

Tuttle, Tucker, and Bontecou each went on to have singularly interesting careers—as the patron saint of modest materials, as founder of the New Museum, and as a case study in career development, respectively. But it is hard not to internalize negative or positive feedback and feelings ranging from anger to euphoria are part of the process of sharing art with audiences.

Aaron Belz

"Critique"

That's not very good.
Try doing that differently.
That's not very good either.
You're not very good at this.[3]

Charles Baudelaire

The best criticism is the criticism that is entertaining and poetic; not a cold type of criticism, which, claiming to explain everything, is devoid of hatred and love, and deliberately rids itself of any trace of feeling, but, since a fine painting is nature reflected by an artist the best critical study, I repeat, will be one that is the painting reflected by an intelligent and sensitive mind. Thus the best accounts of a picture may well be a sonnet or an elegy.[4]

Robert Henri

Don't worry about the rejections. Everybody that's good has gone through it. Don't let it matter if your works are not "accepted" at once. The better or more personal you are the less likely they are of acceptance. Just remember that the object of painting pictures is not simply to get them in exhibitions. It is all very fine to have your pictures hung, but you are painting for yourself, not for the jury. I had many years of rejections.[5]

David Mamet Interview with Andrew Goldman

AG: Do you care about reviews?

DM: Of course you care. I don't read them, but you don't really have to—you know what they are with the way people respond. There's nothing in the world more silent than the telephone the morning after everybody pans your play. It won't ring from room service; your mother won't be calling you. If the phone has not rung by 8 in the morning, you're dead.[6]

Dave Eggers

You simply cannot judge someone, especially someone whose work you have respected, when they disappoint you, superficially, once or twice. Think of the fuckheads who turned their back on Dylan when he started using electric guitars, for Christ's sake. What kind of niggardly imbecile would call Dylan Judas when he plugged into an amp? What kind of small-hearted person wants an artist to adhere to a set of rules, to stay forever within a narrow envelope which we've created for them?[7]

Anya Liftig

I was a serious dancer as a child—one of those munchkins you see each winter and summer on big city stages mingling with the prima ballerinas, crowding around their feet with premature urbane airs. After a show, we would spill out of the stage door in a gaggle, handing out autographs to little girls not much older than we were. This little moment of fame after the performance was one of the tiny rewards in a world that, even at that young age, I understood was all about rejection. As little dancers, we were constantly being criticized and shaped. Sometimes you were too thick in the belly, sometimes you couldn't move fast enough. Sometimes you were sent to the corner because you couldn't understand a complex step. Sometimes the girl whose Daddy was on the Board of Directors of the dance company was chosen for the role. On performance nights, I savored the little drops of recognition from the outside world and tried to make them last on my lips as long as I could. But they were like one of those elusive *Nutcracker* snowflakes, gone in an instant.

Auditions were a constant part of our lives. Numbers were attached to your leotard, clean and pressed, and you were lined up against a wall and told to walk. Crying was not acceptable. Sometimes you were eliminated without even having the chance to dance, just because you were too tall or had the wrong hair color or looked a little cock-eyed that morning. Then the rounds began, numbers were called and the cuts began. It was a painful thrill. Who was called? Who packed their bags? Who got to drink another little drop?

As I grew into adolescence, this awareness of rejection broadened to include an awareness of rejection from and by the opposite sex. Unlike the dance world, rejection from males always felt like a blinding personal attack. I was a bit fascinated by my own inability to handle this pain and the fact that no matter how often I suffered it, it never got any easier, in fact it compounded into something worse. So when in the course of time I learned that there was this thing called conceptual art and that one of the main characteristics of the enterprise was that the path to success was riddled with rejection, I thought myself-well suited for the cause.

Once I finished undergraduate and embarked on the ill-defined path of professional art-making, I resolved to save all of my rejection letters, both professional and personal. The initial decision was just a lark, but twelve years in, I have over 450 of these documents of failure. They have now started to invert themselves; they have become a document of perseverance, a way of making something, anything, out of bad news.

They are a chronicle of not being wanted, over and over again, but they are also a chronicle of possibilities. What would have happened if I had gotten into the Whitney program back in 2003, or published in "I Love Cats Magazine" in 2001? (Which by the way is still on record as having sent the nastiest rejection letter ever...yeah, I'm making a mean cat face at you now...hhhsssttttt!) Would I be forever shooting pictures of cats? I like who I am now, for better or worse. Every artist has to find a way to deal with rejection. My way is to make it part of my work, part of my journey. It is my mental contour drawing of myself. Through negation, I am forged.[8]

Bob Dylan

If I've got any kind of attitude about me—or about what I do, what I perform, what I sing, on any level—my attitude is, compare it to somebody else! Don't compare it to me. Are you going to compare Neil Young to Neil Young? Compare it to somebody else, compare it to Beck—which I like—or whoever else is on his level. This record should be compared to the artists who are working on the same ground. I'll take it any way it comes, but compare it to that. That's what everybody's record should be, if they're really serious about what they're doing. Let's face it, you're either serious about what you're doing or you're not serious about what you're doing. And you can't mix the two. And life is short.[9]

Kay Rosen Interview with Cary Leibowitz

CL: Because your work is so smart and idiosyncratic, and personally gives me a real high when I see it, I am always frustrated when you don't get smart and exciting reviews. What is more frustrating for you—when an "informed" person judges your work aesthetically or when an "informed" person doesn't judge your work aesthetically?

KR: Thank you. Actually I think that some reviews and all of the articles about the work have been smart and exciting, and I've learned a lot from them. I am really happy with anything that an informed person says or writes, aesthetic or otherwise, as long as it's thoughtful and considered. I think that's a reasonable expectation for any artist to have. What frustrates me is when people don't read the work or think about it and then describe it with tiresome old clichés. No one learns anything from that.[10]

David Smith

Do you think acclaim can help you? Can you trust it, for you know in your secret self how far short of attainment you always are? Can you trust any acclaim any farther than adverse criticism? Should either have any effect upon you as an artist?[11]

Jean Cocteau

Listen carefully to first criticisms of your work. Note carefully just what it is about your work that the critics don't like—then cultivate it. That's the part of your work that's individual and worth keeping.[12]

NOTES

1. Hilton Kramer, "Tuttle's Art on Display at Whitney," *New York Times*, Sep 21, 1975.

2. Donald Judd, "In the Galleries," *Arts Magazine* (Jan 1963), from Donald Judd, *Complete Writings 1959–1975* (Press of the Nova Scotia College of Art and Design, and New York Univ Press, 1975), 65.

3. Aaron Belz, "Critique," *Lovely, Raspberry: Poems* (New York: Persea Books, 2010), 2.

4. Charles Baudelaire, in "Introduction," in Martin Gayford and Karen Wright, eds., *The Grove Book of Art Writing* (New York: Grove Press, 1998), xiv–xv.

5. Robert Henri, *The Art Spirit*, Compiled by Margery A. Ryerson (Philadelphia and New York: J.B. Lippincott, 1923), 18.

6. David Mamet, in Andrew Goldman, "Always be Changing," *New York Times Magazine* (May 29, 2011): 15.

7. Dave Eggers, in Saadi Soudavar, "An Interview with Dave Eggers," *The Harvard Advocate* (Apr-May 2000), Reprinted on *Armchair News*, http://www.armchairnews.com/freelance/eggers.html, accessed Aug 8, 2010.

8. Anya Liftig, correspondence to author, Nov 18, 2010.

9. Bob Dylan, in Jonathan Lethem, "The Genius of Bob Dylan," *Rolling Stone* (Sep 7, 2006), 80.

10. Kay Rosen, in "Kay Rosen: 20 Questions, A Project by Matthew Higgs," in *Kay Rosen: Wall Paintings and Drawings, 2002–2006*, Exhibition catalogue (Yvon Lambert Gallery, New York, 2006), n.p.

11. David Smith, "Questions to Art Students," in Karen Wilkin, *David Smith* (New York and London: Abbeville Press, 1984), 112.

12. Jean Cocteau, in David Shields, "It is Much More Important to be Oneself than Anything Else," *Reality Hunger: A Manifesto*. New York (Alfred A. Knopf, 2010), 181.

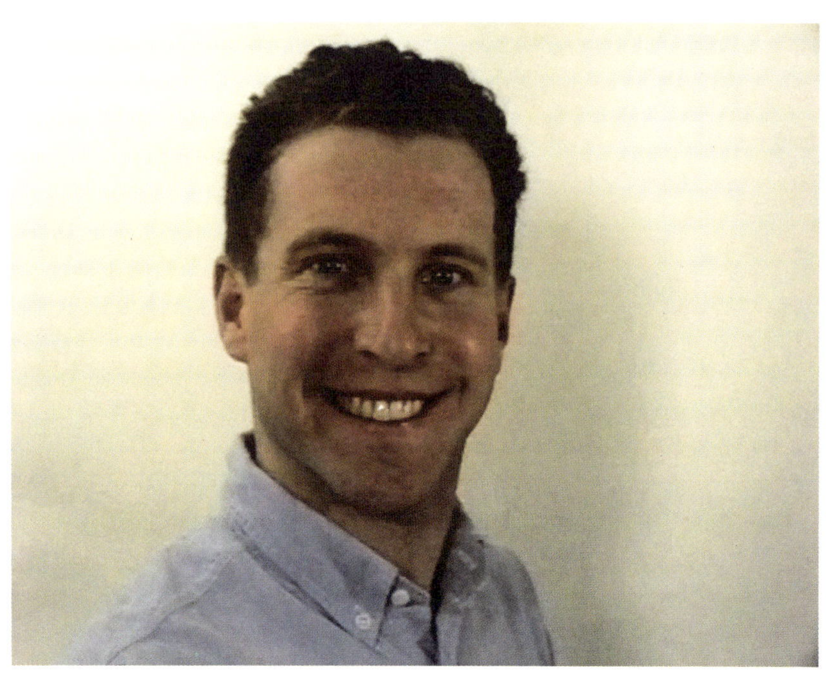

Charles Goldman
Happy To Be Here
1995

11. CAREER

The video *Happy To Be Here* (1995) by Charles Goldman is one example of how a career might feel. The young artist stares into the camera and tries to keep a smile for one hour. His dry mouth and darting eyes reveal the inner struggle to put on a good public face under difficult circumstances. This work seems to say, "I am happy to be here, but that doesn't mean it is easy."

In his 1997 novel *American Pastoral*, Philip Roth describes the difficulties of human interaction. He pinpoints the ways in which we consistently get in our own way, and this may be especially true in situations where we care desperately about the outcome.

> You fight your superficiality, your shallowness, so as to try to come at people without unreal expectations, without an overload of bias or hope or arrogance, as untanklike as you can be, sans cannon and machine guns and steel plating half a foot thick; you come at them unmenacingly on your own ten toes instead of tearing up the turf with your caterpillar treads, take them on with an open mind, as equals, man to man, as we used to say, and yet you never fail to get them wrong. You might as well have the brain of a tank. You get them wrong before you meet them, while you're anticipating meeting them; you get them wrong while you're with them; and then you go home to tell somebody else about the meeting and you get them all wrong again. Since the same generally goes for them with you, the whole thing is really a dazzling illusion empty of all perception, an astonishing farce of misperception.[1]

No one is more aware of what is or isn't happening in their career than the artist. There are the struggles and pleasures of making art, and the parallel frustrations and joys that come with its visibility and reception. I'm sure that many artists have a running mental list of those who don't like their work, what shows they were excluded from (and were obviously perfect for), and what should have happened in a million situations and didn't. I must admit to sharing this curse of awareness, as when I take a tally of who is not at my exhibition openings. But I try to be positive and take pride and satisfaction in who is there and how they are responding.

Artists often say, "The creating is hard enough, do I have to do all the promotional stuff too?" Well, yes, you do, but there are many ways to approach what might seem like hawking one's wares. I'm all for focused ambition, but you don't have to live and breathe your résumé 24/7. Maybe the best strategy for getting ahead is a variation on Henry Wessel's thoughts about the act of taking photographs.

> Part of it has to do with the discipline of being actively receptive. At the core of this reception is a process that might be called soft eyes. It is a physical sensation. You are not looking for something. You are open, receptive. At some point you are in front of something that you cannot ignore.[2]

All of the participants in the art world may experience each other in this way, not knowing which person or situation will bring them the agency and advancement that they seek. To Wessel's notion of soft eyes, one might add open ears and big mouths, because these body parts are directly linked to the "buzz" that energizes the field, whether one is discussing a sculptor fresh out of grad school or a suddenly hot painter who has been around for decades; a particularly thoughtful biennial or an outstanding booth at Art Basel. Careers develop in the best sense of use *value*. We are all mining each other's skills and resources to try and achieve our personal goals. Saul Ostrow once explained his take on the artist's dilemma by posing this question: "I know your work is interesting to you, how does it become interesting to me?"[3] The answer is the process of art leaving its maker to become relevant in other people's agendas.

Dave Hickey

Try Raymond Pettibon's trajectory: grow up in a literary family in a beach house full of books, get a degree in economics, teach math, draw posters for your brother's band (Black Flag), hang out and get discovered. Or Josiah McElheny's trajectory: study sculpture and anthropology as an undergraduate, become interested in single-source traditions like glassblowing, go to Venice to study that tradition, learn to blow glass from the masters and start making art. Or, as a last resort, try the solution my classmate Gilbert Shelton fell upon. Gilbert and his co-conspirators went up to the art department at the University of Texas every day and painted Abstract Expressionism. Every night, they came home and drew underground comic books. When they had enough pages, they founded Zap Comix and moved to San Francisco. Finally, they moved to Paris, where they still draw comics.[4]

David Foster Wallace

There are these two young fish swimming along and they happen to meet an older fish swimming the other way, who nods at them and says "Morning, boys. How's the water?" And the two young fish swim on for a bit, and then eventually one of them looks over at the other and goes, "What the hell is water?"[5]

Mira Schor

To survive in the long run, to continue to function, someone ought to tell you that there is a long run. To survive, it is necessary to stand for something within yourself and yet always doubt your own deepest beliefs. It is necessary to have the agglomeration of terrors and hopes, delights and doubts that make up a soul. Perhaps a soul is culturally bound and determined, but it can be more than a slave to fashion. Trends are fleeting. A lifetime of art cannot be built on a weathervane.[6]

Wallace Shawn

The life of a playwright is tough. It's not easy, as some people seem to think. You work hard writing plays, and nobody puts them on. You take up other lines of work to try and make a living—acting, in my case—and people don't hire you. So you spend your days crossing the city back and forth doing the errands of your trade. Today wasn't any easier than any other day. I'd had to be up by ten to make some important phone calls, then I'd gone to the stationery store to buy envelopes, and then to the xerox shop. There were dozens of things to do. By five o'clock I'd finally made it to the post office and mailed off several copies of my plays, meanwhile checking constantly with my answering service to see if my agent had called with any acting work. In the morning, the mailbox had been stuffed with bills. How was I supposed to pay them? After all, I was doing my best.[7]

Rirkrit Tiravanija

Most of the galleries I work with are generally friends before they are galleries. I don't want to work with people who don't really understand what I do and how I think. The people I work with know this—that they don't know if they are going to make any money from it.[8]

20

DAVID DIAO (b. 1943)

MEAN THINGS, 1990

Signed and titled 'Mean Things, 1990 David Diao'
(on the reverse)
acrylic and vinyl on canvas
56 x 35 inches (142 x 90 cm)
Painted in 1990

Estimate: $80,000- 120,000

$550,000!

PROVENANCE:
Postmasters Gallery, New York

EXHIBITED:
New York, Postmasters Gallery, "1969-1991: a real allegory," October 17, 1991-November 7, 1991
New York, Museum of Modern Art, "David Diao: 25 Years of His Art," August 7, 1993-October 3, 1993
Amsterdam, Stedelijk Museum, "David Diao: 5 Year Plan," February 18, 1994-April 6, 1994
Paris, centre national d'art et culture Georges Pompidou, "David Diao," Paris, May 14, 1994- October 5, 1994

58

David Diao
Auction Result
2011

Hilton Als

The director Elia Kazan asked to see [Jane] Fonda for a film he was casting, *Splendor in the Grass*. The interview consisted of Kazan asking Fonda if she was ambitious. She couldn't say yes. Forty years later, still smarting at having lost the part to Natalie Wood, Fonda said, "You know what I should have said to Kazan? Are you kidding? Of course I'm fucking ambitious!"[9]

David Diao

I have written of my attraction for diagrams, maps and charts. Given their direct presentation of material and statistical information, it becomes a means to short circuit lofty claims for art as spiritual, imaginative, the work of genius. Taking a cue from Courbet's painting of him in the studio surrounded by his supporters and detractors I sought to image how a present-day artist and his surroundings might be rendered as paintings. Curriculum vitae, sales record, reviews in newspapers and magazines, places of life and work, the archival material each and every artist maintains as evidence of having lived became the source for my work.

This recent work, *Auction Result* (2011), is my less than happy response to an auction at Christie's in Hong Kong in 2005. Amateur collectors had put my work up without reserves. Not getting anywhere near the estimated 40-60,000, they were knocked down for a mere 7000 apiece. This was a most destructive act because not only did they ruin my market but they also rendered the other works of mine in their collection worthless. I laid out on canvas, as if printed, a double auction catalog page with the usual information as to artist, title, provenance, estimated value, etc., opposite the image of the work being offered. I gave it an imaginary and highly unlikely high value. Then I came back and wrote by hand an even higher price as the hammer price. It gave me a certain satisfaction to redress even if only in fantasy the debacle of this event. I now plan to also produce pieces revealing the actual lowly 7000 achieved, a continuation of my fact and fantasy approach to my work to join paintings of red dots denoting my checkered record of sales.[10]

Lee Lozano

In 1965 (?) Kasper König said to me:
"You are a good painter and nice girl."

I replied:
"Wrong on both counts. I'm a <u>very</u> good painter and <u>not</u> a nice girl.[11]

Julian Hoeber

Nobody does it by themselves. You know, we all gossip and talk shit, but at the end of the day like, you know I'm pretty careful about who I talk shit about, at least on record! [Laughs] I actually think about these things a lot more than some people, and I know people who are more successful than I am who do not think about this stuff whatsoever. Jim Shaw is a pretty good example. I think Jim just did his thing. But, it just so happens that Jim's thing is to wake up every morning and go to the studio and draw for twelve hours a day, come hell or high water, because if he does anything else he's not happy, you know? And it's like well, that's gonna get you somewhere. I don't think Jim is a social networking kind of guy, but he's incredibly generous and nice. There is not much calculation with him at all. But his work ethic, kindness and his devotion to his ideas have served him incredibly well. And that is a model that has nothing to do with being a shark or being calculating. Only to do with believing in what you believe in, being blessed with some talent, and being secure enough in yourself that you don't have to be a dick to people.[12]

Jon Lapointe Interview with Michael Markowsky

MM: What would you say to people who would say that "going to an art opening and approaching an artist or gallerist, is about the most terrifying thing I can imagine?"

JL: It is the most terrifying thing, but you've got to get over it. Be yourself. Being yourself is not necessarily good advice for some people. [Laughs] If you are an asshole, be someone else! [Laughs] There are a lot of websites out there that teach you how not to be a bore at a party. Ask people questions... That is where personality comes in. A lot of it is self-confidence issues. It takes practice; learning when to shut up; "I'm not going to say anything anymore, because I'm going to dig a hole if I keep talking." It's just getting out there saying, "Hi how are you, nice to see you." That's it. Negotiation is not an event, it's a process. It requires finesse. You can't try too hard because that stinks as well.[13]

David Wojnarowicz

The moment I got validated by a well-known critic, suddenly the pounding on the door was deafening. I remember being extremely angry because I had some pure and naïve notion of what making art was; I wanted to support myself with making art because it always made sense of living for me. I had three shows—nobody would touch the work with a stick and suddenly some critic came along and validated the work and hoards of people were coming left and right to buy things. That kind of acceptance is a double-edged sword. For the first time in my life I had more money than I could ever think of, which brought with it a load of difficulties. Whatever kind of tensions you carry—whatever kind of displacement one feels in their life—when suddenly the one thing that keeps you semi-conscious, such as having to work day in and day out, to suddenly have that taken care of and have nothing but time on your hands because financially you're suddenly free—you can do whatever you want. At that moment all the tensions rise to the top. Everything that you've managed to suppress by keeping yourself exhausted just trying to pay the rent, or getting food on the table—all those tensions surface, and that was very difficult for me.[14]

Andrea Fraser

The question I'm interested in posing is whether art is prostitution—in the metaphorical sense, of course. Is it any more prostitution because I happen to be having sex with a man than it would be if I were just selling him a piece? In fact, I remain much less comfortable with selling the DVDs of *Untitled* than I was with producing the piece. The "normal" sales situation that one has in the art world feels much more exploitive to me than any aspect of my relationship with or the exchange with the participating collector. That's where I lose control of it. That's where the speculation begins.[15]

Dave Hickey

My whole idea in life is to be able to make a living doing what I like to do. I like to write, and I like to write about hard things in the world—I don't usually like to make things up—although I do occasionally. It's fine to make things up at times, because it's so hard to write about things in the world. I am a pretty good writer. I mean some days I write better and some worse, but I have skills, and my view of the world is solid enough that regardless of the topic you give me, I will say some version of the same thing. I wrote a piece called "Earth Scapes, Land Works and Oz" back in '72 for *Art in America* about Land Art and my position has not changed since then. I have spent most of my career writing about Post-Minimalist art. I write about Bruce Nauman, John Baldessari, Ann Hamilton, Robert Gober. Only recently, because of the shift in taste, do I get to write about people whom I have deep temperamental affinities with, like Warhol or John Wesley. For 30 years you couldn't get a job or occasion to write about these people. I like getting assignments, if I didn't get them I would probably not write anything, except maybe Rock N Roll songs.[16]

Paul Shambroom

Sometimes I feel I'm on a mission, that I'm doing something important. But it's good to have this other voice in my head saying, "No, you're not changing the world. You're not going to stop the proliferation of nuclear weapons. You're just a guy taking pictures." I have a dialogue in my head between both of those voices.

In some ways I've become very obsessive and driven: not only is what I'm doing really important but I'm the only guy who can do it. These are definitely delusions of grandeur but I do know how to do these things. With the *Nuclear Weapons* project I had that feeling after I'd been working on it for several years. Going down this path, I know how to do it. No one else knows how to do it. And I'm not going to let anything stop me because if I don't do it, it's not going to happen. I still believe that I came out of that project with something that no one else will ever be able to get because that door is closed now. Whether history will judge it to have value or import is hard for me to tell. It is necessary to my process to have those delusions of grandeur as long as when I come down I realize that's what they are and I still have to wash the dishes at home.[17]

David Rimanelli

Lawrence Rinder's career trajectory has followed anything but a preordained path. After all, who would have wagered that this ripped Studio 54 busboy with a master's degree from Hunter College would have ended up as a curator at the Whitney Museum of American Art in New York? And when he organized the museum's almost universally disparaged 2002 biennial—"the Bland Biennial," in Jerry Saltz's words—and subsequently failed to survive the Max Anderson-to-Adam Weinberg regime change in 2003, who would have thought he'd land on his feet, as dean, no less, of the California College of the Arts in San Francisco before ascending, in 2008, to the directorship of the Berkeley Art Museum and Pacific Film Archive, where he'd begun his career as a curator in the late 1980s? But such has been the art-world boy wonder's charmed life.[18]

Jeffrey Deitch

I have been in the art business my entire adult life. I remember the day after graduation, I drove down to 420 West Broadway and I walked up to Leo Castelli's reception desk and asked for a job. Of course, there was a snooty secretary there and she looked at me, horrified, but I wasn't fazed. I just walked upstairs to John Weber. Their receptionist had just quit and they had nobody. The only problem was that John Weber would in no way accept a man. He had to have a pretty girl as the secretary. I said, "I want to get the experience. Just let me work for free

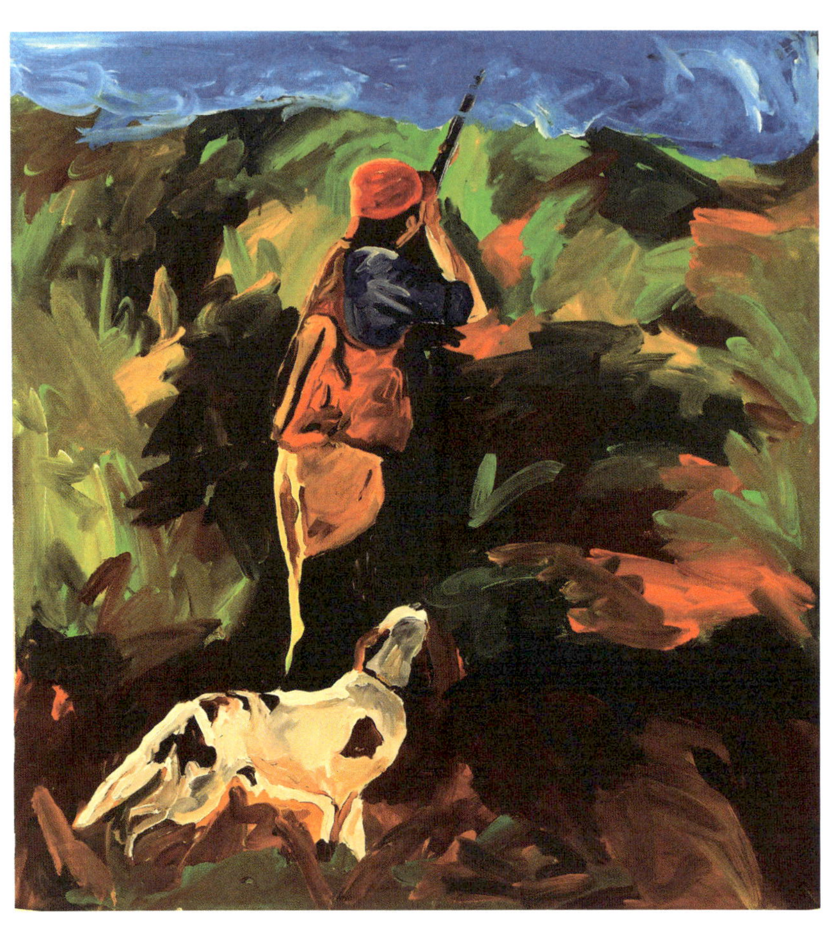

Mike Howard
Field & Stream (Hunter)
1974

for a week, and if I'm good, maybe you can give me a good recommendation after the owner gets back." The director said, "I can't say no to that deal. We need help," so I worked for free. John comes back a week later and sees this guy there at the desk and, of course, he's furious and he calls the director into his office and shuts the door and starts yelling, "Who's that guy sitting there!" I really owe so much to her, the director. She convinced him.[19]

Tad Savinar

Many artists get confused about the reality of the work they are engaged in and their aspirations of where they think it should be exhibited. Obviously, we all think our work is important otherwise we wouldn't be making it. But what if one stands back for a moment and asks themselves, do they want to be the best artist in their family, the best artist on the block, the best artist in their city, the best artist in the state or the best artist in the country? While we would all hope for the best, each of those career trajectories comes with its own set of exhibition arenas, galleries, curators and critics. And while it may be difficult, or even counter-intuitive to acknowledge one's limits, there can be professional value in understanding where you fall for the moment and also worth re-assessing over time. One must always consider the arena in which their work and their skills as an artist are best applied. If you aspire to end up in the collection of The Museum of Modern Art, then most likely you should not aspire to being included in a group show at the local shopping mall.

For myself, I have always considered my work to be within a conceptual, contemporary arena and worthy of being exhibited and critiqued nationally ("the best artist in the country"). And that is what I aspired to with exhibitions across the country and a fair amount of critical response. However, after many years I found that I was placing far too much emphasis on getting shows and less and less time in the studio. After actually quitting the visual art field and working in the theater for a number of years I wandered back into the studio and picked up a brush. But before I completed one new work I had decided that although I wanted my work to be part of a national conceptual conversation, I no longer cared very much about what happened to the work critically or if it was even exhibited very widely. I was surprised to find that when I focused on being the best artist for myself (rather than in the country), the work got more honest, my viewers were more engaged in what I was up to and I actually started selling pretty regularly. In my eyes the work didn't suffer or get soft, rather it got more immediate and exploratory—a result of having been completely separated from endless careerisms.[20]

Nina Katchadourian

The day job stands in the way of "freedom," but is complete freedom necessarily the best climate for productivity? Is the choice to keep the day job a way of imposing some structure on life, to bring discipline to at least one facet of existence, to counter balance the stress of the unpredictable ebb and flow of the studio? And if you chose to work, do you choose a job that's very different from your creative work, so as not to sap energy from it, or do you parlay your artistic abilities into something that you can get paid for?[21]

Mike Howard

I first met Henry Geldzahler in 1970 when I worked for Donald Judd. We were installing some of Judd's pieces at The Metropolitan Museum of Art for the *New York Painting 1940–1970* show. Every day we all went out for lunch and Henry said to stop by and show him my paintings. Four years later, I did. I had just moved into my studio at Rutgers to start grad school. I made twenty 4 ft square stretched canvases using the already primed cheap canvas. I painted in a fast drawing style.

I took slides to Henry and he loved the paintings and said "When you have made 100 more of these, come back and see me." Well, three weeks later I returned with over 100 paintings of everything—Martin Luther King, Jr., JFK, Jesus, men fishing and hunting, my boots. Anything I could grab. About 10 of the paintings were of *Artforum* covers. Henry was impressed (I don't remember if it was the quality or quantity) but he called two people. One was Michael Walls who had just opened a gallery on West Broadway. The second was Charlie Cowles, the owner of *Artforum*. Michael gave me a show and Charlie bought some paintings. I got my first review in *Artforum* of that show at Michael Walls.[22]

Keith Haring

When I go to SoHo, I come away with so many visions of new ideas for my own work that I wonder if that is why I go.

I start to look at the gallery spaces as spaces for my art instead of looking at the art being shown.

I realized today that one of the main reasons I am here is because it is one of the only cities in the world that has gallery space big enough for my anticipated works.

I saw so many spaces today that look like they were made for my art.[23]

Leo Castelli

Most of my artists were young with no prior gallery experience to speak of before joining mine. We grew up together. I place great importance on that connection, and think it has made a bond between us. Also, I've always identified with my artists' needs and problems, financial or otherwise. I never demanded things from them, and while there wasn't much of it around, I tried to advance them all the money I could. Above all, I've never told my artists what to do, especially when it comes to their art. Although sometimes I may be unsure of the new work myself, I encourage them to proceed with it—because I know that there has been a tremendous effort on their parts to do something new, not routine, and that they have struggled to get there.[24]

Janelle Reiring

Ambition is an element I look for in an artist, and I certainly have ambitions as a dealer. I guess most of us are involved in this activity because of certain romantic views about art and artists. But once we're in it, it is a practical, functioning world; it is a business. The same sort of drives and ambitions and instincts function for an artist as they do for other professionals. I don't think that there are good artists out there in obscurity who will not be discovered eventually. The undiscovered genius has become a myth.[25]

Robert Rauschenberg

My career is unknown to me. Other people seem to understand it, but I'm not that interested. I think it's sort of indecent to have things so worked out that they end up like you thought they should. You think I want to be what I am? You just have to expose yourself to more, and see what the consequences are.[26]

Brad Cloepfil Interview with Stuart Horodner

SH: How do you deal with the impact of your career ambitions on your family?

BC: Personal, complete love of the work is always primary. I am happiest and most fulfilled when I'm really in the work. It's taken me 48 years to actually be able to say that to people, and to the people I love. I don't consider that to be a denial of my love for them, but it's an admission of what the work means. And to live with that takes incredible strength. How can you ask someone to live with that? So when you see a movie like *My Architect*, it gives you another view on the dysfunction of it, but the shared truth of it too.[27]

Marina Abramović

I've had so many bad experiences, so that means I want to protect my students from bad experiences.

There was this Turkish girl, and she came to me and said, "There's a gallery that wants to take my work," but the dealer wanted five, like, major pieces to donate to the gallery. I said, "Just say no." And she said, "But this is my only chance." This is exactly how it works because she thinks she will never have a second chance. I said, "Just tell her no." So she goes and tells her no. And then that woman, the dealer, just throws her out of the gallery, and the Turkish girl, she's crying, and I say, "Just wait." The next week, the dealer calls her and says, "Oh, let's talk." And then she asked her to do whatever ... an edition and she would pay or give her one proof. I said, "Say no." (Laughing) Until she really, through the process, learned actually to negotiate because young artists will be used until they get this experience.[28]

Ronald Feldman

In the beginning, I felt enormous pressure to produce money for the artists. I think they were counting on the fact that I would; and in many cases, such as Komar and Melamid, I did. But in many cases I couldn't. There just wasn't an audience to buy what they were making. In the beginning Chris Burden made nothing to sell, and Hannah Wilke's vaginal sculptures, Margaret Harrison's rape paintings, and Mierle Ukeles's touch sanitation pieces are admittedly difficult art. I would not drop an artist because I was unsuccessful in selling the work. That is not the criterion. Sometimes it takes several shows before the audience realizes what the artist is doing and can appreciate the aesthetic.[29]

Rick Rubin

I thought it'd be nice to find the right grown-up artist who maybe is in the wrong place, who I could really do something great with. And the first person who came to mind was John [Cash]. He already had legendary status, and maybe had been in a place where he hadn't been doing his best work for a while.[30]

Alice Neel

When I give lectures to these young people—for instance in Baltimore I was once on a symposium, and all they wanted to do was "to make it." And I said to them: "Don't you know that before you make it, you have to have something to make it with." I think to go to New York and SoHo right off is absurd; you should shop around yourself, see what it is. See what your art is, and then when you think you've made some discovery, go in and do it. [...]

All experience is great providing that you live through it. I would tell these classes of art students, the more experience you get, the better, if it doesn't kill you. But if it kills you, you've gone too far.[31]

Janine Antoni Interview with Stuart Horodner

SH: How do you deal with people looking at you, the fear that they have expectations about the work? You told me once that you feel like you have to hit a home run every time. You have a post-studio practice; things don't evolve out of a daily ritual. The work is project-driven, research is involved, it's collaborative in terms of technical assistance and people you need to help you. How does this affect your freedom? What does it do to your sense of failure or risk?

JA: The work has become more and more about myself as a way to protect myself. The one thing I know and trust is my own experience. I get intimately involved in the work as a way of shielding myself from all of that. I want to make a great work every time as much for myself as anyone else, but I'm much less worried about greatness now. I really believe that you learn most from your failures; you have to allow yourself to fail. Hopefully, it's in the privacy of your own studio, but not always. If I look at an artist's body of work that I really love, the works that I spend most time with are those rare works that didn't get as much attention, the works that don't have the finesse to sweep you away. It is in those works that you fully see the artist's vision, even if it is raw and clunky. These are the works that I really cherish.[32]

Leon Golub

The adventures that you are going to have as artists, as individuals, are going to go in all kinds of ways; they're going to turn back upon each other, they're going to turn upside-down; you're going to recover, you're going to go on the attack, you will retreat, you will make certain investigations of the world in which you are involved. It's never a single road towards achievement, success, or anything else. It's a complex, messy situation. We often have ideal examples shown to us. It means certain artists have very beautiful careers, especially when seen retrospectively. Biographies always tell it to you to make the artist's history look kind of fabulous. However, one of the things you should be aware of, and maybe you are aware, is that the self-consciousness that you will have as young artists and the problems that you face as younger artists are no different than what you will be facing in twenty to thirty years from now. And the problem of success or failure, whatever that means, nobody even knows what those terms really mean, those problems in the arts, and in all of the arts, exist for us continuously. And artists that are internationally famous have the same anxieties as you do as to how they are being treated, where their next exhibition will be, etc. A negative review by someone can throw a well-known artist in a spin that he or she will not recover from in weeks. So they face the same kind of, in a sense, nervous instability for the most part that we all face together. We can almost take this for granted. Of course, it's better to be nervous and extremely successful than to be nervous and unknown.[33]

Mel Chin

I've been called a "mid-career emerging artist." I tried to correct this. They said, "Early, mid-career artist." I said, "Damn. That's a mouthful." I said, "Make it simple. I'm a submerging artist." I truly believe this, because look at it this way. The world I am talking about, that is so tragic, has been shaped by covert forces, political covert forces—business and military. It's always happened. We know this now. Submerging is what I want to do, and you have to make those explorations in that world, being affected by the forces that I'm addressing.[34]

NOTES

1. Philip Roth, *American Pastoral* (New York: Vintage Books, 1997), 35.

2. Henry Wessel, in Philip Gefter, "Henry Wessel: Capturing the Image, Transcending the Subject," *New York Times*, May 21, 2006, http://www.nytimes.com/2006/05/21/arts/design/21geft.html?pagewanted=all, accessed May 17, 2011.

3. Saul Ostrow, conversation with author, Jun 8, 2009.

4. Dave Hickey, "Revision Number Six: Addictions," *Art in America* (Mar 2009): 38.

5. David Foster Wallace, *This is Water: Some Thoughts, Delivered on a Significant Occasion, about Living a Compassionate Life* (New York: Little, Brown and Company, 2009) 3–4.

6. Mira Schor, "On Failure and Anonymity," *Wet: On Painting, Feminism, and Art Culture* (Durham and London: Duke Univ. Press, 1997), 123.

7. Wallace Shawn, in Wallace Shawn and André Gregory, *My Dinner with André*, Screenplay (New York: Grove Press, 1981), 17.

8. Rirkrit Tiravanija, "Providing Free Food," in Linda Weintraub, *In the Making: Creative Options for Contemporary Art* (New York: Distributed Art Publishers, 2003), 103.

9. Hilton Als, "Queen Jane, Approximately," *New Yorker* (May 29, 2011): 58.

10. David Diao, e-mail to author, Apr 27, 2011.

11. Lee Lozano, "May 16, 1969," in "Book #2," in *Lee Lozano: Drawings* (London: Yale Univ. Press and Hauser & Wirth, 2006), n.p.

12. Julian Hoeber, in Michael Markowsky, "Julian Hoeber," *Arts in Store: Rethinking the Relationship between Art and Business* (Self-published, 2009), 46.

13. Jon Lapointe, in Michael Markowsky, "Jon Lapointe," *Arts in Store: Rethinking the Relationship between Art and Business* (Self-published, 2009), 86–87.

14. David Wojnarowicz, in Barry Blinderman, "The Compression of Time: An Interview with David Wojnarowicz," in Barry Blinderman, ed., *David Wojnarowicz: Tongues of Flame*, Exhibition catalogue (University Galleries, Illinois State University, Normal, 1990), 53.

15. Andrea Fraser, in Praxis, "Andrea Fraser in Conversation with Praxis," *Brooklyn Rail* (Oct 2004): 12.

16. Dave Hickey, in Sari Carel, "Dave Hickey with Sari Carel," *Zingmagazine* (2000): 179.

17. Paul Shambroom, in Stuart Horodner, "Process and Perspective: An Interview with Paul Shambroom," in *Paul Shambroom: Picturing Power*, Exhibition catalogue (Weisman Art Museum, University of Minnesota, Minneapolis, 2008), 6–7.

18. David Rimanelli, "Fed with Judgment," *Artforum* (Nov 2010): 101.

19. Jeffrey Deitch, in Adam Lindemann, "The Art Dealer," *Collecting Contemporary* (Koln, Germany: Taschen, 2006), 50.

20. Tad Savinar, e-mail to author, Apr 12, 2011.

21. Nina Katchadourian, "Introduction," *Day Job*, Exhibition catalogue (The Drawing Center, New York, 2010), 8.

22. Mike Howard, e-mail to author, Mar 26, 2011.

23. Keith Haring, "1978," *Keith Haring Journals* (New York: Penguin, 2010), 19.

24. Leo Castelli, in Alan Jones and Laura de Coppet, *The Art Dealers: The Powers Behind the Scene Tell How the Art World Works* (New York: Clarkson N. Potter, 1984), 98.

25. Janelle Reiring, ibid., 295.

26 Robert Rauschenberg, in Calvin Tomkins, "Everything in Sight: Robert Rauschenberg's New Life," *The New Yorker* (May 23, 2005), http://www.newyorker.com/archive/2005/05/23/050523fa_fact_tomkins, accessed Feb 21, 2011.

27. Brad Cloepfil, in Stuart Horodner, "Brad Cloepfil," *Bomb* (Spring 2005): 47.

28. Marina Abramović, in "Conversation: Marina Abramović and Tania Bruguera," in Steven Henry Madoff, ed., *Art School: (Propositions for the 21st Century)* (Cambridge: MIT Press, 2009), 183.

29. Ronald Feldman, in Alan Jones and Laura de Coppet, *The Art Dealers: The Powers Behind the Scene Tell How the Art World Works* (New York: Clarkson N. Potter, 1984), 218.

30. Rick Rubin, in David Kamp, "Letter From Nashville: American Communion," *Vanity Fair* (Oct 2004), http://www.vanityfair.com/culture/features/2010/02/johnny-cash-201002, accessed Feb 21, 2011.

31. Alice Neel, Patricia Hills, "Alice by Alice," *Alice Neel* (New York: Abrams, 1983), 180.

32. Janine Antoni, in Stuart Horodner, "Janine Antoni," *Bomb* (Winter 1999): 53.

33. Leon Golub, "Transcript of the Graduation Commencement Address of the Art Institute of Chicago, May 23, 1982," in Hans-Ulrich Obrist, ed., *Leon Golub: Do Paintings Bite?* (Ostfildern, Germany: Cantz Verlag, 1997), 76–77.

34. Mel Chin, Lecture (transcript), Skowhegan School of Painting & Sculpture, Madison, ME, June 21, 1995.

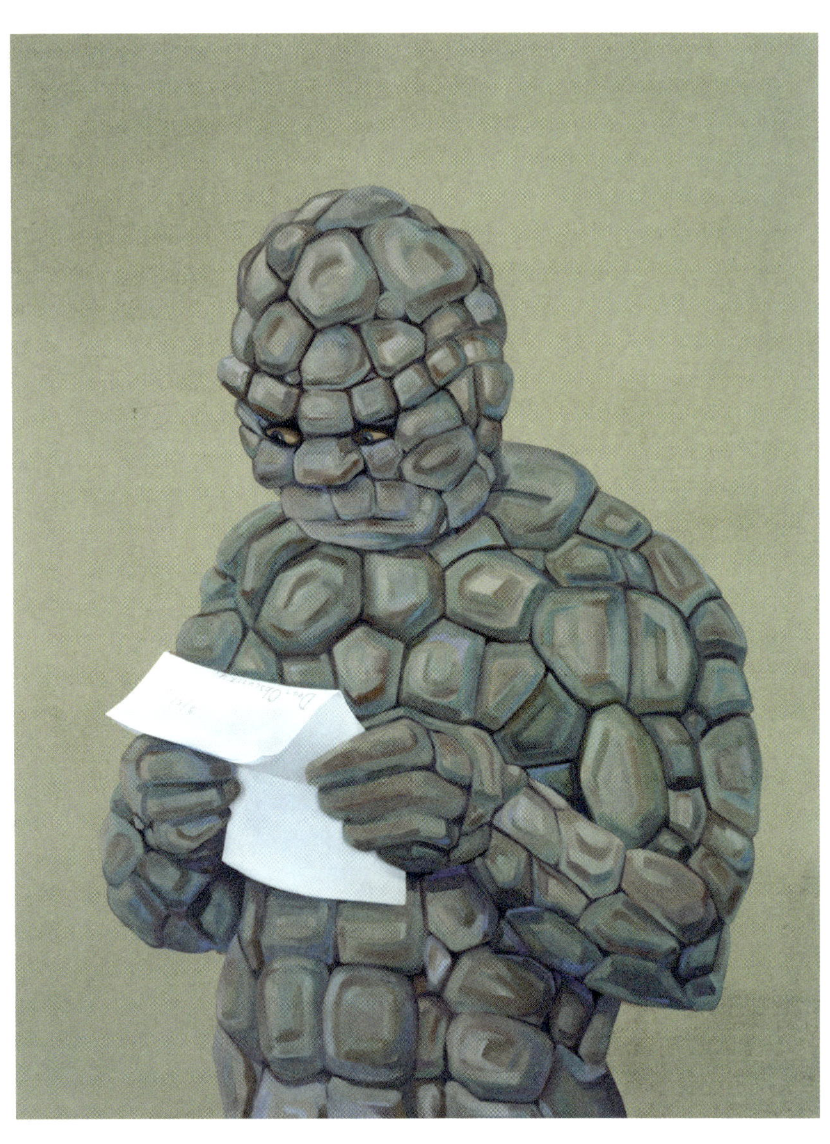

Nicole Eisenman
From Success to Obscurity
2004

12. SUCCESS

How do you define success? Does it have something to do with freedom and time? Would it involve showing with this gallery and having your work bought by that collector and getting invited to all the right parties? Do you need to have a big studio with assistants and exhibitions lined up for the next two years, or would a residency at The MacDowell Colony or The Hambidge Center satisfy you? Do you hunger for full page color ads, or better yet, the cover of a glossy art magazine? Would a great review in *Art Papers* be validation enough or are you holding your breath until Roberta Smith shows up? How about a good teaching job and health insurance?

One goal of all artists, whether they work with clay or sound or film or food, is to create situations that are powerful enough to affect others. Robert Rauschenberg said, "If you do not change your mind about something when you confront a picture you have not seen before, you are either a stubborn fool or the painting is not very good."[1] All you can do is establish your own criteria for personal and professional achievement and meter your progress. John Chamberlain, known for his large-scale sculptures made with crushed automobile parts, has shown his work steadily since the mid-1950s, in important exhibitions and prestigious museums. Recently, he said, "I once had a drink with Billie Holiday, and I smoked a joint with Louis Armstrong. Those are my real claims to fame."[2]

My version of success is being able to do the work I'm most excited about and to make things happen that might not have been possible if I wasn't around. This might best be called the "It's a Wonderful Life" effect.[3] I am satisfied when I see the exhibitions that I've curated listed on artist's résumés, when the letters of recommendation I've written result in residencies or jobs for people I believe in, and when boxes of catalogues come from the printer still smelling of ink. I'm excited when attendance is up and reviews are positive, and when I sense that my next projects will bring increased risks and resources, and greater rewards for all involved.

Leon Golub

There are three things: your work, your livelihood, and your personal life. If any two are going well at the same time consider yourself lucky.[4]

Lane Relyea

Success isn't just quantified in terms of how much a work sells for; it also is measured by how often an artist appears on the visiting-artist roster at art schools, or how often one is commissioned to do site-specific projects at Kunsthallen and contemporary art spaces. Perhaps this relates to why artists themselves draw more attention now than their work; their celebrity has a value of its own, as does their functioning—are they articulate about their work, do they have connections, do they look glamorously arty?[5]

Jean Dubuffet

I do not believe that I have ever encountered a painting which gave me immediately such a strong sense of commotion as the one by Ivan Albright portraying a door; I found it at the Art Institute during my brief stay in Chicago in 1951. It is an unforgettable painting, and it seems to me, a striking example of a work that is worth going to the ends of the earth to see.[6]

Jan Tumlir Interview with Michael Markowsky

MM: Based on your observations, what makes an artist successful? What gives them their first start, what gives them their longevity?

JT: I've always thought that when you have someone in a class and they have a breakthrough, it's always when they get very specific, when they decide that their work is not just about architecture, but about mid-century architecture, and moreover it's about the way that mid-century architecture functions in contemporary advertising, let's say. It's about defining something very specific. Projects that seem to never go anywhere are ones that are maintained in this condition of generalized and totally open-ended possibility. There is a great fear on the part of a lot of young artists to peg themselves to anything.

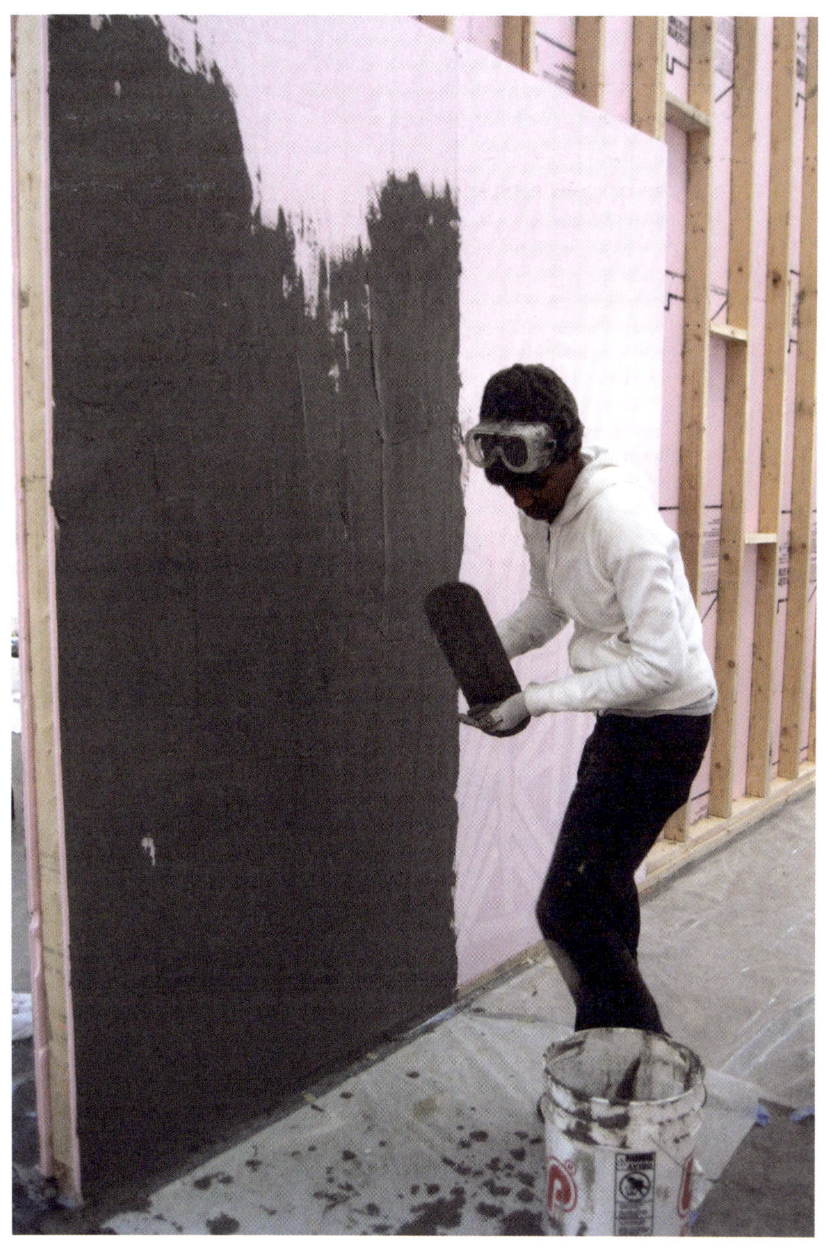

Karyn Olivier
Making *Handball*
2009

On the one hand, it's almost arbitrary what you start with, but since you've already demonstrated some sort of inclination toward it, then to define it further, to become more specific with it, this will only lead you toward what is interesting about it for you. You have to assume, as an artist or writer, that a large part of your experience is unknown to you. You discover it, you discover what you are interested in, you discover what was always there, what your propensities are. I don't think it's necessarily intuitive. The first decision can be almost arbitrary, but by actually working it through in all its specifics, you begin to get closer, I think, to what it is that you are "really" interested in.[7]

Karyn Olivier

I want to be surprised, stunned by art's capabilities. I want to feel ecstatic and comforted by what my works can offer to the world; scared and uncertain whether or not my art will succeed. I think success is developing an ego big enough to grant myself the unsolicited right to make work "for" the public, while remaining humble enough to know that often, it may not be what they asked for. Success for me involves watching and admiring the things of this world—accepting the invitation (or charge, perhaps) to act—to add or shift something I observe, bust it wide open and trust what's revealed will be worthwhile.[8]

Maurizio Cattelan

It's difficult, as an artist, to admit you want to be famous. Being an artist has nothing to do with fame, it has to do with art, that intangible thing needing integrity. Nevertheless, I think one has to confess a desire to be famous, otherwise one is not an artist. Art and fame are the expression of a desire to live forever, two things which are strictly interlinked.[9]

Dave Eggers

First, I was a sellout because *Might* magazine took ads. Then I was a sellout because our pages were color, and not stapled together at the Kinko's. Then I was a sellout because I went to work for *Esquire*. Now I'm a sellout because my book has sold many copies. And because I have done many interviews. And because I have let people take my picture. And because my goddamn picture has been in just about every fucking magazine and newspaper printed in America.

And now, as far as *McSweeney's* is concerned, *The Advocate* interviewer wants to know if we're losing also our edge, if the magazine is selling out, hitting the mainstream, if we're still committed to publishing unknowns, and pieces killed by other magazines.

And the fact is, I don't give a fuck. When we did the last issue, this was my thought process: I saw a box. So I decided we'd do a box. We were given stories by some of our favorite writers—George Saunders, Rick Moody (who is uncool, uncool!), Haruki Murakami, Lydia Davis, others—and so we published them. Did I wonder if people would think we were selling out, that we were not fulfilling the mission they had assumed we had committed ourselves to?

No. I did not. Nor will I ever. We just don't care. We care about doing what we want to do creatively. We want to be interested in it. We want it to challenge us. We want it to be difficult. We want to reinvent the stupid thing every time. Would I ever think, before I did something, of how those with sellout monitors would respond to this or that move? I would not. The second I sense a thought like that trickling into my brain, I will put my head under the tires of a bus.

The thing is, I really like saying yes. I like new things, projects, plans, getting people together and doing something, trying something, even when it's corny or stupid. I am not good at saying no. And I do not get along with people who say no. When you die, and it really could be this afternoon, under the same bus wheels I'll stick my head if need be, you will not be happy about having said no. You will be kicking your ass about all the no's you've said. No to that opportunity, or no to that trip to Nova Scotia or no to that night out, or no to that project or no to that person who wants to be naked with you but you worry about what your friends will say.[10]

Keith Haring

I would like to do a book one day with photos of me all over the world with different children. Many pictures like this exist from every place I have visited. I always have had contact with children on some level during every exhibition in every country.

This is one of the things that I am thinking when I say there are aspects of my life and art that are not duplicated by any other artist that I know of.

I have letters from children from all over the world that testify to this connection. I don't know if it's my funny face or my simple nature that provokes laughter and sympathy between me and them. But we share something that to me is very important to understand the reason for living and meaning of "life," if there is any "meaning" to life at all.[11]

Bettye LaVette

I feel ashamed about the levels that I'm not pleased on. It's because I'm all so old. I didn't grow tired of doing this—they just never let me do it. I'm resentful, but I don't have any real resentments. I'm glad for everything that's happening to everybody—I just wish that it happened to me, too. I don't know that I'd like to be recognized by virtually every living human being. I don't know that I'd like it to be Beatlesque. I'd like it to be more Billy Eckstine-ish.[12]

Dan Cameron

The curator is a kind of medium for artists, so one of the first rules of curatorship is, *The artist must be happy.* It's only logical: artists, who specialize in a visual medium, really cannot be expected to take your ideas seriously unless their spatial (or technological or institutional) needs are addressed. You are not permitted to step back and survey your work with satisfaction until the artists involved are satisfied that their work is being presented to its greatest advantage. This rule has another dimension: as someone who takes the fleeting experience of an exhibition very seriously, your vocation also consists of turning your advocacy of artist's ideas into a public gesture. One of the reasons you became a curator in the first place is that you believe in the way artists think and work; now's your chance to prove it.[13]

Mira Schor

The life of the work, the ecology of the studio is what I am interested in, when the doors are closed on the pressures of the marketplace. And in this life there is always failure, no matter how much money is made.[14]

Chuck Close

The whole notion of success was very different then. If you got your work in front of your peers, maybe got a review somewhere, and sold a piece, that would have been a really successful show. Today there are such raised expectations about what success is that anything short of having a show simultaneously at three galleries, an article in *Vanity Fair*, and a waiting list for your work is not seen as success but is seen as failure. I think it has put a lot of pressure on.[15]

Ad Reinhardt

I haven't done any cartoons or satires for a long time because it doesn't seem possible. The art world is no longer satirizable. I suppose there isn't much going on except business, and that's not very funny. Ten years or fifteen years ago (perhaps it was much longer), it was possible for one artist to call another an old whore. It's not possible any more. The whole art world is whorish and one artist couldn't possibly call another artist an old or young whore. Everyone now wants to be a "howling success" and a celebrity. Everyone wants to be like Elizabeth Taylor. And there isn't anything Elizabeth Taylor can do that's not of great interest to everybody. I've been using the term "selling out"—the way it was used in the twenties and thirties. Everyone else thinks it's a good idea or a good expression. An artist who comes in and says he has sold out his show thinks that's a good thing.[16]

Daniel Pinchbeck

The art world boomed and busted and then moved to Chelsea. New generations of artists rose to the top of the heap. My father kept working in his loft. He moved from rigid rectangles to biomorphic squiggles, flying cigar shapes, shapes that smashed into and interpenetrated one another. He stacked old paintings against the walls. Sculptures made from cardboard, wood, and plaster curled around each other on the floor—bulbous columns and amoebic entities. Art supplies rested on long tables: power saws and staple guns, plaster and chicken wire, tubes of paint piled into cigar boxes. His living area consisted of a desk and a bed in a corner surrounded by paintings—little canvases of spinning shapes watching over him like spirit guardians.

He never lost faith in his art. He rarely lost his good cheer. Despite his lack of success, he knew he had achieved a lot. He had come to New York City alone, knowing no one, with nothing to his name, and he had created himself. Painting infused his life with purpose. He eked out a living, teaching a day or two at Manhattan Community College, renting out part of the studio to a painter friend. Living in a huge loft in one of the wealthiest neighborhoods in the world, he was always poor, his clothes baggy, his jackets smelling of mothballs. Today I remain amazed as well as shocked by his purity, his indomitable effort in the face of such total indifference.[17]

Dave Hickey

How long will I remember this and how precisely? Is this work better than works that are similarly priced? Is it better than the blank wall on which it hangs? Is it better than everything and, if so, how long will I love it? How much do I think about it? How much would I miss it? How often does it surprise me? How many words can I write about it? How much would I pay for it? How much would I sell it for? What would I trade it for? How many people agree with me? Who are they? How complex is the constellation of objects in which it resides? How deep is its historical resonance? How much does it mean and how much does that matter?[18]

Tehching Hsieh

Good work is not a clear concept for me. The criteria could be very subjective. You have to be sincere to yourself, and feel satisfied with the work. Doing work itself is a reward, even if the outside world doesn't accept your work.[19]

John Baldessari

Sol (LeWitt) said his standard for a good work of art would be something he could show to Giotto.[20]

NOTES

1. Robert Rauschenberg, in Lana Davis, "Robert Rauschenberg and the Epiphany of the Everyday," in *Poets of the Cities New York and San Francisco, 1950–1965*, Exhibition catalogue (Dallas Museum of Fine Arts, Dallas, Texas, and E. P. Dutton, 1974), 49.

2. John Chamberlain, in Randy Kennedy, "A Crusher of Cars, a Molder of Metal," *New York Times*, May 9, 2011.

3. *It's a Wonderful Life*, Directed by Frank Capra, RKO Radio Pictures, 1946.

4. Leon Golub, conversation with author, Oct 15, 1999.

5. Lane Relyea, in "Talk: Rainer Ganahl, Paul Mattick, Raymonde Moulin, Lane Relyea, Richard Shiff, Katy Siegel," in Katy Siegel and Paul Mattick, *Art Works: Money* (New York: Thames & Hudson, 2004), 184.

6. Jean Dubuffet, "A Forward," in Michael Croydon, *Ivan Albright* (New York: Abbeville Press, 1978), 7.

7. Jan Tumlir, in Michael Markowsky, "Jan Tumlir," *Arts in Store: Rethinking the Relationship between Art and Business* (Self-published, 2009), 124.

8. Karyn Olivier, e-mail to author, Apr 10, 2011.

9. Maurizio Cattelan, in Barbara Casavecchia, "I Want to Be Famous – Strategies for Successful Living," in Franceso Bonami, et al, *Maurizio Cattelan* (London and New York: Phaidon Press, 2003), 133.

10. Dave Eggers, in Saadi Soudavar, "An Interview with Dave Eggers," *The Harvard Advocate* (Apr-May 2000), Reprinted on Armchair News, http://www.armchairnews.com/freelance/eggers.html, accessed Aug 8, 2010.

11. Keith Haring, "1986," *Keith Haring Journals* (New York: Penguin, 2010), 132.

12. Bettye LaVette, in Alec Wilkinson, "The Music Scene: Long Time Coming." *The New Yorker* (Nov 15, 2010): 73.

13. Dan Cameron, "Why Curate?," in Carin Kuoni, ed., *Words of Wisdom: A Curator's Vade Mecum on Contemporary Art* (New York: Independent Curators International, 2001), 39.

14. Mira Schor, "On Failure and Anonymity," *Wet: On Painting, Feminism, and Art Culture* (Durham and London: Duke Univ. Press, 1997), 123.

15. Chuck Close, in "New York City, February 21, 1994," from William Bartman, *The Portraits Speak: Chuck Close in Conversation With 27 of His Subjects*, Edited by Joanne Kesten (New York: A.R.T. Press, 1997), 120.

16. Ad Reinhardt, in Bruce Glaser, "An Interview with Ad Reinhardt," in Barbara Rose, ed., *Art as Art: The Selected Writings of Ad Reinhardt* (Berkeley and Los Angeles: Univ. of California Press, 1991, First published 1975 by Viking Press, New York), 14-15.

17. Daniel Pinchbeck, "Prince at Greene: Daniel Pinchbeck on Peter Pinchbeck," *Artforum* (Summer 2002): 58.

18. Dave Hickey, "Revision Number Five: Quality," *Art in America* (Feb 2009): 34.

19. Tehching Hsieh, in Barry Schwabsky, "Live Work," *Frieze* (Oct 2009), http://www.frieze.com/issue/article/live_work/, accessed Feb 21, 2011.

20. John Baldessari, in Mel Bochner and John Baldessari, "Outside the Box: Mel Bochner and John Baldessari on Sol LeWitt," *Artforum* (Summer 2007): 102.

LIST OF IMAGES

94 Luis Camnitzer, *This Is a Mirror, You Are a Written Sentence*, 1966–1968, Vacuum formed polystyrene, 19.06 x 24.61 x 0.59 inches, Courtesy the artist and Alexander Gray Associates, New York

104 Nina Katchadourian, *Ten Books I'd Save in a Fire*, 2011, Digital snapshot, Courtesy the artist

112 Collaborative drawing session with David Borchart, David Humphrey, Jennifer Coates, Sharon Mesmer, 2001, David Humphrey studio, New York, Photographs, Courtesy the author

116 Jerald Ordover, *Roberta Smith*, c. 1979, Photograph, 4 x 6 inches, Courtesy Matthew Higgs, New York

116 Jerald Ordover, *Robert Mapplethorpe, Sam Wagstaff*, c. 1979, Photograph, 4 x 6 inches, Courtesy Matthew Higgs, New York

117 Jerald Ordover, *Leo Castelli*, c. 1979, Photograph, 4 x 6 inches, Courtesy Matthew Higgs, New York

117 Jerald Ordover, *Bruce Nauman*, c. 1979, Photograph, 4 x 6 inches, Courtesy Matthew Higgs, New York

120 Horodner Romley Gallery, Guest book, Digital scan, Mar 11–Apr 9, 1994

125 William Pope.L, *My Penis Is Fine How Are You?*, 1995, Postcard, ink, 4 x 6 inches, Collection of the author

126 Paul Ramírez Jonas, *The Commons*, 2011, Cork, pushpins, notes contributed by the public, 126 x 124 x 64 inches, Courtesy the artist and Alexander Gray Associates, New York

129 Group tour of Shana Robbins, *Supernatural Conductor*, Jul 9–Sep 19, 2010, Atlanta Contemporary Art Center, Photograph by Mike Jensen

132 Anya Liftig, Rejection note, c. 2000, Courtesy the artist

138 Charles Goldman, *Happy To Be Here*, 1995, Video, 60 minutes, Courtesy the artist

142–143 David Diao, *Auction Result*, 2011, Acrylic and silkscreen on canvas, 32 x 52 inches, Courtesy the artist and Postmasters Gallery, New York

148 Mike Howard, *Field & Stream (Hunter)*, 1974, Acrylic on canvas, 48 x 48 inches, Courtesy the artist

156 Nicole Eisenman, *From Success to Obscurity*, 2004, Oil on canvas, 51 x 40 inches, Courtesy the artist and Leon Koenig, Inc., New York, Photograph by Bill Orcutt

159 Karyn Olivier, Making *Handball*, 2009, *Make Room*, Feb 5–Mar 29, 2009, Atlanta Contemporary Art Center

Photographs of artists making or installing their work at the Atlanta Contemporary Art Center are courtesy the author.

INDEX OF NAMES

*Participants in exhibitions and educational programs at the Atlanta Contemporary Art Center from 2007 to 2011.

BIBLIOGRAPHY

Adler, Jonathan. "Timeless: Stoked." *New York Times Style Magazine* (Winter 2010): 82.

Allen, Donald, ed. *The Selected Poems of Frank O'Hara.* New York: Vintage Books, 1974.

Allison, Jay, and Dan Gediman, eds. *This I Believe: The Personal Philosophies of Remarkable Men and Women.* New York: Henry Holt, 2007.

Als, Hilton. "Queen Jane, Approximately." *New Yorker* (May 29, 2011): 54–63.

Anker, Suzanne, Susan Bee, Jackie Brookner, Daryl Chin, Jordan Crandall, Bailey Doogan, David Humphrey, William Pope.L, Barbara Pollack, Lucio Pozzi, Jerry Saltz, Mira Schor, and Harriet Shorr. "Forum: On Creativity and Community." M/E/A/N/I/N/G (May 1994): 3–29.

Armstrong, Elizabeth, and Joan Rothfuss. *In the Spirit of Fluxus.* Exhibition catalogue. Walker Art Center, Minneapolis, MN, 1993.

Art21. "Kiki Smith: Learning by Looking: Witches, Catholicism, and Buddhist Art." *Art21.* http://www.pbs.org/art21/artists/smith/clip1.html, accessed May 17, 2011.

Art21. "Kerry James Marshall: RHYTHM MASTR." Art21. http://www.pbs.org/art21/artists/marshall/clip2.html, accessed May 17, 2011.

Ault, Julie. *Come Alive! The Spirited Art of Sister Corita.* London: Four Corners Books, 2006.

Bailey, Stephanie. "Catching up with Matthew Higgs." *Aesthetica* (Sep 9, 2010). http://aestheticamagazine.blogspot.com/2010/09/catching-up-with-matthew-higgs.html, accessed May 17, 2011.

Bartman, William. *The Portraits Speak: Chuck Close in Conversation With 27 of His Subjects.* Edited by Joanne Kesten. New York: A.R.T. Press, 1997.

Bartman, William S., ed. *Vija Celmins.* New York: A.R.T. Press, 1992.

Battenfield, Jackie. *The Artist's Guide: How to Make a Living Doing What You Love.* Philadelphia: Da Capo Press, 2009.

Beckett, Samuel. *Nohow On: Company, Ill Seen Ill Said, Worstward Ho: Three Novels by Samuel Beckett.* New York: Grove Press, 1995.

Belz, Aaron. *Lovely, Raspberry: Poems.* New York: Persea Books, 2010.

Berger, John. *The Shape of a Pocket.* New York: Vintage Books, 2003.

Berger, Maurice. *Adrian Piper: A Retrospective.* Exhibition catalogue. Fine Arts Gallery, University of Maryland, Baltimore, 1999.

Jake Berthot. Exhibition catalogue. Rose Art Museum, Brandeis University, Waltham, MA, 1988.

Bessire, Mark H.C., ed. *William Pope.L: The Friendliest Black Artist in America.* Exhibition catalogue. Institute of Contemporary Art at Maine College of Art, Portland, and Massachusetts Institute of Technology, Cambridge, 2002.

Bhandari, Heather Darcy, and Jonathan Melber. *Art/Work: Everything You Need to Know (and Do) As You Pursue Your Art Career.* New York: Free Press, 2009.

Birnbaum, Daniel, Lynne Cooke, Kathryn Kanjo, Friedrich Meschede, and Richard Wentworth. *Artists at Work: Second Baltic International Seminar, 26–28 October 2000.* Edited by Sarah Martin and Sune Nordgren. Gateshead, Great Britain: Baltic, 2001.

Blair, Dike. "Otherworldly: Interview with John McCracken." *Thing.net* (May 3, 1997). www.thing.net/~lilyvac/writing30.html, accessed Jun 20, 2011.

Blinderman, Barry, ed. *David Wojnarowicz: Tongues of Flame.* Exhibition catalogue. University Galleries, Illinois State University, Normal, 1990.

Bochner, Mel, and John Baldessari. "Outside the Box: Mel Bochner and John Baldessari on Sol LeWitt." *Artforum* (Summer 2007): 101–102.

Bonami, Franceso, Nancy Spector, Barbara Vanderlinden, and Massimiliano Gioni. *Maurizio Cattelan*. London and New York: Phaidon Press, 2003.

Bourdain, Anthony. *Medium Raw: A Bloody Valentine to the World of Food and the People Who Cook*. New York: HarperCollins, 2010.

Brainard, Joe. *I Remember*. New York: Penguin Books, 1975.

Bruggen, Coosje van. *John Baldessari*. Exhibition catalogue. Museum of Contemporary Art, Los Angeles, 1990.

Buchloh, Benjamin H. D., and Judith F. Rodenbeck. *Experiments in the Everyday: Allan Kaprow and Robert Watts – Events, Objects, Documents*. Exhibition catalogue. Miriam and Ira D. Wallach Art Gallery, Columbia University, NY, 1999.

Chris Burden: A Twenty-Year Survey. Exhibition catalogue. Newport Harbor Art Museum, Newport Beach, CA, 1988.

Cabanne, Pierre. *Dialogues with Marcel Duchamp*. Translated by Ron Padgett. New York: Da Capo Press, 1979.

Cage, John. *Silence: Lectures and Writings by John Cage*. Cambridge and London: MIT Press, 1967. First published 1961 by Wesleyan Univ. Press, Middletown, CT..

Carel, Sari. "Dave Hickey with Sari Carel." *Zingmagazine* (2000): 173–182.

Cash, Johnny. *Unchained*. Produced by Rick Rubin. Warner Bros., 1996.

Cixous, Hélène. *"Coming to Writing" and Other Essays*. Edited by Deborah Jenson. Cambridge, MA: Harvard Univ. Press, 1991.

Coggins, David. "Stranger Than Fiction: An Interview with Daniel Bozhkov." *Artnet.com* (Mar 31, 2010). http://www.artnet.com/magazineus/features/coggins/daniel-bozhkov3-31-10.asp, accessed Mar 31, 2010.

Cotter, Holland. "Louise Bourgeois, Sculptor of Psychologically Powerful Works, Dies at 98." *New York Times*, Jun 1, 2010.

Croydon, Michael. *Ivan Albright*. New York: Abbeville Press, 1978.

Csikszentmihalyi, Mihaly. *Flow: The Psychology of Optimal Experience*. New York: Harper Perennial Modern Classics, 1990.

Dargis, Manohla. "Sturges's Travels, A Screwball Tale." *New York Times*, Apr 1, 2005. http://www.nytimes.com/2005/04/01/movies/01stur.html?ref=prestonsturges, accessed Apr 17, 2011.

de Antonio, Emile, and Mitch Tuchman. *Painters Painting: A Candid History of the Modern Art Scene, 1940–1970*. New York: Abbeville Press, 1984.

Debbaut, Jan, Douglas Gordon, and Francis McKee. *Douglas Gordon: Kidnapping*. Edited by Marente Bloemheuvel. Stedelijk Van Abbemuseum, Eindhoven, Netherlands, 1998.

Didion, Joan. "*Why I Write*," *New York Times Magazine* (Dec 5, 1976).

Duguid, Brian. "Tony Conrad." *EST* (Jun 1996), http://media.hyperreal.org/zines/est/intervs/conrad.html, accessed Feb 21, 2011.

Marlene Dumas: Measuring Your Own Grave. Exhibition brochure. The Menil Collection, Houston, 2009.

Dylan, Bob. *Chronicles: Volume One*. New York: Simon & Schuster, 2004.

Ebert, Roger. "Roger Ebert's Journal: Werner & Errol & the Images in Their Caves." *Chicago Sun Times* (Sep 13, 2010). http://blogs.suntimes.com/ebert/2010/09/werner_errol_the_images_in_the.html, accessed Feb 21, 2011.

Farver, Jane. *Luis Camnitzer: Retrospective Exhibition 1966–1990.* Exhibition catalogue. Lehman College Art Gallery, City University of New York, Bronx, 1991.

Fletcher, Harrell. "Ideas from Notebooks." *Harrell Fletcher* website (2001–2003). http://www.harrellfletcher.com, accessed Aug 8, 2010.

Friedman, B. H., ed. *Give My Regards to Eighth Street: Collected Writings of Morton Feldman.* Cambridge, MA: Exact Change, 2000.

Gayford, Martin, and Karen Wright, eds. *The Grove Book of Art Writing.* New York: Grove Press, 1998.

Gefter, Philip. "Henry Wessel: Capturing the Image, Transcending the Subject." *New York Times,* May 21, 2006, http://www.nytimes.com/2006/05/21/arts/design/21geft.html?pagewanted=all, accessed May 17, 2011.

Gilbert & George. *Gilbert & George: The Complete Pictures, 1971–1985.* New York: Rizzoli, 1986.

Gilbert, Elizabeth. "Play It Like Your Hair's On Fire: Tom Waits Would Be America's Springsteen – If America Were A Strange Dispossessed Land Of Circus Freaks." *GQ* (Jun 2002). http://www.tomwaitslibrary.com/interviews/02-june-gq.html, accessed Feb 21, 2011.

Gingeras, Alison M. "John Currin: The Backdoor Man." *Flash Art* (Oct 2002): 70–73.

Ginsberg, Allen. *Howl and Other Poems.* San Francisco: City Lights Books, 1956.

Gladwell, Malcolm. *Outliers: The Story of Success.* New York: Back Bay Books, 2008.

Goldman, Andrew. "Always be Changing." *New York Times Magazine* (May 29, 2011): 15.

Goldsmith, Kenneth. *I'll Be Your Mirror: The Selected Andy Warhol Interviews, 1962–1987.* New York: Carroll & Graf, 2004.

The Graduate. Directed by Mike Nichols. Embassy Pictures, 1967.

Philip Guston: Paintings 1969–1980. Exhibition catalogue. Whitechapel Art Gallery, London, 1982.

Hainley, Bruce, Dennis Cooper, and Adrian Searle. *Tom Friedman.* London: Phaidon Press, 2001.

Halley, Peter. "Wayne Koestenbaum." *Index Magazine* (1999). http://www.indexmagazine.com/interviews/wayne_koestenbaum.shtml, accessed Jun 18, 2011.

Hansen, Beck, and Al Hansen. *Playing with Matches.* Santa Monica, CA: Smart Art Press, 1995.

Haring, Keith. *Keith Haring Journals.* New York: Penguin, 2010.

Heath, Chris. "Mad German Auteur, Now in 3-D!" *GQ* (May 2011): 80–88.

Heiser, Jorg, Willem de Rooij, and Christopher Williams. "As We Speak." *Frieze* (Oct 2010): 179–187.

Henri, Robert. *The Art Spirit.* Compiled by Margery A. Ryerson. Philadelphia and New York: J.B. Lippincott, 1923.

Herrera, Hayden. *Arshile Gorky: His Life and Work.* New York: Farrar, Straus and Giroux, 2003.

Hickey, Dave. "Revision Number Five: Quality." *Art in America* (Feb 2009): 33–34.

——. "Revision Number Six: Addictions." *Art in America* (Mar 2009): 37–38.

Hills, Patricia. *Alice Neel.* New York: Abrams, 1983.

Hilton, Robin. "Tom Waits Interviews Tom Waits." NPR. *All Songs Considered* (May 20, 2008). http://www.npr.org/blogs/allsongs/2008/05/an_interview_with_tom_waits_by.html, accessed Dec 3, 2010.

Hirschberg, Lynn. "Heart to Heart: Michelle Williams & Ryan Gosling." *W* (Oct 2010): 141–143.

Holborn, Mark. "Allen Ginsberg's Sacramental Snapshots." *Aperture* (Winter 1985): 8–15.

Horodner, Stuart. "Brad Cloepfil." *Bomb* (Spring 2005): 40–47.

———. "The F Word." *New Observations* (Spring 1997): 2–4.

———. "Janine Antoni." *Bomb* (Winter 1999): 48–54.

———. "The Language of Stuff: An Interview with Richard Wentworth." *Sculpture* (Apr 2001): 16–23.

Humphrey, David. *Blind Handshake*. New York: Periscope, 2009.

It's a Wonderful Life. Directed by Frank Capra. RKO Radio Pictures, 1946.

Itzkoff, Dave. "Woody Allen on Faith, Fortune Tellers and New York." *New York Times*, Sep 15, 2010.

Jacob, Mary Jane, and Michelle Grabner. *The Studio Reader: On the Space of Artists*. Chicago: School of the Art Institute of Chicago, 2010.

Jianou, Ionel. *Henry Moore*. Translated by Geoffrey Skelding. New York: Tudor Publishing, 1968.

Jasper Johns: Writings, Sketchbook Notes, Interviews. Edited by Kirk Varnedoe, compiled by Christel Hollevoet. New York: The Museum of Modern Art, 1996.

Jones, Alan, and Laura de Coppet. *The Art Dealers: The Powers Behind the Scene Tell How the Art World Works*. New York: Clarkson N. Potter, 1984.

Judd, Donald. *Complete Writings 1959–1975*. Press of the Nova Scotia College of Art and Design, and New York Univ. Press, 1975.

Kakutani, Michiko. "Street Poet, Explores His Life." *New York Times*, Nov 23, 2010.

Kamp, David. "Letter From Nashville: American Communion." *Vanity Fair* (Oct 2004). http://www.vanityfair.com/culture/features/2010/02/johnny-cash-201002, accessed Feb 21, 2011.

Kaprow, Allan. *Essays on the Blurring of Art and Life*. Edited by Jeff Kelley. Berkeley and Los Angeles: Univ. of California Press, 1993.

Katchadourian, Nina. *Day Job*. Exhibition catalogue. The Drawing Center, New York, 2010.

Kaufman, Anthony. "Breaking Von Trier: Jorgen Leth Survives 'The Five Obstructions.'" *Indiewire.com* (May 26, 2004). http://www.indiewire.com/article/breaking_von_trier_jorgen_leth_survives_the_five_obstructions, accessed May 17, 2011.

Kehr, Dave. "Claude Chabrol, Pioneer French Filmmaker, Dies at 80." *New York Times*, Sep 13, 2010.

Kennedy, Randy. "A Crusher of Cars, a Molder of Metal." *New York Times*, May 9, 2011.

de Kooning, Willem. "Letter." *Artnews* (Jan 1949): 6.

Kramer, Hilton. "Tuttle's Art on Display at Whitney." *New York Times*, Sep 21, 1975.

Kuoni, Carin, ed. *Words of Wisdom: A Curator's Vade Mecum on Contemporary Art*. New York: Independent Curators International, 2001.

Lethem, Jonathan. "The Genius of Bob Dylan." *Rolling Stone* (Sep 7, 2006), 74–80, 128.

Letters to a Young Artist. Peter Nesbett, Shelley Bancroft, and Sarah Andress, eds. New York: Darte Publishing, 2006.

Lindemann, Adam. *Collecting Contemporary*. Koln, Germany: Taschen, 2006.

Linn, Judy. "Someone Asked." Artist Statement, Feature Inc., New York, Jun 8, 2005. http://www.feature-inc.com/artist_bios-texts/linn-text.html, accessed on Feb 21, 2011.

Lippard, Lucy R. *Eva Hesse*. New York: New York Univ. Press, 1976.

——. *Six Years: The Dematerialization of the Art Object*. London: Studio Vista, 1973.

Livingston, Jane, and John Beardsley. *Black Folk Art in America 1930–1980*. Exhibition catalogue. Corcoran Gallery of Art, Washington, DC, 1982.

Lee Lozano: Drawings. London: Yale Univ. Press and Hauser & Wirth, 2006.

Lummis, Suzanne. "Charles Bukowski, 1920-1994." *Los Angeles Times* (Apr 10, 1994). http://articles.latimes.com/1994-04-10/books/bk-44148_1_charles-bukowski, accessed Jun 18, 2011.

Madoff, Steven Henry, ed. *Art School: (Propositions for the 21st Century)*. Cambridge: MIT Press, 2009.

Marioni, Tom. *Sculpture and Installations, 1969–1997*. Exhibition catalogue. San Francisico: Crown Point Press, 1999.

Markowsky, Michael. *Arts in Store: Rethinking the Relationship between Art and Business*. Self-published, 2009.

Marsh, Steve. "Black Eyed Peas." *Sky* (Feb 2011): 52–55.

Mayer, Musa. *Night Studio: A Memoir of Philip Guston by His Daughter*. New York: Alfred A. Knopf, 1988.

Miller, John. *Mike Kelley*. Edited by William S. Bartman and Miyoshi Barosh. New York: A.R.T. Press, 1992.

Molesworth, Helen. *Work Ethic*. Exhibition catalogue. Baltimore Museum of Art, and Pennsylvania State Univ. Press, University Park, 2003.

Morphet, Richard, ed. *R.B. Kitaj: A Retrospective*. Exhibition catalogue. Tate Gallery, Millbank, London, 1994.

Morse, John D., ed. *Ben Shahn*. New York: Praeger Publishers, 1972.

Myles, Eileen. *The Importance of Being Iceland: Travel Essays in Art*. Los Angeles: Semiotext(e), 2009.

——. *Inferno (A Poet's Novel)*. New York: O/R Books, 2010.

The New American Painting. Exhibition catalogue. The Museum of Modern Art, New York, 1959.

Obrist, Hans-Ulrich, ed. *Leon Golub: Do Paintings Bite?* Ostfildern, Germany: Cantz Verlag, 1997.

O'Hara, Frank. *Art Chronicles: 1954–1966*. New York: George Braziller, 1975.

——. *Robert Motherwell, with Selections from the Artist's Writings*. New York: The Museum of Modern Art, 1965.

O'Hara, Frank, and Norman Bluhm. "Poem Paintings." *Lingo* (1997): 10–18.

Ono, Yoko. *Grapefruit*. New York: Simon & Schuster, 2000. First published 1964 by Wunternaum Press, Tokyo.

Pamuk, Orhan. *Other Colors: Essays and a Story*. Translated by Maureen Freely. Toronto: Alfred A. Knopf Canada, 2007.

Phair, Liz. "Stray Cat Blues." *New York Times Book Review* (Nov 14, 2010): 11.

Phillips, Tom. *A Humument: A Treated Victorian Novel*. London: Thames and Hudson, 1980.

Picabia, Francis. *I am a Beautiful Monster: Poetry, Prose, and Provocation*. Translated by Marc Lowenthal. Cambridge and London: MIT Press, 2007.

Pinchbeck, Daniel. "Prince at Greene: Daniel Pinchbeck on Peter Pinchbeck." *Artforum* (Summer 2002): 57–60.

Platow, Raphaela. *Dana Schutz: Paintings 2002–2005*. Exhibition catalogue. Rose Art Museum, Brandeis University, Waltham, MA, 2006.

Poets of the Cities New York and San Francisco, 1950–1965. Exhibition catalogue. Dallas Museum of Fine

Arts, Dallas, Texas, and E. P. Dutton, 1974.

Porzio, Domenico, and Marco Valsecchi. *Pablo Picasso: Man and his Work.* Secaucus, NJ: Chartwell Books, 1973.

Powell, Padgett. *The Interrogative Mood.* New York: HarperCollins, 2009.

Praxis. "Andrea Fraser in Conversation with Praxis." *Brooklyn Rail* (Oct 2004): 12–13.

Prose, Francine. "Thomas Nozkowski." *Bomb* (Fall 1998), http://bombsite.com/issues/65/articles/2171, accessed Feb 21, 2011.

Arnulf Rainer Self-Portraits. Exhibition catalogue. Galerie Ulysses, Vienna, Austria, and Ritter Art Gallery, Florida Atlantic University, Boca Raton, 1986.

Rappolt, Mark. "Ed Ruscha." *Art Review* (Oct 2009): 72–77.

The Return of the Cadavre Exquis. Exhibition catalogue. The Drawing Center, New York, 1993.

Rilke, Rainer Maria. *Letters to a Young Poet.* Translated by M.D. Herter Norton. New York and London: Norton, 1934.

Rimanelli, David. "Fed with Judgment." *Artforum* (Nov 2010): 101.

Rose, Barbara, ed. *Art as Art: The Selected Writings of Ad Reinhardt.* Berkeley and Los Angeles: Univ. of California Press, 1991. First published 1975 by Viking Press, New York.

Kay Rosen: Wall Paintings and Drawings, 2002–2006. Exhibition catalogue. Yvon Lambert Gallery, New York, 2006.

Martha Rosler Library. Edited by Paul Domela and John Byrne. Exhibition catalogue. Liverpool School of Art and Design, Liverpool, UK, 2008.

Ross-Ho, Amanda. *Absolutely Everything, Volume 1: Invisible Opponent.* Fall 2004–Spring 2005. Text given to author, Aug 23, 2010.

Roth, Philip. *American Pastoral.* New York: Vintage Books, 1997.

Safdie, Sylvia. *John Heward: A Portrait.* Video, 2008.

Sandler, Irving. "In Conversation: Jerry Saltz with Irving Sandler." *Brooklyn Rail* (Sep 2008). http:// www.brooklynrail.org/2008/09/art, accessed May 17, 2011.

Saunders, Wade. "Making Art, Making Artists." *Art in America* (Jan 1993): 70–95.

Schnabel, Julian. *CVJ: Nicknames of Maitre D's & Other Excerpts from Life.* New York: Random House, 1987.

Schor, Mira. *Wet: On Painting, Feminism, and Art Culture.* Durham and London: Duke Univ. Press, 1997.

———. "Postcard Post." *A Year of Positive Thinking* (Aug 8, 2010). http://ayearofpositivethinking.com/2010/08/08/postcard-post, accessed Aug 8, 2010.

Schwabsky, Barry. "Live Work." *Frieze* (Oct 2009), http://www.frieze.com/issue/article/live_work/, accessed Feb 21, 2011.

Schwarz, Dieter, ed. *Agnes Martin: Writings.* Verlag, Germany: Hatje Cantz, 1992.

Serota, Nicholas. *Experience or Interpretation: The Dilemma of Museums of Modern Art.* London: Thames and Hudson, 1996.

Paul Shambroom: Picturing Power. Exhibition catalogue. Weisman Art Museum, University of Minnesota, Minneapolis, 2008.

Shawn, Wallace, and André Gregory. *My Dinner with André.* Screenplay. New York: Grove Press, 1981.

Shelley, Mary. *Frankenstein; or, The Modern Prometheus.* New York: Bantam Books, 1967. First published 1818.

Sherman, Sam. Thomas Nozkowski Interview. *KultureFlash*, 2003. http://www.kultureflash.net/archive/67/priview.html, accessed Aug 8, 2010.

Shields, David. *Reality Hunger: A Manifesto.* New York: Alfred A. Knopf, 2010.

Siegel, Katy, and Paul Mattick. *Art Works: Money.* New York: Thames & Hudson, 2004.

Simblist, Noah. "Concreteness and Circumstance: In Conversation with Walead Beshty." *Art Papers* (Mar/Apr 2010): 32–36.

Simon, Joan. "An Interview with Jonathan Borofosky." *Art in America* (Nov 1981): 156–167.

Smith, Patti. *Just Kids.* New York: HarperCollins, 2010.

Soudavar, Saadi. "An Interview with Dave Eggers." *The Harvard Advocate* (Apr–May 2000). Reprinted on Armchair News. http://www.armchairnews.com/freelance/eggers.html, accessed Aug 8, 2010.

Stiles, Kristine, and Peter Selz, eds. *Theories and Documents of Contemporary Art: A Sourcebook of Artists' Writings.* Berkeley and Los Angeles: Univ. of California Press, 1996.

Stillman, Steel. "Luc Tuymans." *Art in America* (Feb 2010): 76–83.

Storr, Robert. *Philip Guston.* New York: Cross River Press, 1983.

Strauss, Neil. "The Broken Heart & Violent Fantasies of Lady Gaga." *Rolling Stone* (Jul 8–22, 2010): 66–74.

Sweeny, Kevin W., ed. *Buster Keaton: Interviews.* Jackson: Univ. Press of Mississippi, 2007.

Sylvester, David. *Interviews with Francis Bacon.* New York: Thames and Hudson, 1975.

Talese, Gay. "Onward and Upward with the Arts: High Notes: Tony Bennett Sings with Lady Gaga." *The New Yorker* (Sep 19, 2011): 62–68.

Thurman, Judith. "Walking Through Walls: Marina Abramovic's Performance Art." *The New Yorker* (Mar 8, 2010). http://archives.newyorker.com/?i=2010-03-08#folio=024, accessed Aug 8, 2010.

Tomkins, Calvin. "Everything in Sight: Robert Rauschenberg's New Life." *The New Yorker* (May 23, 2005). http://www.newyorker.com/archive/2005/05/23/050523fa_fact_tomkins, accessed Feb 21, 2011.

Wallace, David Foster. *This is Water: Some Thoughts, Delivered on a Significant Occasion, about Living a Compassionate Life.* New York: Little, Brown and Company, 2009.

Warhol, Andy. *The Philosophy of Andy Warhol: From A to B and Back Again.* San Diego, New York, and London: Harcourt Brace Jovanovich, 1975.

Weintraub, Linda. *In the Making: Creative Options for Contemporary Art.* New York: Distributed Art Publishers, 2003.

Wilkin, Karen. *David Smith.* New York and London: Abbeville Press, 1984.

Wilkinson, Alec. "The Music Scene: Long Time Coming." *The New Yorker* (Nov 15, 2010): 68–75.

Wilson, MaLin, ed. *The Hydrogen Jukebox: Selected Writings of Peter Schjeldahl, 1978–1990.* Berkeley and Los Angeles: Univ. of California Press, 1991.

Wright, Beryl J. *Jack Whitten.* Exhibition catalogue. Newark Museum, Newark, NJ, 1990.

Acknowledgements

The Art Life: On Creativity and Career would not exist without the generous support of the Emily Hall Tremaine Foundation. Since 2002, they have funded our *Artist Survival Skills* series, and its next iteration, *Creative Lives & Careers*, which have both sought to empower artists with practical and philosophical knowledge. This publication is the natural extension of the numerous workshops, lectures, panel discussions, and portfolio reviews that were made possible by their funding. Our sincere thanks go to the Foundation and their staff, especially Nicole Chevalier and Ashley Sklar, who have been real champions of our mission and methodology.

The Andy Warhol Foundation for the Visual Arts has provided significant grants for our exhibitions in recent years, allowing us to bring consequential artists to Atlanta. Many of their thoughts about the realities of art-making today are featured in this book. We are grateful to the Foundation, and Joel Wachs, Pamela Clapp, James Bewley, and Rachel Bers, in particular, for their support of our institution and so many others in the field.

Recognition and thanks go to the foundations, government agencies, and funders that support the programs of the Atlanta Contemporary Art Center: City of Atlanta Office of Cultural Affairs, Artadia: The Fund for Art and Dialogue, Canadian Consulate, The Community Foundation for Greater Atlanta, Forward Arts Foundation, Fulton County Arts Council, Georgia Council for the Arts and its partner agency, the National Endowment for the Arts, LUBO Fund, Massey Charitable Trust, Metropolitan Atlanta Arts Fund, The Sara Giles Moore Foundation, Perennial Properties, Possible Futures, The Rich Foundation, Tim and Lauren Schrager Family Foundation, Taylor Family Fund, WISH Foundation, and Women's Caucus for Art of Georgia.

Special thanks to Sean Elwood and Donna Wingate who were both very encouraging and helpful in getting *The Art Life: On Creativity and Career* to the attention of Todd Bradbury at D.A.P., who enthusiastically committed to be our distributor. Todd has been a thoughtful collaborator in this project, believing in our approach to the content and in the potential audience for it.

Much appreciation goes to all of those individuals and institutions who gave their permission to use previously published materials: Alexander Gray Associates; Andrew Kreps Gallery; Artist Pension Trust; Christopher Rauschenberg and Blue Sky Gallery; Betsy Sussler and *Bomb Magazine*, New Art Publications; Peter Nesbett and Darte Publishing; Scott and Teddi Dolph; Hudson and Feature Inc.; HarperCollins Publishers; Independent Curators International; Kavi Gupta Gallery; Leo Koenig, Inc.; Lyons Wier Gallery; Michael Markowsky; Maureen Paley, Inc.; Persea Books; Regen Projects; Skowhegan Lecture Archive at Ernest G. Welch School of Art and Design, Georgia State University; and Matthew Higgs and White Columns. We apologize for any inadvertent errors or omissions in recognizing individuals, publishers, or galleries.

Byron Kim and Lisa Sigal hosted a lovely dinner for me at their home, so I could discuss this publication with Janine Antoni, Nina Katchadourian, Dave McKenzie, and Paul Ramírez Jonas. Their generosity and ideas were both inspiring and clarifying.

David Humphrey, Wayne Koestenbaum, Mira Schor, and Katherine Smith each read a version of this manuscript. Their emotional and critical feedback is much appreciated.

Thanks go to the following colleagues, friends, and family for their advice and support: Regine Basha, Michael Coffey, Louis Corrigan, Craig Drennen, Laurel Gitlen, Barbara Horodner, Ben Horodner, Larry Horodner, Scott Ingram, Mike Jensen, Jess Laskosky, Rose Marcus, Jen Mergel, Helen Molesworth, Saul Ostrow, Amy Pleasant, Nancy Popp, Ingrid Schaffner, Jena Sibille, Joe Sola, Linda Sorkin, and Erin Wright.

A huge debt of gratitude goes to my co-editor and colleague Stacie Lindner. She has contributed her profound care and consideration to every detail of the researching, editing, and proofing of this publication. She deserves serious recognition and a vacation.

Current and previous board and staff members of the Atlanta Contemporary Art Center have provided encouragement and understanding during the evolution of this publication. Thanks to Melanie Beal, Saskia Benjamin, Jennifer Long, Jennifer Price, Tim Schrager, Jonathan Shils, Susan Tarnower, and Alana Wolf.

Susan Bowman has designed several publications for our institution. It is always a professional pleasure to work with her and, once again, she has aligned form and content beautifully. Kirk Sils at Davis Direct provided great assistance in shepherding this book from design through printing. Much appreciation goes to these collaborators.

We are indebted to all of the individuals whose words and images make up the content of this publication. Their efforts make the strongest possible case for wanting and maintaining a creative life.

Stuart Horodner